information security

Strategies for successful management

S.J. Gaston, FCA

CA

Canadian Cataloguing in Publication Data

Gaston, S.J. (Stephen James), 1943 –
Information security – Strategies for successful management

ISBN 0-88800-459-1

1. Data protection. 2. Computer security. 3. Business – Data processing.
I. Title. II. Canadian Institute of Chartered Accountants.

HF5548.37.G37 1996 658.4'78 C96–990023–6

The Canadian Institute of Chartered Accountants
277 Wellington Street West
Toronto, Ontario
M5V 3H2

Printed and bound in Canada

Preface

Too many organizations still consider their information security as an administrative cost, something that is done in the back office and in the nature of an insurance policy.

But information security is much more than that. It is the way we ensure the integrity of our data and protect the privacy and confidentiality of our competitive information and the data entrusted to us by our customers and employees. It is how we ensure that computer systems will be continuously available so that we can manage our business and serve our customers. Effective information security allows us to drive the information highway while avoiding the thieves, highway robbers and drunk drivers that lurk along the way. It sets the scene for an organization to participate in the fast-growing world of electronic commerce in all of its shapes and facets. In all, it is a vital part of the competitive advantage challenge facing virtually every organization.

Information security is truly everybody's business. As our customers often interface with us through our computer systems, information security is part and parcel of the goods and services that we offer. It must be included in product and service design. It must also be part of a robust and healthy system of internal control that protects our assets and ensures the integrity of our data while protecting our computer systems against disaster. On top of all of this, we must make sure that we meet customer expectations in all of these regards and ensure that the increasing amount of data and information we provide them in electronic form is complete and accurate and that the information they provide us is held private and confidential.

In today's highly competitive economy, we must offer our customers the right goods and services at the right price. In managing security costs, management walks the razor's edge. On the one hand, enough resources and money must be devoted to information security so that its crucial objectives are achieved. On the other hand, we must always avoid being wasteful as we strive to reduce costs and sharpen our efficiency wherever possible.

As a senior Information System Risk Management (ISRM) specialist for Price Waterhouse and the firm's lead consultant for information integrity services, I have had a unique chance to explore information security policies and structures in dozens of Canadian and international corporations and to debate these issues with top specialists and senior client officials. Based on this experience, I have found that there are some basic principles in the design and implementation of information security that successful organizations follow. Whenever I've communicated these principles to my clients, together with strategies for putting them into practice, the vast majority of my clients have been able to improve the efficiency, effectiveness and competitiveness of their information security structures.

This is the second book in my evolving series of Strategies for Management of Information Technology in which I share the principles that can help management successfully deal with information technology issues. The series is written for management, not for technical specialists. My previous book, *Getting the Right Systems at the Right Price*, was designed to help senior management get executive control of the organization's information systems and effectively manage IT acquisitions, implementation and inevitable changes. In this book, I focus on the appropriate policies and standards necessary to mobilize effective information security: how to integrate security into your customer services and your overall systems of internal control and the ways in which you manage information technology generally. It is designed to help you gain the knowledge and background understanding of information security issues you need to be able to work effectively with information systems security specialists, and more importantly, direct this work rather than follow what the "specialists" tell you.

Whether you are a director, senior manager, chief financial officer, head of major operating department or a senior internal or external auditor, this book provides the pragmatic, "real world" principles and strategies that can help you achieve information security success.

I would like to thank my many clients who over the years have given me fascinating assignments and who have taught me so much. In particular, I extend special thanks to two clients who were especially helpful and kind in sharing their knowledge with me while I was developing this book: Mr. Brian McPhedran, Director of Information Security and Control for the Canadian Imperial Bank of Commerce, and Mr. Paul Wing, Vice President of Systems Security and Controls for the Bank of Nova Scotia.

I am grateful to The Canadian Institute of Chartered Accountants (CICA) for its leadership in publishing this book and in supporting the still developing series of publications, Strategies for Management of Information Technology. I thank Kathleen Aldridge, B.A., B.Ed., for her extensive help and advice; without her editorial assistance and patience this book could not have been produced. I would also like to thank Peter J. Hoult, CA, Associate Director of the CICA Professional Services Group and the many other staff at the CICA who have been so helpful in the development and publication of this book.

Finally, I am deeply indebted to my partner, Graeme Booth, and all of my colleagues at the ISRM group in the Toronto Office of Price Waterhouse. The fascinating assignments and knowledge gained from them could not have been obtained without their skills, enthusiasm and support.

Contents

The book in summary

Introduction – The vital role of information security 1

Presents the author's thesis: information security is far too important to leave in technical hands; it is everyone's concern and responsibility as it is part and parcel of the product or service the organization is selling. This section introduces concepts such as "PACES" and "believed systems" that will be explored in the chapters that follow as well as explaining how different members of the management team can use the book to get on top of security issues.

Chapter 1 – Focusing the goals of information security 11

Reviews information security from an overall perspective and shows how it contributes to achieving broad corporate goals. This chapter explains how information security is part of an overall system of internal controls and discusses how the access rights and privileges of customers and other third parties as well as employees need to controlled. The chapter includes an overview of information security from a management perspective, providing an executive level of understanding of security principles so that security issues may be addressed in a consistent and logical manner in keeping with broad corporate goals and issues. A similar overview is provided for the Internet and its particular security challenges.

Chapter 2 – Putting information security in its place 69

Discusses how information security should be addressed as part of an overall corporate-wide information resources management policy. The chapter reviews how information security should be built to interface with overall systems of internal control so that the two together provide for integrity, privacy and confidentiality and disaster recovery planning. The possible formation of an information security steering committee to help develop and maintain information security policies, standards and procedures is also discussed.

Chapter 3 – Mobilizing the organization for information security success 101

Provides an overview of the entire process to define, implement and maintain information security processes. Following this, the roles of all departments in the organization right from top management through operating departments and the information security speciality group are discussed.

Chapter 4 – Creating the information security policy (including networks, microcomputers and the internet). 175

Looks at an overall strategy for information security including the policies, standards, procedures and practices which are required. The chapter reviews the process which senior management should use to develop new or revised information security policies and supporting standards and gain acceptance for their use throughout the organization. The chapter provides discussion, commentary and rationale on each section of a sample policy as it is developed. The sample information security policy is then provided in its entirety in the appendix of the chapter.

Chapter 5 – Tailoring security measures to the organization's needs 273

Focuses on the nature of information security standards which should be developed to implement the policy and describes the content and purpose of these standards from a management perspective. The chapter also provides suggestions as to how to best organize for the development and on-going maintenance of these standards and how to put effective transition plans in place to implement changes to information security policies and supporting standards.

Introduction

The vital role of information security

This book is the second in a series of books on Strategies for Management of Information Technology published by The Canadian Institute of Chartered Accountants. Like the first book, *Getting the Right Systems at the Right Price*, this second book, *Information Security*, focuses on strategies and is written for management rather than technical staff.

The introduction to *Getting the Right Systems at the Right Price* states that information systems are too important to the critical success of the organization to leave solely in the hands of the information systems specialists. Information systems are part and parcel of what the organization provides to its customers and vital to its critical success.

The same is true of information security. As a vital part of information technology, information security is far too important to leave in the hands of the information security specialist.

Think about it from a customer's point of view. As customers, we are not going to do business with an organization that can't keep track of its relationships with us, be that in the sense of money owing, account balances, open orders, status of the delivery of goods and services, the making of reservations or the movement of cash between us. *Such information integrity cannot be achieved without good information security.* As customers, we will be reluctant to provide the data and information an organization needs to serve us well unless we know that it will remain private and confidential. *But privacy and confidentiality is not possible without good information security.* As customers, we want to know that our supplier is there for us to provide us with goods and services whenever we need them and that they will deliver goods and services on time as promised. *Continuity of goods and services is not possible without good information security that ensures that our systems and data will be there for us to get the job done.*

Information security is also vital from an internal point of view. We have to have good control systems to manage risk. But we cannot do this so thoroughly and completely that we spend a fortune or make our systems so secure that employees and customers cannot quickly get at them. We need to create a balance in these competitive times; we need the right amount of security at the right price.

Information security is not some separate thing that gets tagged on as an afterthought or operates by itself. It needs to be part of the business process that is used by our employees and customers to do business. Once, again, it is management that knows the business process, not the technical employees.

For all these reasons and because information technology is part of what all of us do and touches all our business lives, information security must be everyone's concern and responsibility.

This book is designed to give you the understanding of information security you need as a member of management. It will enable you to help develop the policies and strategies on information security that your company needs to compete in today's electronic market place. It will give you the knowledge you need to define information security as part and parcel of the company's business processes. It will assist you to balance information security with the needs of your employees and customers for relatively easy access to systems and information to do business with you or to do their jobs. It will allow you to take complete and secure advantage of technologies by putting information security through its PACES:

P **Protect** information assets. Ensure the value and availability of the organization's data and information.

A **Assure** quality. Ensure the right things are done by the right people, those who have the requisite skills and authority.

C **Compete**. Support competitive advantage by protecting confidentiality yet allowing customers and other third parties to deal with the organization in a relatively easy and secure manner.

E **Eliminate** unnecessary expense through careful consideration and balancing of risk and the amount of security actually required.

S **Serve** customers. Good information security is part of the goods and services we sell when customers can easily do business with us electronically in a secure manner.

Why securing information assets is becoming increasingly more important to all organizations

Information security is far more than a necessary cost or evil but rather is a road to competitive advantage. It is good, cost effective information security that allows the company and its employees to drive the information highway. Without good information security, the organization cannot compete in the fast-growing world of electronic commerce.

Customers want to be able to deal with us electronically, to view our merchandise or services, to find out our prices, to order goods or schedule services, to track the status of their orders, and to determine their balances and financial transactions with us. This is true whether we have wholesale customers or retail customers, whether our customers want to connect with us business computer to business computer, through the Internet, through the telephone and telephony or through ATM and banking machines or the soon to be widespread smart cards and stored value cards. And customers want to do this easily and quickly, without muss or fuss, while at the same time feeling that their dealings with us are private and confidential and that any exchange of funds is secure from fraud.

When we are the customer, we want to do these same things ourselves with our suppliers. Our systems, for the sake of efficiency and effectiveness, must enable us to do this.

None of the above is possible without good information security that:

- allows us to know with some degree of certainty who we are communicating with or receiving messages and data from
- protects the integrity of our stored data and information and the data and information we send to and receive from others
- ensures the privacy and confidentiality of the information our customers and employees entrust to us, and
- ensures that our computer systems and information will be continuously available, because without them we cannot meet our commitments in the market place.

Thus it is obvious why securing information assets is becoming increasingly more important to all organizations. As we make greater use of information systems to conduct and account for business activities, we become more reliant on the continuing availability and integrity of computerized data. As we reduce layers of administration and approval authorities and empower individuals, we increase our reliance on information systems and the controls surrounding them.

Today, many information systems have become "believed systems", whereby organizations will accept transactions or transfer money based on computerized data *without further checking or verification.* Customers also seek to treat our systems as believed systems, and judge the quality of service they receive in considerable measure on the quality and availability of data they can obtain from us.

At the same time, threats to information assets are on the rise. With more and more business being conducted electronically, the opportunity to commit fraud and profit from it is increasing. The threat of malicious acts, which destroy files and programs, is also growing. So are the number of people who have the knowledge to commit such actions.

If this were not enough, there is plenty of helpful information on the Internet on how to hack into computer systems. Electronic mail is being used to exchange information on dial up numbers, logon IDs and passwords. Programs are now available on the Internet that will help the user create viruses, logic bombs and time bombs and to search out inherent weaknesses in many computer system configurations. At this time, the publishing or sharing of this information is not illegal in Canada or most other countries. Strange isn't it, when you consider that you can be arrested for possessing burglary tools!

A few years ago it took some skill and finesse, or at least some brain power to be a first class hacker or computer criminal. But with all the information and software tools available today from so many places, computer criminals are more like common thieves and muggers and appear all over the place.

The computer environment increases in complexity with each passing day. Most computer systems are being connected to other computers and receive and send data in electronic form. More and more, organizations are venturing into the Internet world to reach the 35 million individuals who belong to it. Some are starting to use the Internet not only to share information but to conduct business. Inside the organization, the dispersal of systems on LANs and wide area networks strains management and security frameworks, while at the same time it puts important computer processes into the hands of departmental management who may not have professional information systems skills. Large declines in the costs of telecommunications and the increasing availability of new and better tools are giving rebirth to the large centralized system. As a result, organizations have or are developing a veritable pantheon of computer structures and networks.

How this book is organized

Each chapter in the book is organized around a set of principles for information security, principles that management should follow in order to gain competitive advantage through information security that is efficient, effective, risk responsive and tuned to customers' and employees' needs.

As each of these principles is discussed, "Strategies for Success" which are helpful in putting the principles into action, are developed and highlighted. At the end of each chapter, the principles and related Strategies for Success are repeated. This serves both as a summary for the chapter and a rough checklist for management of the principles and the strategies needed to put them into action.

While it is, of course, not the job of management to perform technical tasks, management does need an overall grasp of what information security is and how it works. Given the growing interest in electronic commerce, they also need this understanding from the point of view of the Internet. *Chapter 1*, Focusing the Goals of Information Security, provides this understanding, and also discusses how information security is part of the larger, overall system of internal control.

In *Chapter 2*, Putting Information Security in its Place, we explore how information security should be dealt with as part of the overall management and corporate governance of information technology. A summary of overall information resources management policies is provided, and the manner in which information security might best be managed within it is discussed. This chapter also reviews how information security contributes to integrity, privacy and confidentiality and continuity and availability of information.

No activity can be carried out successfully unless all the players understand their roles and responsibilities and how they should best work together. Thus *Chapter 3*, Mobilizing the Organization for Information Security Success, spells out the roles of all departments in defining, creating, designing, implementing and then maintaining efficient and effective processes for information security.

Chapter 4, Creating the Information Security Policy (including Networks, Microcomputers and the Internet), presents a sample information security policy and the describes the reasons for and the thinking behind each section of the suggested sample policy. In keeping with design principles for good policies in any area, the sample policy is as short and succinct as possible and focuses on principles and the overall manner in which information security should be managed.

Standards can be thought of as the activities that are required to effectively implement the principles set forth at the policy level. *Chapter 5*, Tailoring Security Measures to the Organization's Needs, describes the standards that should be put in place to support the information security policy. As this book is for management and not technical personnel, only a brief description of the purpose and content of each of the many standards listed is provided. However, the description is sufficient to enable the reader to understand the areas that each standard should address, and the options and challenges that exist in each area.

How different members of the management team can benefit from this book

All members of management

All members of management need to have a basic grasp of the nature and purpose of information security and know fundamentally how it works. Without this, they cannot participate in determining how information technology might best be used to advance the critical success factors in the company's operations for which they are responsible.

This book is specifically designed to meet these needs.

Members of boards of directors and audit committees

The CICA studies on Criteria of Control point out how important it is to have proper Board oversight of the proper control environment and to have appropriate policies in place for the overall design and implementation of internal controls. As this book clearly illustrates, information security is a major component of internal control.

Thus directors may wish to review *Chapters 1* and *2* which explain how information security is part and parcel both of an overall system of internal control and of the overall corporate governance and risk management of information technology. Furthermore, they may find the sample policy in *Chapter 4* to be of use to evaluate the information security policy of the organization to see whether it addresses all of the areas that should be covered.

The chief executive officer and other members of top management

Executive management is charged with establishing proper policies and standards in all areas, not the least of which is information security. Thus the entirety of this book will be useful to them, first in understanding enough about information security to lead these activities from a top management perspective, and then in seeing that appropriate and effective information security policies and standards are created.

The chief financial officer

The chief financial officer or CFO will be helped by this book in the same way as any other member of top management. In addition, the CFO has special responsibilities for internal control, to see that assets are protected and that accounting records are complete and accurate. This book will be of major assistance in these areas.

The CFO is also responsible for assessing the business cases for major expenditures, including those related to information security. The principles set forth in this book will help the CFO in defining and then reviewing business cases for expenditures that are driven by or have major information security components.

Each department head

Each department head owns or is responsible for the computer systems that support his or her business processes, including their information security aspects. This business process owner, acting as the systems owner, needs to define cost effective information security processes as an integral part of an efficient and focused business process that serves the needs of both the company and its customers.

This book will help department heads in doing all of these things and provide the understanding needed to work with the information systems department and information security specialists when doing so.

The information systems department and information security specialists

Information technology specialists always face the challenge of gaining the active participation of the users of computer systems. Unfortunately, senior management as well as department heads often do not understand their important roles in creating appropriate policies and standards which both they and the information technology specialist will use as they work together. Users often do not understand the important role of senior and departmental management in defining systems requirements in detail, including those related to information security. Often they do not understand that information security is only part of an overall system of internal control which needs to contain procedures and steps carried out by personnel in their departments, as well as procedures performed by technical personnel and by software.

This book will help bridge this understanding gap with users and assist all information and information security specialists to communicate to users the help and cooperation they need from them during all phases of the process.

Internal auditors

Today internal auditors more and more need to focus on the sufficiency of policies and standards. It is no longer good enough to issue findings on individual systems and projects without tracking down the cause of these problems, which are often rooted in insufficient or out-of-date policies and standards. Indeed, today's best internal audit practice includes an ongoing review of all policies and standards to see that they are appropriate and up-to-date and that they provide a good control framework to manage change, including the acquisition of new systems and technologies.

Thus this book will be of major assistance to internal auditors in their ongoing efforts to add value to the organization they serve, helping them evaluate and recommend improvements to information security policies and standards.

External auditors

External auditors need to evaluate the control environment of a company in carrying out an audit under generally accepted auditing standards. This can often include the review of policies and standards, which have a major impact on all controls as they contain the principles and practices under which all detailed internal controls are designed and maintained.

Further, a review of information security policies and standards will often enable the external auditor to make value-added suggestions and recommendations to the client.

Management consultants

More and more companies are turning to an outside consultant, not just to help them with individual projects but to put in a framework of policies and standards that will help the company manage matters more effectively on an ongoing basis. This book will be of considerable help to management consultants as they assist clients to create or improve their information security policies, standards and processes.

Chapter 1

Focusing the goals of information security

For every organization and its senior management, the goal of securing information assets is a vital concern. It is also one of the fastest growing corporate costs. As organizations make greater use of information systems to conduct and account for business activities, they become more reliant on the continuing availability and integrity of computerized data. As computer technology reduces the layers of administration and approval authorities, individual employees are empowered. Threats to information assets are on the rise and opportunities to commit fraud and profit from it are increasing. So are the number of people who have the knowledge to commit malicious acts that could destroy files and programs.

Throughout this book, the focus is on the development of senior management's insights and strategies for securing information assets in an increasingly complex environment. Ultimately, the book is designed to help you learn proven principles for obtaining the right amount of security at the right price.

This chapter provides an overview of information security and the various key elements that need to be addressed as part of a corporate-wide approach to data security structures and architectures. It is specifically directed at enhancing your conceptual understanding of information security. With this knowledge, you can maximize the benefits to be gleaned throughout the book and more important, develop winning strategies for determining the level of data security that your or your client's organization requires.

The last section of this chapter provides a succinct but high level overview of information security from a technical point of view, including the particular challenges of the Internet and an organization's Intranet. Of course, it is not the role or responsibility of senior management to deal "hands-on" with technical matters. However, a conceptual understanding of the technical aspects of information security is essential groundwork for making the best overall management decisions and communicating and working with information systems management.

This chapter discusses the principles:

1.1 Senior management should view information security from an overall perspective, recognizing its contribution in achieving the organization's broader goals.

1.2 Information security should be viewed as a part of the overall system of internal control.

1.3 The access rights and privileges of customers and other third parties should be adequately controlled.

1.4 The differences between data and information should be recognized and provided for in the information security policy.

1.5 "Believed systems" must be recognized and carefully provided for from an information security perspective.

1.6 As the organization's dependency on information security evolves and grows, the information security policies and standards must be periodically revisited and strengthened where necessary.

1.7 Information security should be viewed from a customer's perspective to ensure the organization provides the security and ease of use the customer expects when dealing with the organization electronically.

1.8 Senior management should obtain an executive level understanding of basic security principles to ensure security issues are addressed in a consistent and logical manner and in keeping with broader corporate issues and goals.

1.9 Senior management should have a basic understanding of the Internet and its security challenges and opportunities.

The basic goals of information security

Quality information systems and quality data and information are vital to the achievement of many key corporate goals. Information security is one of the keys to achieving this quality.

Information security should be responsive to the needs of both customers and employees and cover all of the organization's information systems processes, whether these processes are performed by customers, employees or computer programmers. Information security must be dealt with, whether the organization operates the systems or delegates their operation to an outside service bureau or facilities manager. In all instances, the organization should achieve a proper balance amongst the need to protect information assets, the costs of information security and the relative ease of access which customers and employees require. As shown in the exhibit below, all of these factors interact with each other and need to be brought into balance within each business process.

Exhibit 1.1

Balanced information security

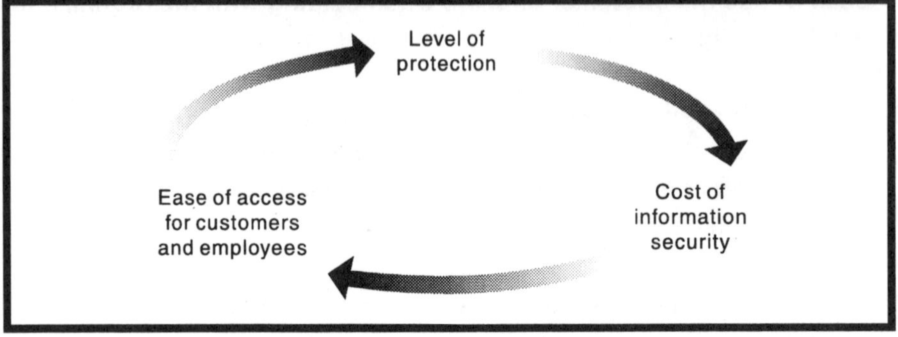

As we strengthen information security, we tend to drive up costs and make it more time-consuming for customers and employees to obtain the access they require. On the other hand, spending too little on information security or providing overly simple means to access the system can result in loss of security.

More than an insurance policy

In many ways, information security is like an insurance policy: *We need the right amount of coverage at the right cost.* Similarly, for each business process, we need to determine the amount or degree of information security we require. Too much security wastes money and creates inconvenience; too little runs the risk of unacceptable losses to the organization's financial health, its reputation as a stable supplier and its ability to serve customers.

But information security is much more than mere insurance; it is part and parcel of the goods and services we sell and a key element of competitive advantage.

Direct benefits of information security

Information security can provide many important benefits to the organization. It can serve to:

- protect the organization's large investment in information assets, including confidentiality of information and competitive advantage

- promote quality assurance, ensuring that only authorized individuals can perform or approve certain acts and transactions
- support competitive advantage by allowing customers to transact business with the organization electronically in an acceptably secure manner
- reduce administrative costs by providing a secure environment that permits the organization to computerize controls and functions and empower individuals, and
- enable the organization to deliver quality service by ensuring that information needed by customers and employees is readily available with a minimum amount of "administrative interference".

Indeed, as the computer environment increases in complexity with each passing day, securing information has become vitally important to an organization's very survival. More succinctly, the exhibit below outlines the goals of information security.

Exhibit 1.2

Putting information security through its PACES

The right amount of information security can help the organization:

P **Protect** information assets. Ensure the value and availability of the organization's data and information.

A **Assure** quality. Ensure the right things are done by the right people, those who have the requisite skills and authority.

C **Compete**. Support competitive advantage by protecting confidentiality yet allowing customers and other third parties to deal with the organization in a relatively easy and secure manner.

E **Eliminate** unnecessary expense through careful consideration and balancing of risk and the amount of security actually required.

S **Serve** customers. Good information security is part of the goods and services we sell when customers can easily do business with us electronically in a secure manner.

The last point, related to service, is highly important. Without proper information security, we will not be able to communicate electronically with our customers or be able to do business with them electronically.

Thus, inadequate information security puts the organization at a competitive disadvantage. On the other hand, good information security *enables* the organization to provide a host of information electronically to the market place and to transact business electronically.

With the growth of electronic commerce, we need to have information security that enables us to do as much, if not more, electronically than our competitors.

This area is of such importance that it is discussed in detail later on in this chapter under Principles 3 and 7.

THE FIRST PRINCIPLE

1.1 Senior management should view information security from an overall perspective, recognizing its contribution in achieving the organization's broader goals.

As stated in the introduction, information security is a means to an end and not an end in itself. In a very real sense, we need to ensure that all information used to conduct and manage the business, to form part of the goods and services sold, to receive and disburse money and to protect assets is authentic and continuously available. We want to protect this information from unauthorized alteration, whether by accident or on purpose, and maintain our competitive advantage and the confidence of our customers by protecting confidentiality. Information security is the primary means to accomplish these goals.

Defining and communicating information security needs

We have seen that information security should be an integral part of all of our business processes. This requires that the role of information security in meeting corporate objectives be understood by all departments throughout the organization. It also requires that many departments work together to design and implement effective information security. As always, the role of senior management is to see that the right things get done the right way. It is senior management who should ensure that:

- information security requirements are set from an overall business perspective by those who are responsible for running the business
- an organizational structure is in place that can effectively and efficiently meet these requirements, and
- all departments understand their roles and responsibilities in defining, implementing and successfully managing information security on a day-to-day basis.

Information security contributes to all of the organization's goals for information. As explained below, sometimes it is the primary way to achieve the goal; other times, it is only a contributing factor, albeit a significant one.

STRATEGIES
FOR SUCCESS

Good information security provides much more than security. It also makes a significant contribution to quality assurance, competitive advantage and cost control.

Senior management should establish appropriate policies to promote the development and implementation of effective information security.

Purpose of information security

The basic purpose of information security is to ensure that data, information and programs can only be read, added to or altered by authorized persons using authorized programs. Through its information security, the organization seeks to ensure that:

- the operating systems, applications, and information are protected against unauthorized alteration

- the computer processes and information are continuously available to help conduct and manage the business, and
- should a disaster occur, these can be recovered within an acceptable time frame.

The degree of protection afforded, and thus its cost, should be commensurate with the importance of the information and technology process to the organization. Put another way, the amount of information security should be proportionate to the damage the organization would suffer should confidentiality or integrity be compromised. Damage includes loss of customer confidence or ability to provide service, financial loss and loss of competitive advantage should others gain access to the organization's data and business plans.

STRATEGIES
FOR SUCCESS

The management responsible for each business process must have the primary responsibility to define and communicate the nature and degree of information security they require.

The importance of information security in achieving goals

Against this overall background, we can now look at how information security contributes to the achievement of the traditional goals all organizations have for their information. The table below lists each of these goals and indicates the contribution information security makes to achieving it. These are then discussed in detail as follows.

With reference to the chart, in weighing a goal's importance:

- low indicates that there is a role for information security, but it is supportive only – the goal is basically achieved by other means
- medium indicates that information security makes a significant contribution to the goal, and
- high indicates that the goal is primarily, but not exclusively, achieved through information security.

Exhibit 1.3

Information security and the achievement of corporate goals

The goal	Description	Information security contribution
Quality assurance	computer sites, systems and the data and the information they contain have been subjected to defined quality assurance processes	medium
Completeness	data (and the information derived from it) reflects all events and transactions the organization has entered into	low
Accuracy	data (and the information derived from it) has the degree of accuracy needed for *all* the purposes it is used for	low
Timeliness	data is recorded promptly	none to low
Authorization	the recording of data and information and access to it are restricted to those authorized	high
Privacy and confidentiality	the competitive advantage that an organization has in its data and information is appropriately protected by restricting access to it; customers' expectations regarding privacy and confidentiality are respected	low, medium, or high, depending on the specific business of the organization
Authentication	the identity of the person or party accessing data is reasonably assured and can be subsequently determined	high
Continuity and availability	computer systems and the information they contain will be available as required to conduct and manage the business	high
Logicality	computer systems function correctly to produce logical data and information in accordance with specifications	medium

Let's now examine each of these information security goals in greater depth.

Quality assurance

Information security and the achievement of corporate goals		
Quality assurance	computer sites, systems and the data and the information they contain have been subjected to defined quality assurance processes	medium

In the context of this book, quality assurance is concerned with computer sites, systems, networks and programs and the information they contain or create. There are, of course, many procedures required to properly manage quality assurance.

Information security reinforces the quality assurance procedures by ensuring that:

- changes to all systems and application software as well as changes to networks go through quality assurance procedures, and
- computer sites are managed to protect data integrity and reasonably assure continuity and availability.

In other words, information security is used to make sure that all changes of defined types are forced through a "quality assurance gateway" where a quality assurance function can take steps to ensure the change has been subjected to the entirety of the organization's quality assurance process, before the change is put into operation. This is basically achieved by requiring a separate password in the possession of a change control group to be used to put all changes into actual use.

In practice, adherence to quality assurance processes is much higher when it is enforced through information security processes.

Information security also plays a large role in ensuring the quality of information. As explained below, quality of data can be thought of in terms of its completeness, accuracy, timeliness and other factors, for all of which information security makes some kind of contribution.

Completeness

Information security and the achievement of corporate goals		
Completeness	data (and the information derived from it) reflects all events and transactions the organization has entered into	low

Completeness is basically achieved by establishing a set of internal control procedures that help ensure that all transactions and events that the organization enters into are captured and then recorded. The key controls that help achieve this goal include:

- assigning responsibility for initiating and then recording transactions
- using batch controls and balancing
- agreeing control totals to the total of detailed records, and
- other "people-performed" procedures.[1]

The fundamental contribution of information security to completeness is in ensuring captured data is not lost or altered once it has been recorded. This is accomplished by ensuring that data can only be changed or deleted by the owners (usually the originators) of the data, and thus cannot be altered by others, including the information systems department and people outside the organization such as hackers.

1 Further information on these and other procedures that help ensure the completeness, accuracy and timeliness of data can be found in the CICA publication *Managing and Controlling Small Computer Systems Including LANs*, also written by Jim Gaston. The means of obtaining complete, accurate and timely data are the same regardless of the size of the computer system or the size of the organization.

Accuracy

Information security and the achievement of corporate goals		
Accuracy	data (and the information derived from it) has the degree of accuracy needed for *all* the purposes it is used for	low

The contribution of information security to accuracy goals is very much the same as that for completeness. It ensures:

- information can only be created or altered by those with the knowledge to do so correctly and only by using authorized application programs.

The concept of authorized application programs is essential to achieving these goals.

Generally speaking, authorized programs are the application programs of the organization. These applications can and should be designed to produce control reports or listings of transactions and other data recorded so that accuracy may be reviewed and checked if considered necessary. As well, applications frequently have built-in edit routines that can check data for accuracy and completeness. We want generally to ensure that all data is recorded through the use of these applications, rather than by other means. In this way, we know that the data has gone through tested applications which accurately record all data submitted and produce the necessary control reports such as transaction lists or batch controls for manual checking and internal control.

Authorized application programs are in contrast to special systems software programs or utilities that can be used to add or alter data in an uncontrolled way. These special or utility programs have the power to alter or add data of any type or format in any file or database. They do not contain any edit routines and usually do not produce any control listings describing the nature and extent of the data that has been added or altered.

As we shall see later on in the book, it is necessary to have special systems or utility software programs available to deal with emergencies or to handle technical problems that cannot be effectively resolved by other means. However, their use should be tightly restricted and controlled.

Information security also contributes to accuracy through the enforcement of the quality control process for new programs and changes to existing programs. This can include making all changes to programs go through a "change control door" that is staffed and guarded by a quality assurance function (typically information systems personnel), as well as making sure that all testing of new and amended programs has been satisfactorily performed before they are put into use. In this way, management can gain assurance that programs function in accordance with specifications.

Timeliness

Information security and the achievement of corporate goals		
Timeliness	data is recorded promptly	none to low

The goal of timeliness is to ensure that:

- the information itself is recorded and made available on a sufficiently timely basis.

This is quite different than availability, discussed below, which revolves around the systems' and the data's availability for use.

Information security has little, if anything, to do with the timeliness of data. This goal is achieved through the design of real time or online computer systems as required in conjunction with people-performed procedures that help ensure that all transactions are promptly recorded.

Authorization

Information security and the achievement of corporate goals		
Authorization	the recording of data and information and access to it are restricted to those authorized	high

This, of course, is one of the major reasons why information security exists. The authorization process should be designed to ensure that:

- all accesses to information, whether to add or alter data or merely to read or copy it, are restricted to authorized individuals, and
- each individual can only access the information needed to perform his or her job. (Or each customer can only record or view information in accordance with the access rights defined for that customer.)

From an information security point of view, all accesses to data are "*transactions*", including accesses that are only to read or copy data. This broader view of access and transactions is necessary to ensure that confidentiality issues are addressed.

"Extra transactions" are one of the most difficult challenges in information security. For example, say Mr. X has the authority, and thus the access rights via his password, to enter purchase invoices into the system. Nothing in the information security process itself prevents Mr. X from accidentally or purposefully recording additional purchases that are fictitious or altered. No piece of paper or form is required to input data. Thus, by the very nature of his job and the access rights he has been given, Mr. X is in a perfect position to enter "extra transactions." Research has shown that a majority of computer frauds occur at the input stage due to this "extra transaction" problem.

The problem is very broad in scope. It exists for *each and every type of transaction* that the organization has, i.e., cash receipts, credit notes, sales invoices, journal entries, adjustments, cheque requisitions, etc. It also applies to data and transactions which at first glance may not appear to have financial consequences, such as names and addresses of suppliers, employees and other parties. But these are used to prepare and mail cheques. The problem also exists for customer-initiated transactions, discussed under the third principle in this chapter.

Extra transactions also are a problem from a confidentiality perspective. Employees who are authorized to read information may, simply out of curiosity, browse records of customers or other employees. Or, these employees may be selling copies of client lists, sales data and business plans to competitors for cash bribes.

While information security can provide some control over extra transactions, these concerns need to be covered as part of the overall system of internal control. The three-step and best defense is to ensure that:

- the system logs each transaction and the password used so that accountability is fixed and there is a trail of who has done what
- each application prints out a list of all transactions that have been recorded, either for review by someone else and/or for balancing with a previously determined control total established before the transactions were handed over for data capture, and
- a proper division of duties exists that prevents individuals who are authorized to record transactions from being responsible for initiating those transactions.

In all cases, recorded transactions should be reviewed and/or balanced to independent control totals by someone else, or equivalent procedures applied.

These procedures are generally only employed for the recording and alteration of data. Their extension to cover the reading or copying of data is administratively burdensome and is used only in the most unusual or demanding of circumstances. This is one reason why we say below that information security, in many instances, only makes a small contribution towards privacy and confidentiality.

STRATEGIES
FOR SUCCESS

Information security by itself will not prevent employees, customers and other third parties from making "extra transactions", those which are additional but unauthorized transactions of the type and nature the system allows them to do. There must be other procedures in the system of internal control to prevent or quickly detect and act upon such transactions.

Privacy and confidentiality

Information security and the achievement of corporate goals		
Privacy and confidentiality	the competitive advantage that an organization has in its data and information is appropriately protected by restricting access to it; customers' expectations regarding privacy and confidentiality are respected	low, medium, or high, depending on the specific business of the organization

The contribution information security makes to achieving the organization's objectives for privacy and confidentiality will vary from low to high, depending on the specific business of the organization.

Specifically, privacy and confidentiality include:

- restraining access to information which would harm the competitive position of the company should it become available to others, and
- meeting the expectation of customers and other third parties as well as employees that data concerning them will only be used for the purpose for which it was supplied and will otherwise remain confidential.

In many jurisdictions around the world, laws concerning privacy are currently under development or firmly established. Thus another dimension of confidentiality is that senior management should ensure there are processes in place to ensure the organization is fulfilling its legal responsibilities.

Privacy and confidentiality are challenging areas in which to create a balance between information security on the one hand and ease of access and cost control on the other. First, there are many more accesses to information to read or copy it than there are accesses to change or add to it. While many employees need access to create or alter data, many more employees need what is called "read access" to systems. Many employees and indeed members of management want access to an entire database for information purposes or want copies of this data on their local area networks or even portable lap tops for financial and business analysis purposes.

When it comes to the ability to record or alter data, most companies are willing to pay the costs of controlling access very tightly and to put in additional procedures to guard against the extra transactions we just discussed. But it is unusual for organizations to go to the trouble and expense of logging all "read accesses" to data and then having procedures in place to review them to see if each access or copying of data is necessary and justified. Even if we performed such procedures, they would not provide any control over how the data was used once it had been read or copied. The risk often does not seem to justify this cost, especially considering how widespread and frequently read accesses are used. Thus for privacy and confidentiality, we tend to rely more on preventative controls such as the use of passwords to restrict who can read what data or information.

Overall approaches which may be valuable include looking for employees who seem to be accessing data more frequently than needed and tightly restricting read accesses to specially sensitive records such as management remuneration, sales data for the organization's largest customers, etc.

The most common approach to protecting critically sensitive data is, of course, to tightly and rigorously restrict access to information such as business plans, budgets, trade secrets etc. If necessary, this data can be placed on stand-alone microcomputers which have no network connections and access to this hardware and software can be physically restricted through location, locks and normal password safeguards.

STRATEGIES
FOR SUCCESS

It is important to carefully think through the mechanisms, if any, which an organization may need to monitor the actions of employees and others who are reading or copying computerized information.

As it is difficult to monitor "read access" to data, extra care should be taken to limit the number of people who can read or copy sensitive information.

Authentication

Information security and the achievement of corporate goals		
Authentication	the identity of the person or party accessing data is reasonably assured and can be subsequently determined	high

Authentication revolves around determining the degree of certainty required as to the identification of the individual who is making or requesting a particular transaction. Keep in mind that the concept of a transaction includes reading or copying data as well as accesses by third parties and employees.

Authentication is important from two points of view. First, the more certain we are that the access requester is genuine, the more secure our systems and data are. Second, today a lot of business is transacted computer to computer. In this way, organizations allow customers to initiate their own transactions. The user authentication process may need to be strong enough to prove that a particular third party authorized or initiated a transaction so that collection or acceptance of the results can be enforced. However, as we increase authentication procedures, we drive up costs and indeed customer inconvenience.

In reality, the approach needs to be a balancing act that takes into account:

- the need for customers and third parties to feel there is enough security that they are willing to transact with us electronically
- the need to avoid an excessive security process that is so inconvenient that it could drive customers to competitors, and
- the need to balance all the above plus related costs to the need we have to positively identify individuals or our ability to accept losses in event of a dispute.

We have all experienced the other side of these matters when we use our ATM/debit cards or telephone calling cards. As senior management, we now have to turn this point of view around to determine our organization's security needs.

Authentication is a key matter to address as electronic commerce will continue to increase. We have to think about electronic commerce, including electronic data interchange, electronic funds transfer, just-in-time inventory systems, the ability of customers to initiate transactions with us through the telephone (sometimes termed "telephony") and, of course, the rapidly growing use of the Internet.

Whether for employees or third parties, the basic approach to authentication is to provide each individual with a unique password. However, our password structures and standards can be set to provide varying levels of certainty that we have "verified" the user. But no matter how well we set them and manage them, passwords are subject to limitations. They can be lost, stolen or shared. They can be guessed or intercepted. For these reasons, we may need to bolster our password safeguards by combining them with other techniques, such as smart cards, one time passwords, biometric devices that identify the user's voice or fingerprint, or the use of encryption including non-repudiation signatures.

STRATEGIES
FOR SUCCESS

The approach used to authenticate an individual's identity inside or outside the company has to balance costs and ease of use on the one hand with the need to appropriately authenticate users and restrict losses on the other. Senior management must take the lead in balancing these factors and in communicating their requirements.

Losses arising from disputes and concessions to customers and other third parties as to the transactions they have initiated electronically need to be captured and reviewed. In addition, authentication methods must be continuously reviewed in the light of these costs, recognizing that passwords alone may not be sufficient.

Continuity and availability

Information security and the achievement of corporate goals		
Continuity and availability	computer systems and the information they contain will be available as required to conduct and manage the business	high

All of our systems and data are of little value unless they are available to help us conduct and manage the business. These objectives address:

- how continuously in a given business day we need to be assured that our systems and data are available, and
- in the event of a disaster, determining how long we can survive without our systems before we suffer unacceptable consequences, and procedures to ensure our computer resources and data can be replaced or restored within acceptable time frames.

Availability relates to the risk of day-to-day operations in the computer site. As problems can and do occur in the routine operations of the computer and its programs and files, systems and data can be unavailable for short periods of time during individual days. Senior management should define their needs in this regards, both in terms of how long such "outages" can last as well as how frequently they can be tolerated. Invariably, as we reduce the time period for outages and decrease the likelihood of this problem occurring, costs rise. Senior management needs to be involved directly in stating the needs of the business and in balancing these factors.

Continuity refers to the need of the business to recover its information systems capabilities in the event of a major disaster to one or more computer sites. This is referred to as disaster recovery planning. Once again, it is incumbent upon senior management to define the time period within which the organization must be able to recover its computer capabilities. Of course, the shorter the time of recovery, the greater the cost of disaster recovery arrangements.

STRATEGIES
FOR SUCCESS

Information security policies should cover the needs for continuity and availability of the organization's information systems and the information they contain.

Logicality

Information security and the achievement of corporate goals		
Logicality	computer systems function correctly to produce logical data and information in accordance with specifications	medium

This goal was already discussed under quality assurance but there is another important factor that must be managed: Computer programs, like people, create, read and record data. *This means that access to computer programs, in the sense of changing programs that exist or putting new programs into use, is in fact access to data.* Thus we need a set of procedures to control access to the computer programs themselves as part of our overall information security efforts.

The basic thought to keep in mind is that while computer programs are often written to help record data, computer programs can also be written to create or change data without any human intervention. Thus we need to make sure that computer programs are logical and correct through a quality assurance process.

The ability of programs to create and alter data, if properly used, is a highly important and efficient function. It is by this means that we create and calculate sales invoice values and produce salary payrolls and cheques from data that has already been stored. But like any other capability, it can be used for malevolent purposes. Consider the following types of instructions that can be easily written into any computer program:

- if the employee number is xxx, then multiply the salary by 2
- if the vendor number is yyy, change the payee name on the printer spool, used to print the cheque, to John Brown, and

- if the date on the computer's clock is 06/06/96, then erase the database.

These are just some examples of how programs can be used both to commit fraud and to perform malicious acts.

STRATEGIES
FOR SUCCESS

Information security policies and standards need to reflect the reality that computer programs create, record and alter data. Information cannot be secured unless all programs are secured as well.

THE SECOND PRINCIPLE

1.2 Information security should be viewed as a part of the overall system of internal control.

Like beauty, internal control and its purpose is in the eye of the beholder. For an accountant, comptroller or financial auditor, internal control is a series of processes and procedures designed to safeguard assets and to ensure complete and accurate accounting records. And of course, information integrity is part of this process. For general management, internal control helps ensure that staff adhere to corporate policies in accepting and managing business events and all information of any type is sufficiently reliable for its intended purposes.

Thus it is evident that the goals of internal control systems are much broader than simply ensuring the integrity of information. Indeed, in the discussion above we saw that information security by itself is *not* sufficient to achieve these goals.

It follows from all of this that information security is *part of a system of internal control* and therefore it should be designed to fit into an overall internal control framework. Put another way, it is an integral part of an overall business process.

Furthermore, we cannot have effective policies and procedures for information security unless there are policies for the design, implementation and day-to-day management of overall internal controls!

For example, one of the major goals of information security is to limit the access rights of all employees to those that they require to perform their jobs. In other words, it enforces an overall division of duties within the organization. But how can we do this unless we have already decided, as part of our overall internal control design, who is allowed to initiate, record, read, approve or balance transactions for a particular business function? And how do we decide on this division of duties unless we have designed the overall internal controls for this business function and its transactions?

The discussion at the end of this chapter underscores that there is no such thing as a perfect or truly secure set of information security controls. No matter how well information security is designed, there will always be a handful of individuals doing key technical jobs who are in a position to do damage, either accidentally or purposefully. A truly completely secure information process would be so tightly controlled that customers and employees could not make use of it without unacceptable inconvenience. Moreover, the cost of such an environment would be prohibitive.

Amazingly, a number of large and sophisticated organizations do not have any policy framework for the design of internal controls. There is no policy setting forth who is responsible for the overall design of internal controls for each area or business process. There is no framework defining the role of various departments such as finance, accounting, information systems and the department in charge of the business area in defining, designing, implementing and managing internal controls. Perhaps it is for these reasons that so many organizations are struggling with the concepts of corporate governance. The key concept is: The organization should first address the design and effective implementation of overall internal control processes; internal control is the bedrock on which corporate governance is based.

STRATEGIES
FOR SUCCESS

Effective corporate governance requires the design and effective implementation of overall internal control processes.

Often when we set out to create or improve information security policies and standards, we must deal with a host of issues that should have already been addressed through policies on internal control.

It is well beyond the scope of this book to explain how to address corporate governance issues or how to create and implement overall policies for internal control. However, the process would have many similarities with that described in this book for information security, but would, of course, be applied with a wider view.

STRATEGIES
FOR SUCCESS

Information security for any business process is only part of an overall system of internal control for that process.

The goal in designing information security is to minimize the total costs of the security procedures, including the losses which the organization shall inevitably incur.

Information security should be created, designed and implemented in harmony with the policies and procedures within the organization for the design and implementation of overall internal control systems.

An organization should ideally have a framework of established policies and standards for the design of overall systems of internal control before seeking to create or amend its policies and practices on information security. Where this does not exist, such control policies should be created whenever possible, often as a key element in the overall corporate governance process.

THE THIRD PRINCIPLE

1.3 The access rights and privileges of customers and other third parties should be adequately controlled.

An organization has to manage all of the information it uses, no matter how it is obtained. Thus, accountability must be fixed for all data, including data that is initiated or recorded by customers. In turn, this means that responsibility for defining and managing the access rights given to customers and other third parties should also be fixed.

The previous discussion examined the importance of authenticating identity when customers and other third parties initiate or record transactions. It is equally important to have a process to review and monitor the transactions they initiate. This responsibility should be allocated and discharged and as part of information security.

Like many other control goals, those of review and monitoring are usually accomplished by both software and people-performed controls. The software-performed controls usually include edit routines that limit the size of individual transactions or total transactions per day that a third party can initiate. Software can also look for patterns of abnormal activity in third party initiated activities and either cut the customer off or issue a warning for some employee to investigate. Larger value transactions can be reported for individual human review and approval before they are accepted and acted upon. This may include contacting the customer directly.

We have all experienced these kinds of controls when we use ATM, debit or credit cards. Such procedures, albeit in a different form, are common controls for well designed EDI (electronic data interchange) systems so that the organization does not inadvertently act on false sales orders or orders that are wrong due to data capture errors by customers.

The frequency and variety of these kinds of third party computer interactions will continue to grow. In order to have any degree of utility and longevity, an information security policy should address these computer to computer interactions. For example, in addition to today's EDI and EFT (electronic funds transfer) transactions, organizations may soon have to deal with orders or transactions received through E-mail and the Internet or initiated by customers through telephony, if they are not already doing so.

An important consideration is whether our present computer hardware and software have the necessary security capabilities to support electronic commerce, including the positive identification of the customer and the ability to provide supporting evidence to settle disputes as to whether the transaction requests were genuine. The hardware and software should also be capable of providing the necessary level of protection against hacking.

All of this supports the importance of the following strategy for success.

STRATEGIES
FOR SUCCESS

Responsibility must be assigned for the integrity of all customer-initiated transactions and data, including responsibility for determining customer access rights and privileges and for reviewing transactions in total or individually as required.

Appropriate use should be made of the capabilities of software to monitor transactions individually and in total for patterns that could indicate errors or fraudulent activities of hackers.

THE FOURTH PRINCIPLE

1.4 The differences between data and information should be recognized and provided for in the information security policy.

Recognizing and providing for the differences between data and information are very important aspects of designing an effective overall system of information security.

From a security point of view, data can be thought of as individual pieces that enable us to conduct individual business transactions or manage individual economic events, for example, a particular sales order, sales invoice, the wage rate or job category for a particular employee or the number of units of inventory on hand for one particular product. Clearly, all of this data is primarily used to conduct business with third parties or to manage individual economic events on a day-to-day basis.

On the other hand, information can be thought of as aggregated data that is used *not* to conduct business but rather to manage the business and make overall business decisions. For example, we summarize sales orders into overall sales information to help monitor sales results and to set sales and marketing targets and strategies; we summarize inventory quantities and values to help us manage supplier relations and inventory levels, etc.

Of course, all of the information we use does not come from aggregating data, but a key part of it does.

Overall, data is used to enter into transactions and conduct business day-by-day and information is used for management decision-making purposes. Because information in large part is derived from data, we need reliable data to have reliable information, but the converse is not true. Furthermore, to the extent information is derived from data, if it is incorrectly altered or accidentally destroyed, the underlying data still exists and the information can be re-generated.

From the above, it is clear that the relative importance of the goals discussed earlier is different for data than for information. Of course, all of the goals are relevant to both data and information; it is the relative weight of their importance that differs.

Exhibit 1.4

Data versus information

Data	Information
• used to enter into transactions and conduct business day-by-day • includes economic events • critical goals: completeness, accuracy, integrity, availability.	• used for management decision-making purposes, e.g., reports • can be re-generated from data if its integrity is lost • source of competitive advantage • critical goals: confidentiality, availability, appropriateness.

Data

We have to tightly control who can add or amend data and ensure data is accurate and in balance. These controls are essential because we will use this data to pay or receive money, to enter into transactions with third parties or to keep track of our assets. We are also highly concerned about data availability because if our data and supporting systems are not available, the organization may lose track of its assets or be unable to serve customers promptly on a continuous basis.

However, while we have to respect the valid privacy concerns of our customers, a loss of confidentiality concerning a few sales orders or some customer data (as distinct from someone obtaining a copy of our entire sales database from which they can generate information) is a relatively lesser concern.

Information

With information, we need to be highly concerned about confidentiality. When we have information or access to an entire database to create it, then we are dealing with competitive advantage and information which must be kept confidential. We are less concerned with the availability of the information as we can always re-create it from the underlying data. We are less concerned about restricting the ability to change the information, as anyone doing so maliciously would unlikely be able to benefit from such a change. Even if this did occur, once again, the information can be re-created.

Thus our major, as distinct from only, concern surrounding information is one of privacy and confidentiality. This is an important distinction, as microcomputers and their local hard drives (i.e., the hard drive built into the microcomputer itself) usually contain information rather than the official data of the organization. Alternatively, executives dialling in to the host systems in an organization are usually only given access to information and not to data.

The above discussion relates to information which we have created and which can be re-created from data. But there are other kinds of information such as word processing documents, E-mail, etc. With these kinds of information, we should pay more attention to the other goals described earlier in this chapter. Of special concern is its availability; we do not want to have this valuable information lost or destroyed. The best way to ensure its availability is to store it all on a local area network, or LAN, which then can be properly backed up by the LAN administrator.

From all of the above, we can derive an important concept. We should have a defined "corporate" repository for all data and for all information that cannot be derived from data. This gives us a source that we can always go back to re-generate any information that becomes lost or loses its integrity.

In our discussions throughout the following chapters, we will use the word "information" to refer to not just information but also the data from which it is derived.

STRATEGIES
FOR SUCCESS

The computer sites where the organization's data resides should be properly secured with regard to all the goals for the integrity of data.

For computer sites, systems and microcomputers that contain only information that can be re-generated from the underlying data, information security centres around privacy and confidentiality concerns.

THE FIFTH PRINCIPLE

1.5 "Believed systems" must be recognized and carefully provided for from an information security perspective.

A "believed system" is one where we transact business based solely on information supplied by our computer applications and do no further checking before entering into a transaction or exchanging funds. In some cases, we may view the verification that might be done by a third party as part of our system of internal controls. We believe that the potential error rates are so low that the financial loss and inconvenience are more than offset by the administrative savings we gain. As consumers and customers, we may also trust the system of another party as a believed system. The following example expands on this concept.

The bank systems that support the use of ATM machines are a good example of believed systems. If the bank's database shows that you have sufficient funds on hand to support a withdrawal, then you are given the money. No further checking is done by the bank in regard to your withdrawal; if the computer records say that you have the money, then it is provided to you.

The bank does this for two reasons. First, the ready access to funds is a major convenience to the customer. Second, the process significantly reduces the bank's administrative costs. The bank does not pay a teller to count the money for you. You do the data capture for the bank and through a service charge, you actually pay the bank for this privilege. Of course, the banks do incur fraud losses through their ATMs, but these are offset by the cost savings.

Note also that the bank limits its risks in these regards. Knowing that cards do get stolen and frauds do occur, the software limits the amount of cash a customer can withdraw in any one day to typically $1,000. In addition, the bank's systems may be able to look for patterns of unusually high withdrawals from a particular customer over a number of days or from a particular ATM machine in a short time frame.

Thus the bank has a believed system in its ATM machine software, carefully balanced to maximize the sum total of competitive advantage through enhanced customer convenience, reduced administrative costs and relatively controlled losses.

An organization's believed systems

Most companies have believed systems. A common example is an accounts payable system where the cheques are printed by the computer software and either laser-signed on the printer or put through a cheque signing machine. In other words, organizations have computerized the cheque issuance process and are now willing to pay funds based on the amounts stored in their computer application. Often, the risk is minimized with the requirement that cheques over a certain dollar values be manually signed.

EDI systems, again usually for transactions below a certain dollar value, are also often treated as believed systems. Customers submit orders electronically and the organization's software edits these transactions to determine if they are reasonable and whether the credit limit is sufficient and then proceeds to process or reject the order. Usually, management sees only summaries of such individual orders of a routine nature and, of course, exception reports.

Where believed systems are used, the information security procedures are a much larger and more significant part of internal control. As these transactions or exchanges of assets proceed without further verification, we need greater certainty as to who has access to the system, the means we use to authenticate their identity and the limits of what they can do. We need to be far more careful that there is good information security over the application software itself, as errors in the software are much more likely to cause significant loss before they are detected. Thus we want to make doubly sure that program changes go through all the quality control procedures; information security is the one means to ensure these quality control procedures are followed.

Few of us verify our routine electric bills beyond a cursory review for reasonableness. While an organization may check its telephone bills to ensure that the calls were actually made and that they were made for business purposes, rarely will an organization actually check the correctness of the rates on the bills. In believing in the suppliers' systems, many organizations have severely minimized the procedure of checking the mathematical correctness of purchase invoices from well known suppliers.

When both ourselves and our customers "believe the system", at least to some extent, this means that errors and irregularities can go on for a longer period of time before they are detected. Thus any losses or upsets that do occur tend to be widespread and expensive before they come to light.

STRATEGIES
FOR SUCCESS

Where transactions are accepted or assets exchanged based on computerized data and without further verification, make sure that information security procedures have been designed in light of the greater reliance that is being placed on such a "believed system".

THE SIXTH PRINCIPLE

1.6 As the organization's dependency on information security evolves and grows, the information security policies and standards must be periodically revisited and strengthened where necessary.

Organizations are always looking for ways to gain further competitive advantage from their computer systems. This includes looking for ways to further computerize functions and to interface computer systems with the systems of third parties. It also includes expanded use of electronic commerce. As we succeed in these endeavours, we increase our dependency on information systems and our plans for information security, including disaster recovery arrangements, may become inadequate.

Thus we have to put a process in place that periodically reviews our information security policies and standards, including disaster recovery arrangements. As we add more data that requires a higher level of protection or allow third parties access or increased access to our computer resources, we may need to strengthen our information security in a particular area.

STRATEGIES
FOR SUCCESS

A formal process for periodic reviews of the adequacy of all information security policies and standards should be established and the responsibility for this activity assigned.

The methodologies and processes used to enhance systems should provide for revisiting all information security arrangements for those systems and their data, including disaster recovery arrangements.

THE SEVENTH PRINCIPLE

1.7 Information security should be viewed from a customer's perspective to ensure the organization provides the security and ease of use the customer expects when dealing with the organization electronically.

The importance of this principle has already been introduced earlier, but it is so important it bears highlighting as a separate principle and some more discussion.

All sorts of pressures are causing us to make our computer systems accessible to our customers as this access is part and parcel of the services that we sell. This trend is readily apparent in the banking industry's efforts to offer more and more services through automated teller and banking machines (ATMs and ABMs) and the growing number of ways we can interact with banks to conduct a variety of transactions, both personally and commercially. It is also evident in the growing use of the Internet for providing marketing and other information and doing business transactions. Other examples are the increasing uses of voice response systems and telephony.

Another compelling reason for this growth is cost reduction. Whenever we allow customers to initiate transactions with us electronically, we transfer the data capture costs to the customer and allow customers to directly obtain information on the status of their orders or other transactions with us themselves, rather than tying up our personnel in answering queries. Through this process, we also cut down on the efforts needed to reconcile balances with customers, as there is now little, if any, difference in timing or value of transaction recording.

Assign responsibility

Someone in the organization should be responsible for the access rights of customers and for the integrity of customer-initiated data.

As regards access rights, the responsible person should:

- decide which transactions and information a customer may create or read
- define the administrative process for granting, changing and cancelling customer access rights, and

- define the process for creating contractual arrangements with customers and for approving any exceptions to standard customer contracts.

As regards customer-initiated data, the responsible person accepts these transactions on behalf of the organization. The need to so fix responsibility does not change because this process may be done principally or exclusively for routine transactions of a routine amount by computer software. It does mean that the responsible person should:

- define and be responsible for the adequacy of these software performed procedures
- decide on the level of transactions that require manual intervention and approval before they are accepted
- define software procedures to search for and report unusual transactions and patterns, and
- put a process in place to perform these tasks.

STRATEGIES
FOR SUCCESS

The organization must both recognize and respond to the customers' need for security and ease of use when dealing with the organization electronically. Creating the correct balance between these factors is a critical success factor.

Someone in the organization must be directly responsible for:

- *the nature of access rights for customers and the process for administering customer access, and*
- *the acceptance, integrity and correctness of customer-initiated transactions.*

THE EIGHTH PRINCIPLE

1.8 Senior management should obtain an executive level understanding of basic security principles to ensure security issues are addressed in a consistent and logical manner and in keeping with broader corporate issues and goals.

While it is the job of senior management to set policy and to mobilize the organization to effectively follow it, senior management does not typically perform detailed or technical tasks. However, effective leadership of information security demands a high level *understanding* of the technical tasks involved so that they can appreciate the implications of the policies they set and the standards that are referred to them for approval. Moreover, when senior management has an overall conceptual understanding of the technicalities, it enhances their abilities to communicate effectively with information systems and security specialists.

The following discussion provides a high level overview of the technical aspects of information security and is intended to assist senior management in gaining the perspective they need to set policy and mobilize the organization to address security issues.

The ways that different environments and operating systems implement information security vary as do the quality and level of security protection that different operating systems are able to provide. Thus through necessity, the following discussion is generic and does not necessarily match the way any particular hardware and software systems work. What is most important here is the principles that are illustrated. Generally, these can be implemented in most environments, albeit by using a variety of technical means and different procedures and techniques. Thus an organization should be able to fundamentally implement security on LANs, WANs, midframes and mainframes in the manner suggested by the description given below.[2]

---

[2] Information security for individual microcomputers and laptops is addressed as a separate topic in *Chapter 4* of this book.

Not all operating systems are alike in their ability or functionality to provide a security environment. Often the operating systems have to be supplemented by additional programs (called security software) purchased from third party suppliers. It should be the responsibility of the technical staff in the information systems department to assess the various operating environments and their capability to meet the information security requirements for a particular business function or set of circumstances. Certain kinds of business practices require a higher level of security than certain operating systems can provide, and thus for security reasons, some processes should be placed on different computer hardware which can use an operating system and supplementary logical security software that provides a better security capability. We will return to this topic in the next chapter when we discuss enterprise architectures and data security architectures in greater detail.

Physical and logical security

Before launching into the high level overview of the technical issues, we'll first examine two foundation terms you've likely heard security specialists mention: physical security and logical security.

Physical security relates to controlling access to the computer site and its peripheral equipment as well as the disks and tapes that are stored there. Its purpose is to protect computers and files against accidental or purposeful physical damage or theft. Thus physical security is mainly concerned with the goal of availability.

Logical security refers to the use of operating systems and security software to restrict and control access to the actual data and programs. This logical security supports all the other goals we have for information as discussed earlier in this chapter.

Logical security is itself a computer program. In some environments, it is part of the operating system and in other environments, it is a separate program. Often information system departments will buy other logical security programs that will work with and strengthen the security functions within the operating system.

Logical security is able to restrict a password holder's rights to one or more of the following three categories or types of access:

- *read access*
  the ability to read the contents of a file, but does not permit you to alter or add to those contents. Note also that if you need to copy a file, then you must have "read" access to that file. The reverse is usually also true – someone who has read access will also have the ability to copy a file.

- *write access*
  the ability to alter the existing contents of a file or add more data to it. In most but not all security software, if you are given the ability to write, you are also given the ability to read.

- *execute privilege*
  the right to execute a particular program but are not the right to read the code within that program or write (i.e., alter) it.

The execute privilege is an important reminder that, from a security point of view, a program is just another file to be defined and protected in much the same way as any other file. And that applies to the operating system and the security software itself and all applications which are also programs. We now get some insight as to why effectively installing logical security is so difficult; the operating systems and security software have to protect themselves!

The operating system itself is all powerful in its ability to perform its functions which include:

- loading programs into memory
- getting the data from databases and files that application programs need to work on
- storing the revised or new data that the application program creates
- creating files or instructions for information to be printed, and
- storing values in internal registers and temporary files to do its work (and these also can be altered!).

All of these functions are needed for the operating system to be able to fulfil its role in tying the central processing unit of the computer together with keyboards, screens, networks, databases, terminals and printers so that the computer can be used. As well, organizations often buy additional programs supplied by a variety of third party vendors to improve the capabilities of the operating system in these regards or to make it operate more efficiently.

Systems software

The operating system and all these additional tools, including databases and telecommunications networking software, are referred to as systems software. From a security point of view, these additional systems software tools often have the same kinds of wide powers and capabilities as the operating system and have to be managed in the same way as the operating system itself. Systems software does not directly perform any business tasks; rather it provides the environment for the applications systems, which perform the real work, to function.

While they can be technically created in many ways, application programs are like people in that they need access rights to do their job.[3] For example, a program that is designed to create sales invoices has to have the ability, i.e., access, to read shipping and pricing data and the ability to write on the sales invoice file.

To understand the power of an operating system and systems software, consider all things you can do on your personal computer through its installed operating system. Whether the platform is DOS, Windows or Windows 95, the operating system allows you to add and delete programs, copy or delete any data or files or use additional utilities that you can install to go directly to any file and change individual characters and numbers, leaving no trail that you have done so. You can also go in and alter the directories, showing a revised date and time for the

---

3 In some systems, these access rights are given to the person who is executing the program rather than to the program itself. When the person enters his or her password, this is shared around the operating system or security software and allows the programs to get at the files it needs. However, conceptually it all comes back to the same thing: From a security point of view, giving the access rights to the person is not as strong as directly giving these rights to the program. When the individual holds these rights, he or she can use other, unauthorized programs to alter data – and this is yet another risk to be managed.

file's creation. All of these capabilities exist to even a greater extent in the more powerful operating systems used on LAN file servers, mid range and large scale computers.

From this discussion, we can see there are many ways in which the data in our systems can be read, written on, or altered. This is summarized in the exhibit below.

Exhibit 1.5

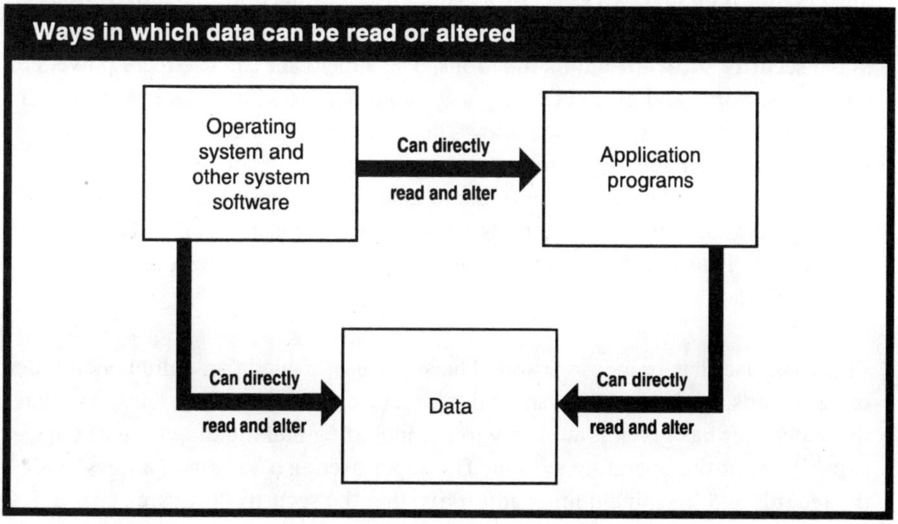

If I think of myself as a hacker, here are some routes I can use to alter data:

- I can use the operating system or systems software to directly alter data, or add new systems software programs that will enable me to do so
- I can alter application programs or add new application programs which will enable me to read, write on or alter data, or
- I can use the existing application programs to fraudulently record transactions or enter adjustments as if I were an employee performing these tasks as part of my job.

As this discussion proceeds, we will see how logical security should prevent me from doing these things. The first step is to see how security software should be used to create passwords.

Whether it is part of the operating system, a separate package or a combination of the two, all systems software sets contain some form of security software. It is the security software that provides the first base layer of logical security.

The super user

To provide a means for setting up and getting jobs done, the security software must permit high level accesses by a "super user". It may be called by various names, but that function always has to be present. The super user has total access to the security software and its functions. The super user can use these powers to create passwords and give access rights to all other individuals and programs. In addition, most security software allows the super user to share some of these powers with other security administrators; for example, another security administrator could be given the rights to hand out passwords and access rights over a particular sub set of programs and files that are used in his or her department. Thus security administration can be either centralized or de-centralized.

The super user has immense power. The super user can add an unlimited number of passwords, each of which can read, write, or execute any file or program that the super user has given it authority to do, including making direct use of the capabilities of the operating system. The super user also has direct access to all the records and logs, including audit trails, that the security software generates. These logs are an important record of who did what with their password at what time. It is through these that we can fix accountability for all accesses and what each password holder has done and investigate actual attempted security violations. But if you have access to these logs, then you can erase the record of any violation or unauthorized activity you may have performed!

Setting up individual access rights

When the super user or some departmental security administrator sets up access rights for an individual, there are typically three ways that individual gains access rights.

First, there is a universal category or group. All users who have a valid password have the access rights included in this universal definition. So, for example, the ability to use the E-mail software might be included in the "universal group" and *all* passwords are defined as belonging to this group. Also, the ability to read marketing material or price lists might be included in this universal group.

Second, security software allows us to define groups and then give access rights to that group. If need be, a person can belong to more than one group. Of course, we need to be vigilant in ensuring that a person is not given conflicting duties from an internal control perspective. So, for example, we might establish a group called "sales order clerks" and anyone who is given this job function can be joined to the sales order clerk group.

It is very important to define groups and decide on access rights by job profile. If this is not done, the task of assigning and administering access rights becomes most unwieldy and time-consuming and we can quickly lose control over who has access to what. This approach is also in keeping with the need, as part of an overall system of internal control, to decide on the division of duties among various job functions. When for a particular system we create a chart of all job functions and the access rights of each job function, this is called an access matrix. We will see in later chapters that access matrices are one of the most important ways in which operating departments communicate their security requirements to systems developers.

This approach also supports the idea of decentralizing security administration. We can limit the ability of departmental administrators so that they are only able to give access rights to employees by assigning them to pre-defined groups. The assignment of additional individual access rights or the creation of new groups would have to come back to the overall data security officer, thus strengthening control over non-routine actions.

Third, individuals can be given additional individual or personal access rights to any other programs or data that they may need to do the job. For example, if a sales order supervisor is also be responsible for preparing summary reports on sales orders, he or she may be given additional rights to execute certain programs that prepare those reports.

Exhibit 1.6

The three types of access for an individual customer or employee
1. Universal category or group – all passwords
2. Defined groups – passwords relate to job functions or particular customer groups
3. Individual or personal – passwords allow additional rights, e.g. access data for report preparation.

Application software and access controls

On closer inspection, we will discover that the overall security software within or attached to the operating system is often only able to restrict the access rights of users at a fairly high level. In other words, at the operating system level, we can restrict an individual to the use of a particular application program. What they can do within a particular application or with a particular database has to be further restricted by the application or database management system in question. In buzzword terms, security is more "granular" or finer at the application system level, meaning that it further restricts what the password holder is able to do.

These more finely-tuned security capabilities often need to be built right into the application programs. Usually they take the form of setting up screens defining the various functions that the application can perform; then the ability of a particular user is restricted by only permitting him or her to access various screens within the application. The following example and the illustration that follows will help to clarify these layers of security.

An example of an access route

The operating system or overall security software examines the password I have entered and sees that I am authorized to use the sales and receivable system. All the operating system can do is determine that I have a valid password to allow me into the system in the first place, and then restrict me to the applications I am allowed to use. What I can do within the application then has to be controlled by the application itself.[4]

The application may require that I enter a separate password once I am in communication with it, or more commonly, the operating system will pass along the password I entered in the first place to the application.

The application (or application software layer) looks at my password and relates it to a table of the screens or functions that I am allowed to access or transactions that I am allowed to perform.

In defining my responsibilities as a sales order clerk, the organization has granted me the authority and thus the access rights to:

- record sales orders
- run reports summarizing sales orders
- read details such as the customer's credit limit but not alter it, and
- read the status of past sales orders so that I can answer customer queries.

My access rights are restricted to the above. I do not have any other capabilities such as the ability to record cash receipts, initiate credit notes, make adjustments to sales prices, etc., as the application software or application layer prevents my accessing these capabilities.

---

[4] Technically, this may also be done by defining transactions to a part of the operating system called a TCP or telecommunications protocol or through a database management system. In terms of logical security, this is all the same. One layer of software decides what applications I can use and then another layer further restricts me to specific transactions or actions within that application.

Exhibit 1.7

Security software – tracking a user's route

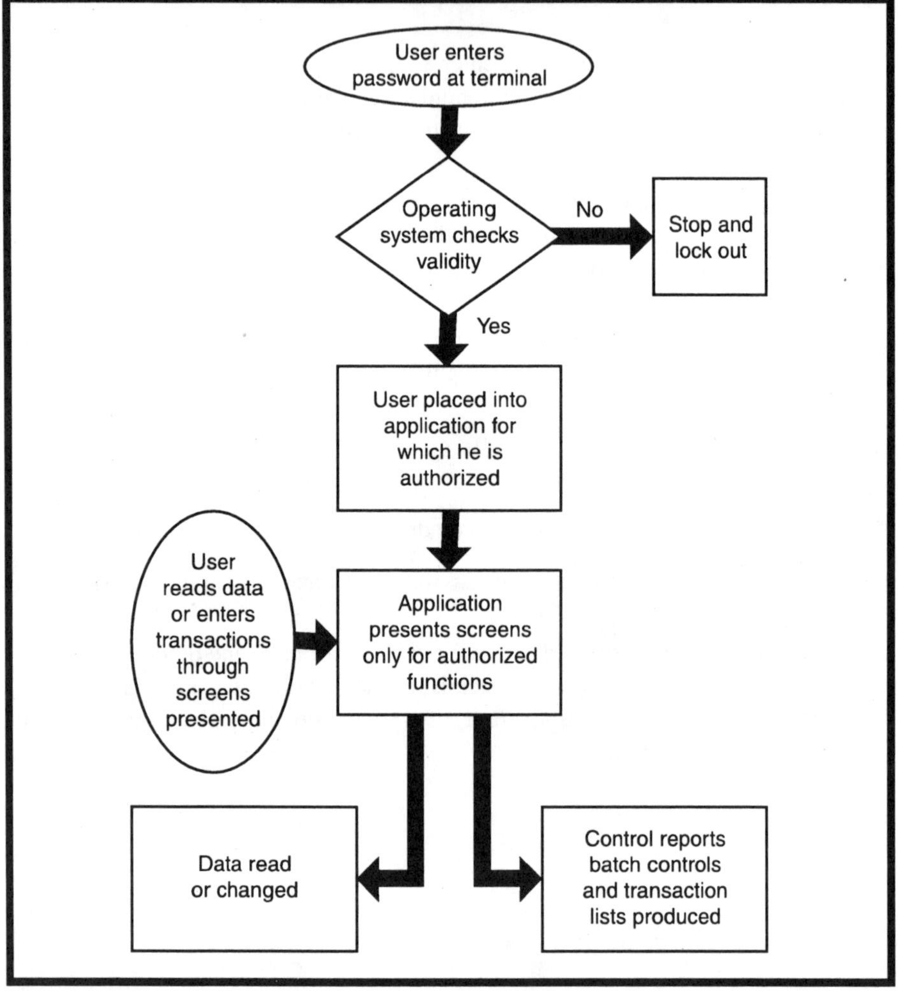

Note that throughout this chapter we have referred only to passwords, which are the most common way of authenticating the identity of a user and finding what that user may do once given access.

The same approach is used when we combine passwords with other access means to more surely identify users and to keep out imposters and hackers. Thus we may use smart cards with encrypted codes, encrypted digital signatures, biometrics such as fingerprints and voice prints, etc., to supplement the password, requiring the user to present two items (the password and something else) to identify himself. But the nature of the process remains the same.

This example illustrates how we deal with access rights for application users as well as for customers and other third parties. The steps involved include:

- making use of the overall security software to determine that the password (or other means of user authentication) is valid and thus the user should not be totally locked out, and
- passing the user on to a particular application that further decides or restricts what the user may do.

Note that the goal of the security software has been to restrict the user or customer into using an application. We cannot risk having users tramping around the operating system and system software and using all of its powers or adding their own programs that perform tasks. The goal is to allow users inside and outside the company to use only authorized application programs and keep them completely away from any other capabilities.

Overall, the example above underscores the need to clearly define, design, implement and test the functions and transactions that are available to each employee or customer group. The development of access rights should be approached in the same manner as *any other requirement* that is part of the development process for any application.

STRATEGIES
FOR SUCCESS

The access rights of each employee or customer group should be defined, designed, implemented and tested as part of the systems development process.

Access rights should be based on job profiles, rather than being individually designed for each employee.

Access rights of information systems department

The previous discussion explained the importance of managing the development of access rights for customers and employees. But this concept becomes far more complicated for dealing with the technical employees in an information systems department. As explained earlier, these are the people who need powerful accesses to the operating system and systems software to do their jobs.

On one level, the approach is very much the same as that described for users outside the information systems department. We should define the access rights that are required by each job function within the information systems department (e.g., database administrator, senior operator, systems programmer, application programmer, database technician, tape librarian, etc.). We can then design access rights for each of these groups which are commensurate with a proper segregation of duties for internal control purposes. If individuals need additional access rights beyond those set for their job functions, these should be true exceptions and should be carefully reviewed and approved at a senior level.

After this process, however, we will still have a few remaining individuals who have a great deal of power and access rights. Because of their job responsibilities, they are empowered to use the operating system, change application programs, or directly access files and data in a manner that leaves no audit trail of exactly what changes they have made. How does senior management address these risks?

In simple terms, we can set the security software to report whenever these powerful privileges are used and then have the data security officer obtain an explanation as to what was done and why from the password holder. We may supplement or replace passwords by using smart cards, fingerprints or other techniques, thus making it more difficult to gain unauthorized access to these dangerously powerful privileges. We can also take some comfort from the division of duties we have created in the first place, so that in the normal course of events no one individual alone has ownership of, or can make changes to, any program or data without the involvement of someone else, even if this is after the fact in case of an emergency.

Again, keeping in mind that information security is only part of a total internal control process, we can also rely on the overall controls that the user departments in the organization use. These controls also work on an overall basis to protect assets and guard information integrity and include those used to balance data, spot and investigate unusual values, send confirmations of transactions and balances to third parties, etc.

The key points are:

- There is no such thing as absolute security. There are only systems that provide varying degrees of security.
- If we try to approach "perfection" in preventing unauthorized access, costs will escalate geometrically.

For these reasons, information security procedures should also include detective controls. These are controls that are designed to detect unauthorized activity and alert us to take steps to remedy the situation before unacceptable losses or damage occur.

Put another way, information security, like any other system of internal control, requires a balance of preventive and detective procedures. Any other approach is built on the fallacy that preventive controls are "foolproof." We should also balance the cost of controls and the cost of losses as an overall total. When we try to balance either of these factors in isolation, we spend too much money without getting the level of protection we need.

STRATEGIES
FOR SUCCESS

A balanced and cost effective system of preventive/detective controls serves to:

- *prevent losses of a level that are unacceptable to the business, either in terms of financial loss or in terms of customer relations,*
- *ensure losses, either from accidental or purposeful acts, are discovered quickly enough so that the losses or damage we suffer are restricted to an acceptable level, and*
- *in the event of a mishap, provide pre-defined procedures for stemming the losses and strengthening the controls to prevent further loss or damage occurring in the same way in the future.*

Information security is only part of an overall system of internal controls and by itself cannot protect assets or ensure the integrity of data and information.

The key point throughout this chapter is again: All data security, including preventive and detective controls, is part of the overall system of internal controls. *We cannot rely on information security alone to protect our assets or to ensure complete, reliable and accurate data.* There can and should be other controls in the overall system that will serve to protect assets and safeguard the integrity of information.[5]

THE NINTH PRINCIPLE

1.9 Senior management should have a basic understanding of the internet and its security challenges and opportunities.

To help senior management understand what the Internet is and its current security implications, this section provides a brief overview of the Internet and the Intranet (as it is called when an organization uses the Internet internally).

At the time of publication of this book, the Internet is not secure and providing even a reasonable level of security is a very challenging technical task. Even as security capabilities increase over time, management of information security for the Internet will remain a daunting technical task. Thus, we should take appropriate measures to ensure that the Internet is only used in those circumstances where sufficient security can be provided.

What is the internet?

In essence, the Internet is a public telecommunication network. It is not really owned by anybody or managed by anybody. The only real coordinating body is a body which internationally assigns Internet addresses and names for Internet servers. Thus, a corporation that wants to establish an Internet site will apply to

---

5 For a detailed discussion of controls, refer to *Managing and Controlling Small Computer Systems Including LANs.* The concepts are the same regardless of the size of the computer system in question.

this body for an Internet address. This Internet address is then used on a worldwide basis to access the corporation's Internet server, interacting with it, obtaining messages from it, or sending messages to it.

Individuals who want to be able to work with the Internet go to a third party supplier who has already established an Internet server and purchase from them access to that Internet site. It is through this site that they can use E-mail, contact other Internet sites and perform all other activities on the Internet and the worldwide web.

The Internet network (and the worldwide web which is part of it) works through the telecommunications protocols established for its use. These protocols, called TCP/IP protocols, provide all of us with an easy way to get through the telecommunication network to reach a particular network server out of the tens of thousands which now exist. It also provides the protocols necessary for the exchange of messages with that Internet site.

While in essence the Internet is a telecommunications network, from a business perspective, we need to look at the use of the Internet as an extension of our enterprise architecture and its impact on our management of information security.

From the viewpoint of using the Internet for business purposes, we have three major activities:

- establish an Internet server which is really just a specialized computer site
- write applications for the Internet which will reside on this server, and
- make use of the Internet network to provide access through the Internet to and from our Internet server.

We will now look at these three aspects of our "Internet Enterprise Architecture" in more detail.

The internet server

As previously mentioned, the Internet server is really just a specialized computer site. It contains the application programs that we have created, plus the telecommunication systems software and operating systems necessary for it to function as part of the Internet. Thus, all of our policies and standards relating to the assignment of computer site ownership and the standards for internal control for all general and environmental controls at a computer site can and should apply to our Internet server.

The challenge is that Internet servers are generally based on the UNIX operating system and, of course in the telecommunication layer, must make use of the Internet telecommunication protocols (see below).

Because the Unix operating system and the TCP/IP telecommunication protocols are not well designed from an information security perspective, they present challenges in properly securing the site against outside hackers or indeed employees.

After all, both the UNIX operating system and the TCP/IP telecommunication protocols were originally designed to provide for an open and free exchange of information on a public basis. In their origins, these protocols and operating systems were never designed to provide any large degree of information security. While over the years efforts have been made to "tighten up" these operating systems and telecommunication protocols to provide greater information security, they still fall short of what we would normally wish to have in an operating system or in a telecommunication network that supports commercial activities.

Firewall protection

The vast majority of Internet servers are protected by "firewalls". Firewalls sit in front of the server and are designed to protect it from malicious attacks of any nature. In essence, a firewall is just another computer operating as a server, using a stripped down version of an operating system which, as it provides less functionality, is harder to misuse for malevolent purposes. The firewall talks to the outside world on the one side and then passes through data or messages on the other side to the real "Internet Server" that contains programs and data. When the Internet server wants to send a message back, it sends the message to the firewall which then communicates it onwards into the world. Thus, the firewall acts as a narrow doorway through which all exchanges of data and messages to and from third parties must pass.

While firewalls can provide an additional measure of security, we should keep in mind that they can be and indeed are often broken through. Unfortunately, the Internet itself is the source of many of these problems; not only does it provide the means by which the breakthrough occurs, but also supplies the information to break in. There are now rich amounts of information and even software tools available freely on the Internet that can be used by would be hackers to break through fire walls and enter Internet servers of all types, shapes and descriptions. Thus, our potential hackers not only include technically sophisticated people with training and knowledge but now encompass many individuals who can mount sophisticated attacks by using the software and the knowledge provided for them on the Internet itself.

The telecommunications network

There is a big difference between using the Internet for telecommunications and even using a public telephone network. Generally, when we use a public telephone network, we dial up from our computer site to another computer site through the telephone system, establish a connection and then exchange messages and data. Of course, these arrangements are subject to penetration; the data and messages may go through many switches in the telephone companies' long distance service, including the switches of other telecommunications companies. While we have some comfort that these switches are professionally managed and offer some reasonable degree of appropriate information security and internal controls, our telephone lines can be tapped and our messages and data copied. Indeed, the private switching networks which we have in our company could be compromised so that our messages could be read or perhaps even altered.

Most of this is also true when we use the Internet, but there are other further complications. In the Internet, our messages and data may go through many servers on the Internet en route from us to the ultimate destination. Typically, they may pass through 5 or 10 other Internet servers. The key points here are:

- we do not know who owns these other servers, and
- we need to recognize that these other servers are powerful computer systems which can intercept, copy, read and indeed alter the contents of our messages and data very easily.

For example, our electronic mail can be read, its contents or the name of the sender or receiver changed or others can send messages masquerading or pretending to be us. This is also completely true of messages that we receive from others. Indeed, it is even possible for another server on the network to pretend to be our server and then third parties send and receive messages to this outside third party falsely thinking they are in communication with your company!

Thus, we need to consider all of these factors when we use the Internet in any way. Where we are simply allowing customers to come in to our Internet site and obtain information on our products and services, most companies would accept these risks. However, if we wish to E-mail any confidential information across the Internet, we need to carefully consider encryption which will help ensure the confidentiality of our messages and data and make it very difficult to alter them without this being readily detectable.

At this particular time, there is a high degree of reluctance to actually transact business over the Internet as distinct from sharing information about the company with customers and potential customers or, in some cases, doing a minor amount of business which is carefully monitored and reviewed and where the individual transaction values are extremely low. In this latter case, it is becoming common to use encryption for the exchange of the related data and messages, sometimes with the companies providing the necessary encryption software to customers or potential customers to set the scene for such an encrypted exchange. Also, many electronic mail systems today make provision for the encryption of messages, using different cryptographic protocols of varying strength and value.

As we can see, the control of messages and data and all of the internal controls related to networks and telecommunications clearly apply to the Internet environment. The only difference is the environment is far more complex and challenging to secure to any reasonable degree. Developments in these regards are fast and rapid and statements made today may not be true three months from now.

The applications

The applications that sit on a company's Internet server are really just like any other applications that we might acquire or develop. Of course, there are now specialized tools which are available to create web pages and web sites, to add information to them, etc. These applications can pass and exchange data with other applications within the company, either on the Internet server or elsewhere on some other computer site. Thus, Internet applications are the same as any other applications; we simply have some new programming languages which assist in the creation of the application. All the processes mobilized by our information security policies and standards regarding how we define and then implement the detailed requirements for internal control generally and for information security in particular when acquiring or amending applications still apply.

How will all this evolve?

Undoubtedly, we will continue to see progress through the availability of additional security controls to tighten and further protect our Internet sites and their firewalls from a logical security perspective. However, it is doubtful whether this will ever be enough.

The main efforts being made today are to develop cryptographic methods which are simple enough on the one hand and complex and robust enough on the other to provide for the wide spread use of encryption by customers and businesses when exchanging messages, exchanging data or doing business over the Internet. Indeed, there is some hope on the horizon that there will be cost effective ways to also encrypt the data which resides on computer sites. If we were able to encrypt all the data on the computer site, then we would present a hacker with another set of challenges to overcome before breaking into our computer site would be of any benefit (although of course plain, malicious damage might still be possible).

Advantages of encryption

Such a widespread use of encryption both in message exchange and at the computer site would provide many advantages. It would:

- protect the privacy and confidentiality of messages and data
- alert us immediately if any of our messages or data had been altered, and
- provide us with a means to authenticate the identity of the person of whom we are in communication or who is performing an action.

These encryption techniques would not replace all of the information security procedures and processes we have today; rather they would supplement them in order to make the use of public networks such as the Internet more secure and thus able to support a much greater variety of business events.

The intranet

Much is written today about the use of the Intranet to provide for electronic mail and shareware within a company. Using this approach, the company would set up one or more Internet servers and then provide a way for all employees using this internal Intranet to exchange electronic messages, share files, set up discussion groups for various topics, access text databases containing company policies and standards, etc.

Companies that use an Intranet do so for a variety of reasons, ranging from the fact telecommunications are cheaper within an Intranet (as it uses the Internet for wide area communication) through to the attitude that employees will be learning the Internet anyway and thus might as well have a common tool and interface when working within the office environment.

All of the discussions above concerning use of the Internet apply with equal force and value to any Intranet that your company may establish.

STRATEGIES
FOR SUCCESS

An organization's Intranet should be managed in the same manner and with the same care as use of the Internet.

Overview

Chapter 1 – Focusing the goals of information security

The principles discussed in this chapter include:

1.1 Senior management should view information security from an overall perspective, recognizing its contribution in achieving the organization's broader goals.

1.2 Information security should be viewed as a part of the overall system of internal control.

1.3 The access rights and privileges of customers and other third parties should be adequately controlled.

1.4 The differences between data and information should be recognized and provided for in the information security policy.

1.5 "Believed systems" must be recognized and carefully provided for from an information security perspective.

1.6 As the organization's dependency on information security evolves and grows, the information security policies and standards must be periodically revisited and strengthened where necessary.

1.7 Information security should be viewed from a customer's perspective to ensure the organization provides the security and ease of use the customer expects when dealing with the organization electronically.

1.8 Senior management should obtain an executive level understanding of basic security principles to ensure security issues are addressed in a consistent and logical manner and in keeping with broader corporate issues and goals.

1.9 Senior management should have a basic understanding of the Internet and its security challenges and opportunities.

STRATEGIES
FOR SUCCESS

Good information security provides much more than security. It also makes a significant contribution to quality assurance, competitive advantage and cost control.

Senior management should establish appropriate policies to promote the development and implementation of effective information security.

The management responsible for each business process must have the primary responsibility to define and communicate the nature and degree of information security they require.

Information security by itself will not prevent employees, customers and other third parties from making "extra transactions", those which are additional but unauthorized transactions of the type and nature the system allows them to do. There must be other procedures in the system of internal control to prevent or quickly detect and act upon such transactions.

It is important to carefully think through the mechanisms, if any, which an organization may need to monitor the actions of employees and others who are reading or copying computerized information.

As it is difficult to monitor "read access" to data, extra care should be taken to limit the number of people who can read or copy sensitive information.

The approach used to authenticate an individual's identity inside or outside the company has to balance costs and ease of use on the one hand with the need to appropriately authenticate users and restrict losses on the other. Senior management must take the lead in balancing these factors and in communicating their requirements.

Losses arising from disputes and concessions to customers and other third parties as to the transactions they have initiated electronically need to be captured and reviewed. In addition, authentication methods must be continuously reviewed in the light of these costs, recognizing that passwords alone may not be sufficient.

Information security policies should cover the needs for continuity and availability of the organization's information systems and the information they contain.

Information security policies and standards need to reflect the reality that computer programs create, record and alter data. Information cannot be secured unless all programs are secured as well.

Effective corporate governance requires the design and effective implementation of overall internal control processes.

Information security for any business process is only part of an overall system of internal control for that process.

The goal in designing information security is to minimize the total costs of the security procedures, including the losses which the organization shall inevitably incur.

Information security should be created, designed and implemented in harmony with the policies and procedures within the organization for the design and implementation of overall internal control systems.

Responsibility must be assigned for the integrity of all customer-initiated transactions and data, including responsibility for determining customer access rights and privileges and for reviewing transactions in total or individually as required.

Appropriate use should be made of the capabilities of software to monitor transactions individually and in total for patterns that could indicate errors or fraudulent activities of hackers.

The computer sites where the organization's data resides should be properly secured with regard to all the goals for the integrity of data.

For computer sites, systems and microcomputers that contain only information that can be re-generated from the underlying data, information security centres around privacy and confidentiality concerns.

Where transactions are accepted or assets exchanged based on computerized data and without further verification, make sure that information security procedures have been designed in light of the greater reliance that is being placed on such a "believed system".

A formal process for periodic reviews of the adequacy of all information security policies and standards should be established and the responsibility for this activity assigned.

The methodologies and processes used to enhance systems should provide for revisiting all information security arrangements for those systems and their data, including disaster recovery arrangements.

The organization must both recognize and respond to the customers' need for security and ease of use when dealing with the organization electronically. Creating the correct balance between these factors is a critical success factor.

Someone in the organization must be directly responsible for:

- the nature of access rights for customers and the process for administering customer access, and
- the acceptance, integrity and correctness of customer-initiated transactions.

The access rights of each employee or customer group should be defined, designed, implemented and tested as part of the systems development process.

Access rights should be based on job profiles, rather than being individually designed for each employee.

A balanced and cost effective system of preventative/detective controls serves to:

- prevent losses of a level that are unacceptable to the business, either in terms of financial loss or in terms of customer relations,
- ensure losses, either from accidental or purposeful acts, are discovered quickly enough so that the losses or damage we suffer are restricted to an acceptable level, and
- in the event of a mishap, provide pre-defined procedures for stemming the losses and strengthening the controls to prevent further loss or damage occurring in the same way in the future.

Information security is only part of an overall system of internal controls and by itself cannot protect assets or ensure the integrity of data and information.

An organization's Intranet should be managed in the same manner and with the same care as use of the Internet.

Chapter 2

Putting information security in its place

Information security is a means to an end and not an end in itself. Security needs to be integrated into other activities, including strategic planning and overall management of internal controls before it can add value. Senior management needs to understand these relationships and then promulgate policies that respect and reinforce them. This includes establishing and communicating clear policies and assigning responsibilities for key activities, such as information systems and information security that cross departmental boundaries. This chapter focuses on the nature of such policies; the assigning of responsibilities to achieve these goals is discussed in *Chapter 3*.

This chapter discusses the principles:

2.1 Before addressing information security policy, senior management should first develop and implement a corporate-wide Information Resources Management (IRM) policy to provide an overall framework for all of the organization's information technology activities, including information security.

2.2 Information security policies should reflect the relationships between information security and overall internal controls, privacy and confidentiality and business continuity planning.

2.3 Careful consideration should be given to the formation of an information security committee to help ensure that the information security policies, standards and procedures continually meet the changing needs of the organization.

2.4 Regardless of where and by whom information is created, stored or processed, information security must be managed.

Creating paper does not create change. Top management must be visible in their support and in their demands for cooperative efforts throughout the organization on all information technology matters, including information security.

Information technology is critical to the success of all organizations and its successful deployment requires active participation and cooperation across departmental boundaries. Thus all policies regarding information technology need to emanate from top management, and top management should see they are effectively implemented and followed.

Chapter 1 presented the underlying concept of the entire book: *Information security is not a goal in itself, but rather an essential contributor to overall information systems and internal control goals.* In other words, information security is a basic requirement for ensuring the integrity, confidentiality and ongoing availability of systems and data. As such, it should be addressed in an integrated manner with all other interrelated policies and standards. Information security is also part of the larger challenge to get the right systems at the right price.

Information security considerations should be integrated into all key information systems management activities, including strategic planning for information systems, the definition and acquisition of new systems and the balancing of the costs of systems with the benefits they produce.

The first step to achieving this goal is to consider how information security fits into and should be managed as part of the overall process to strategically manage the organization's information systems. This overall strategic governance of information systems sets the scene for ensuring information security is managed consistently and successfully. The first principle below addresses this strategy for overall management of information technology, including security matters.

THE FIRST PRINCIPLE

2.1 Before addressing information security policy, senior management should first develop and implement a corporate-wide Information Resources Management (IRM) policy to provide an overall framework for all of the organization's information technology activities, including information security.

The previous book in this series[1] discusses the role of senior management in setting the policies, framework and culture that are vital for ensuring information technology directly supports the critical goals of the organization. The book stresses the importance of developing an overall infrastructure of hardware, systems and networks that support the organization's goals and critical success factors and presents the principles that will help senior management direct the management of these resources. The information security policy, the focus of this book, is just part of the organization's information technology activities.

The following briefly summarizes some of the key issues discussed in the former publication as a background for building on the concepts specific to information security in itself and in the context of the broader framework of the overall technology infrastructure.

---

1 For an in depth discussion of the IRM policy, refer to *Getting the right systems at the right price – Strategies for senior management.*

The information resources management (IRM) policy

The information resources management (IRM) policy is an overall policy that serves to ensure that all information resources are viewed and treated as corporate assets and managed appropriately and effectively throughout the organization. The IRM policy is the framework for ensuring that the whole organization contributes its talents to defining the information systems the organization requires to achieve its goals and that each department contributes to the corporate-wide goal of getting the right systems at the right price. Most important, the IRM policy communicates senior management's view that information systems are a broad-based corporate challenge together with their clear expectation that all departments will work together to ensure information technology resources contribute to the strategic goals and critical success factors of the organization.

STRATEGIES
FOR SUCCESS

The information resources management (IRM) policy serves to communicate senior management's view that information systems are too important and too costly to be left solely in the hands of the information systems department.

Because the IRM policy will affect the whole organization, it should be developed by a group representing all major departments of the organization and then issued by and actively supported by senior management.

The IRM policy and the standards and activities that support it should be revised from time to time. Also, it is a document that should be continuously improved as experience shows the need to amend our policies and practices in the light of what works best for us. We also need an overall mechanism to see that our policies are being followed in practice; that is, we need a forum to monitor compliance with them.

Many organizations create a top management committee of three or four senior officers to oversee all key decisions and manage corporate strategy. This group sometimes acts as the IRM committee as one of its responsibilities. Other organizations create a separate IRM committee to both own and monitor IRM policies and to perform other important roles for information systems, such as reviewing major information systems investments and the annual information systems budget.

STRATEGIES
FOR SUCCESS

Overall responsibility for reviewing and amending IRM policies and practices should be fixed. Often, this is assigned to a top corporate management committee as part of a portfolio of responsibilities or to a separate IRM committee with senior cross-departmental representation.

The following exhibit illustrates, at a high level, the contents of the IRM policy.

Exhibit 2.1

The IRM policy – overview of possible contents
1. The requirement for a strategic information systems plan (SISP)
2. The need for adherence to an overall enterprise architecture[2]
3. The role of a chief information officer (CIO)
4. The means by which the organization will monitor information technology developments
5. The roles and responsibilities of the IRM committee, or other means to manage IRM policy and practices issues
6. Approvals required for major systems investments
7. The business case analysis for individual major systems investments
8. The responsibility for the control of costs and achievement of the benefits of information technology
9. The approach to be used to measure the information systems return on investment
10. The approach to be used for the definition, acquisition and implementation of new systems, and the responsibility to be accepted by each area of the company in the process
11. The concepts of systems ownership and data ownership
12. The requirement for an information security policy
13. The requirement for a disaster recovery plan.

As addressed throughout this book, information security includes both data security and disaster recovery planning.

---

[2] An enterprise architecture can be thought of as the overall collection of hardware, systems software and connecting networks within the organization and to the outside world that enables the organization to make overall use of information technology.

The IRM policy establishes the basis for the creation of an information security policy. It defines the major roles of systems developers, systems owners and data owners in all aspects of information technology, including their information security responsibilities. The IRM Policy should require that information security is addressed in an integrated manner at every step in the overall acquisition and management of information systems and resources. By defining the key roles of systems and data owners, it links the security activities of the specialists in the information systems department with those of the operating departments in their roles as systems and data owners.

Exhibit 2.2

Objectives of the IRM policy from an information security perspective

The IRM (information resources management) policy establishes the basis for the creation of an information security policy. Specifically, the IRM:

- defines the major roles of systems developers, computer site owners, systems owners and data owners
- ensures information security is addressed in an integrated manner in the acquisition, implementation and ongoing use of information systems, and
- links security activities of the specialists in the information systems department with those of the operating departments in their roles as systems and data owners.

STRATEGIES
FOR SUCCESS

The IRM policy should set out the policies and standards that will ensure information security is dealt with in an integrated manner with all other activities in the acquisition and management of information technology. Through defining the responsibilities of systems owners, data owners, systems developers and computer site owners on all matters, it establishes the framework for cooperation on information security matters across departmental boundaries.

If an IRM policy or its equivalent does not exist, the company should give careful consideration to creating one. As a minimum, the information security policies would have to be broadened in the absence of an IRM policy to deal with all the important interfaces just described.

Chapter 3 discusses the responsibilities of all the ownership roles discussed above from an information security perspective and illustrates how they should be communicated in an information security policy.

THE SECOND PRINCIPLE

2.2 Information security policies should reflect the relationships between information security and overall internal controls, privacy and confidentiality and business continuity planning.

Chapter 1 established that information security could not by itself ensure data integrity, completely deal with privacy and confidentiality or ensure that the company could always remain in business to serve its customers. In creating information security, we need to remember that security has to fit in with all of the other corporate policies and standards.

Under this principle, we will first explore how policies and standards need to be created to manage all aspects of internal control. We will then see how information security fits into this wide definition of internal control.

A comprehensive view of internal controls

As shown in the exhibit below, internal controls need to address three major areas.

Exhibit 2.3

A comprehensive view of internal controls

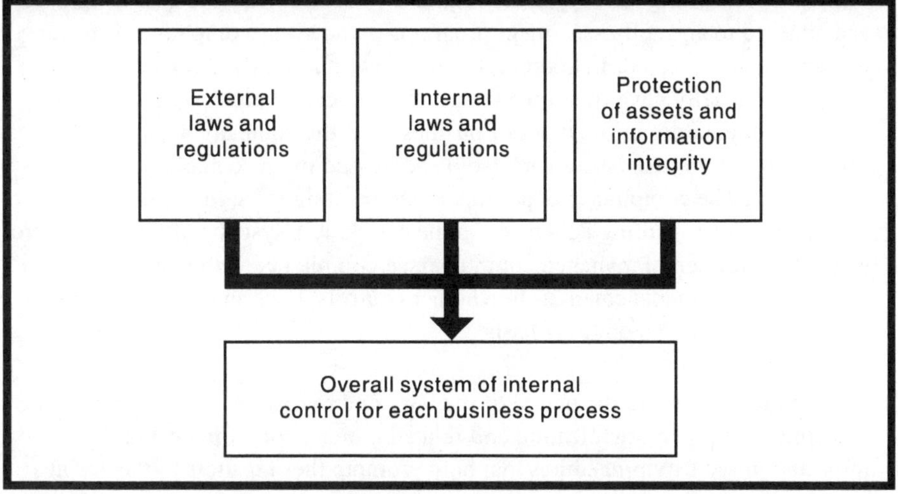

All three areas need to be built into integrated business processes for each of the company's major activities such as sales, accounts receivables, purchases and accounts payable, inventory management, etc. Each area of control is described below.

External laws and regulations

Many organizations are subject to laws and regulations as to the nature of the internal controls they must maintain and how they must respect the privacy of third parties. Some may also have to follow complex laws and regulations in regard to environmental protection, safety in the workplace and many other areas. Pressures in these areas are only going to increase, given the current interest in increasing the accountability of large public companies, concerns about privacy and the threat of integrated computer systems and their vast amounts of data, and the focus on the environment.

Often, these laws address the privacy and confidentiality of customer information, the length of time that electronic files need to be kept for inspection by tax auditors and others, and other matters that affect information technology.

In replying to these increasingly complex circumstances, many companies have set up a compliance department to promulgate knowledge throughout the company concerning how legal and regulatory requirements must be monitored and adhered to and self assessment programs on how this compliance is being managed and respected. In addition to these external laws and regulations, companies usually have their own codes of conduct and policies on corporate ethics and the nature of the types of business that the company wants to attract and will accept. These issues can also be addressed by the compliance department. The compliance department may be assigned significant responsibilities regarding adherence to the company's systems of internal control, helping departmental management to oversee compliance with controls and reporting to top management as to whether controls, laws and regulations are being respected on an ongoing basis.

We need to understand the nature of the laws and regulations, codes of conduct and ethics within an organization and related issues in order to design information security procedures that help promote these matters to the extent possible. While the contribution that information security can make may be minor, nonetheless there should be effective liaison with the compliance department or whatever department is responsible for these matters.

STRATEGIES
FOR SUCCESS

There should be appropriate liaison between those who are creating any information security policies and those responsible for adherence to external laws and regulations policies on corporate conduct.

Internal laws and regulations

Internal laws and regulations refer to the policies and standards relating to the nature of the business the organization wants to accept and the terms and conditions under which it will accept and conduct business.

Thus in this area we define the nature of the products/services we sell, establish sales prices and terms of payment, set forth the commissions we may be willing to pay to third parties, etc. On the supply side, we define the terms and conditions we wish to put in place in dealing with suppliers, the form of the purchase orders, etc.

Indeed this concept of internal laws and regulations, expressed in policies and standards that define the business we wish to accept and the terms and conditions under which we will accept business and fulfil our business obligations, applies to virtually every business process.

STRATEGIES
FOR SUCCESS

Internal control procedures and activities should be designed to help ensure adherence to internal policies and standards, regarding the nature of business to be accepted and how business is to be conducted.

Protection of assets and information integrity

This is the traditional and indeed central role of internal control. For each business process, we need to define internal control procedures and activities to safeguard assets and to ensure data and information integrity. We explored these areas in some detail in *Chapter 1* and saw that information security, as in all other areas, can make a major contribution towards these goals but by itself alone cannot achieve them. Instead, we need to think of information security as part of a broader system of internal controls which achieve these goals.

STRATEGIES
FOR SUCCESS

A broad set of internal control procedures and activities, including information security procedures, is needed to protect assets and ensure information integrity.

We have now discussed the three major areas that systems of internal control must address, as illustrated earlier in Exhibit 2.3. The question now is: How do we set these internal control systems for each business process?

All companies need overall internal control processes to risk manage each business process. Policies and standards should be in place to fix accountability for and guide the development, effective implementation and ongoing adherence to such overall internal control processes. Within this broader control framework, we can then ensure that information security is properly and cost effectively designed as part of these overall internal controls to assist in ensuring data integrity. As shown in the exhibit, the need to develop these integrated business processes should be established by executive management and then implemented by all departments.

As we design overall controls for a particular business process, we will be able to gauge and understand the relative importance of information security procedures to ensure complete, accurate and authorized data and determine the division of duties that we want to enforce through security software. In short, we will be able to design information security as a cost effective part of an overall system of internal control.

The goal of senior management in this endeavour is to consolidate information security into the overall control processes used to:

- ensure adherence to laws and regulations
- accept business from third parties (e.g., internal laws and regulations)
- record these economic events
- exchange monetary assets, and
- fulfil all our accounting requirements.

(e.g., protection of assets and information integrity)

We cannot accomplish all of this unless we have an effective framework of policies and standards for the development, implementation and adherence to effective systems of internal control over business processes. It is essential that this policy framework set forth clearly the responsibilities of system developers, systems owners and other key players in this process. Without this, there is no really effective basis for dealing with information security as there is no way of managing the whole picture.

Overall policies for internal controls are essential. It is astounding how many otherwise well-managed companies have failed to put these controls in place. At a time when we are so busy re-engineering processes to do more with less and striving to empower our employees to serve customers more effectively and do their jobs more efficiently, at a time when society expresses so much concern for proper corporate governance, the lack of internal control policies as a cornerstone for corporate governance is difficult to understand. It is a fit subject for a book on information security, as we cannot manage the security part without a vehicle to manage the overall controls process.

There are many compelling arguments for the creation of internal control policies. The regulators in Canada are waking up to this, as witnessed by the Standards Assessment and Reporting Program (SARP) issued by the Canada Deposit Insurance Corporation (CDIC) in 1994. The document sets out the requirements for assessment and reporting with respect to whether member institutions are following CDIC's Standards of Sound Business and Financial Practices, made law in August of 1993. The Standards Assessment and Reporting Program requires members to complete an annual self-assessment which focuses on three questions:

- Does the member have a well-defined program of policies and procedures in place with respect to internal control, liquidity, interest rate and foreign exchange risks, credit risks and securities, real estate appraisals and capital management?
- Is the program sound and prudent?
- Is the program in practice being adhered to?

In a broader context, the work being done by the CICA's Criteria of Control Board (CoCo) addresses control issues as they affect all organizations. Established in 1992, the CICA's Criteria of Control Board (CoCo) has a mandate to issue guidance on designing, assessing and reporting on the control systems of organizations. CoCo offers a framework for making judgments about control in the hope that committees, managements and others concerned with effective control will use this guidance on a voluntary basis.[3]

---

3 The first public documents from the CICA's CoCo, *Guidance on Control* and *Guidance for Directors – Governance Processes for Control,* were released late 1995.

In other countries, such as the United Kingdom and the United States, these regulatory requirements are much more advanced and Boards of Directors are being given direct and clear responsibilities in these regards.

Striking a balance

More important than the march of regulation is the need in these competitive times to strike a balance between controlling costs and protecting the organization and thus its stakeholders through effective control processes. Unless there are internal control policies and standards in place for overall systems of internal control, it is hard to see how this can be accomplished.

While the development of criteria for controls and corporate governance requirements for society as a whole, written in a manner that can be reasonably applied by all concerned, is a huge challenge, it is a far less daunting task for companies to create these policies for their own individual use.

STRATEGIES
FOR SUCCESS

The organization's internal control policies and supporting standards must clearly fix accountability for and guide the development, implementation and monitoring of effective adherence to overall internal control processes for each business process.

Senior management must ensure each individual and every department throughout the organization understands that information security is only part of an overall internal control process that should exist over each business process.

The information security policy should include appropriate references to the relationships between overall internal controls and information security.

Discussions in *Chapter 1* as well as the last few pages have set the scene for understanding how information security contributes to each of the four pillars illustrated below.

Exhibit 2.4

The four pillars of information risk management

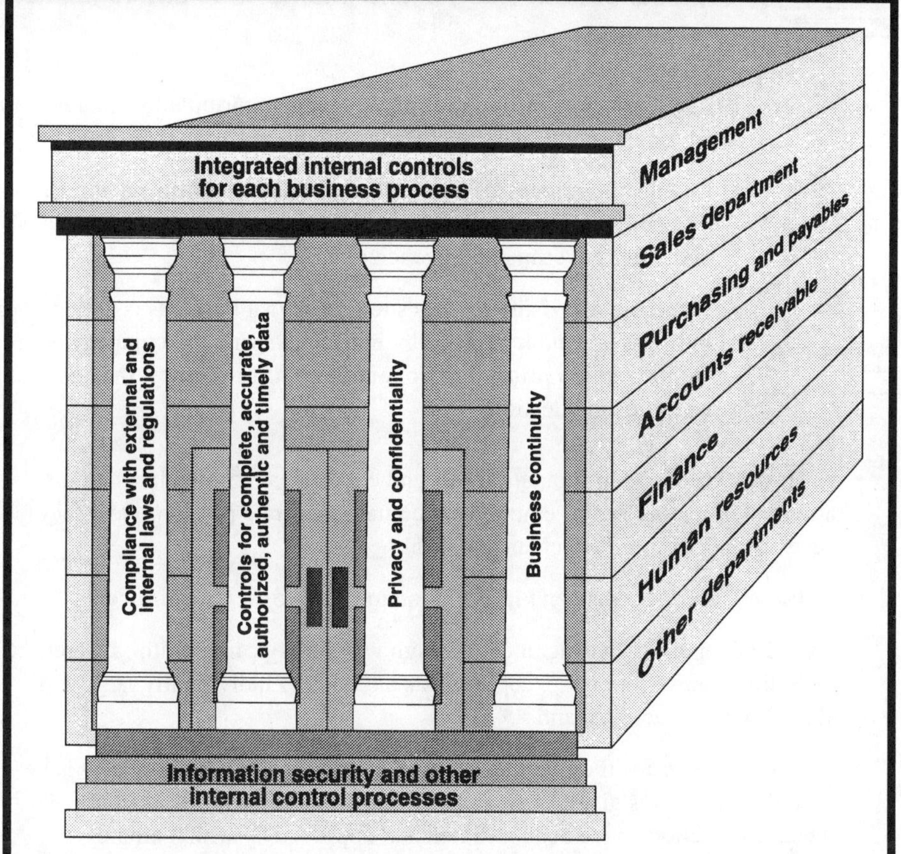

Each department needs to implement information security, overall internal controls, privacy and confidentiality measures, a business continuity plan and compliance with laws and regulations into an overall risk management structure. Clearly there are many overlaps between the four pillars and activities under one pillar will often contribute to one or more other pillars. Thus each department needs to put into place a coordinated set of procedures and activities to achieve these pillars in a cost effective manner. This requires first that all of the related policies, including information security policies be written in a manner that respects these inter-relationships, and second, that departments understand these relationships when they design and implement their procedures to respect each of the pillars. Let's now look at how information security contributes to each of these pillars.

Compliance with external and internal laws and regulations

Examples of how information security can contribute to adherence to legal requirements and "internal laws and regulations" include:

- establishing processes that ensure that data and information are retained to meet records retention requirements of tax authorities and other governmental agencies
- enforcing a division of duties to ensure that business is accepted or business is conducted only by individuals who the company has authorized to initiate the economic events or perform the business activities in question
- ensuring exceptions to standard terms and conditions or procedures require approval of a more senior employee who has a separate password and set of access rights to signify such an approval
- restricting access to data and information to meet privacy requirements
- providing reports to management through which they can monitor adherence, including control reports, exception lists and lists of individually large and significant transactions, and
- setting the scene for the accountability of all employees, i.e., how they have used the authorities given them as determined through audit trails that record which transactions have been initiated and approved by which employee.

It is clear from the above that while information security can assist in ensuring compliance with external and internal "regulations," most of this assurance will come from other sources including:

- the establishment of an environment by senior management that requires and expects sound internal controls and adherence to them
- cultivation of responsibilities to keep abreast of the requirements of external laws and regulations and to design controls for adherence to them
- the same approach as above for internal laws and regulations
- overall management and supervisory controls which permit the management of each department to assess departmental employees' adherence to internal controls on an ongoing basis, and
- the promulgation of policies on corporate conduct.

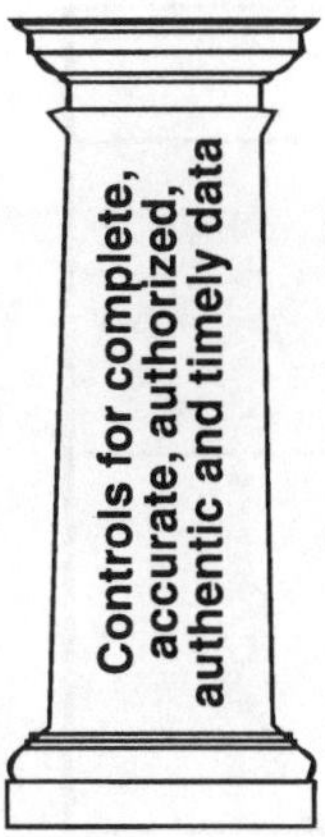

Controls for complete, accurate, authorized, authentic and timely data

In *Chapter 1*, we reviewed the contribution that information security can make to these goals as well as the nature of other internal controls which are usually required to meet these integrity objectives. This contribution is illustrated in the following exhibit, taken in part from Exhibit 1.3 in *Chapter 1*.

Exhibit 2.5

Information security and the achievement of corporate goals		
The goal	**Description**	**Information security contribution**
Completeness	data (and the information derived from it) reflects all events and transactions the organization has entered into	low
Accuracy	data (and the information derived from it) has the degree of accuracy needed for *all* the purposes it is used for	low
Timeliness	data is recorded promptly	none to low
Authorization	the recording of data and information and accesses to it are restricted to those authorized	high
Authentication	the identity of the person or party accessing data is reasonably assured and can be subsequently determined	high

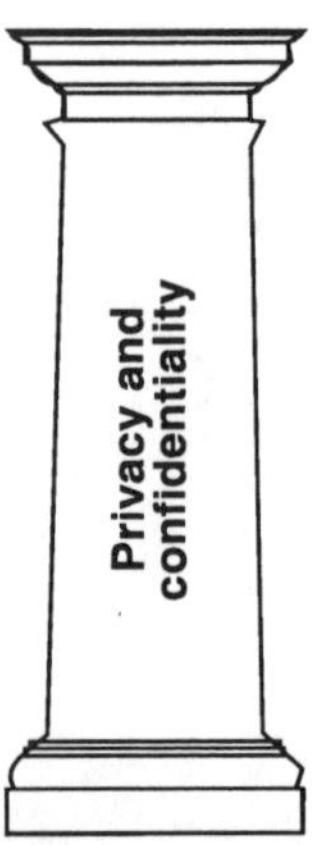

Privacy and confidentiality

The objective of privacy is to keep the information provided by customers and employees private, while for confidentiality, it is to guard information about the company in order to protect competitive advantage. As the approach to achieving both these objectives is similar, these subjects are usually discussed together.

In *Chapter 1*, we saw that information security can only make a minor contribution to achieving confidentiality and privacy. Information security policies normally only protect data and information in machine-readable form and do not address the many documents and printouts existing in any organization. Thus, if privacy and confidentiality objectives are to be properly addressed, separate policies that are cross-referenced to the information security policies are needed.

The relative importance of privacy and confidentiality varies greatly from organization to organization. All of us are concerned about confidentiality. We do not want our business plans, customer lists and "trade secrets" to be available to our competitors. Some of us may have additional concerns, for example, a need for strong protection of competitive advantage methods, processes and trade secrets.

As regards privacy, every organization is concerned with protecting the privacy of employee and customer information given to it for business purposes only. While the protection of private employee information generally does not vary a great deal from company to company, there can be a much greater variance with customer information. For a company they has have little information about its customers that would not be publicly available in any event, privacy is a minor issue. But in other organizations such as banks and trust companies, insurance companies and health service providers, a vast amount of their data about customers is not available to others. And rightfully, their customers or clients assume this data will be guarded and remain private. Companies may also be subject to laws and regulations as to how they can even use this information within their own businesses or for marketing purposes, and may have to create "walls" to fulfil their responsibilities. In addition, professional firms of accountants and lawyers have other, special responsibilities to respect the privacy and confidentiality of information supplied by their clients.

Some companies may be able to address confidentiality and privacy concerns by providing brief codes of conduct to their employees and putting some kind of awareness program in place to draw employees' attention to them. Other organizations may need elaborate codes of conduct and detailed guidance to address these issues; in some instances, they may even need a compliance department and other procedures to see that the rules and policies are adhered to.

STRATEGIES
FOR SUCCESS

Separate policies and codes of conduct are needed to manage the organization's privacy and confidentiality responsibilities. These policies need to be integrated with information security policies. Also, processes are needed to deal with paper-based information.

Business continuity

Organizations need to make plans that will ensure they can stay in business or get back into business as soon as possible after being hit with a natural disaster or other catastrophe that could disrupt its ability to provide goods and services to customers. Being out of the marketplace and unable to provide goods and services for an unreasonable amount of time can permanently damage a company's reputation and market share.

The policies, standards and procedures for reducing the risk of such a catastrophe occurring or recovering from such an event in an acceptable time frame is called a business continuity plan or business resumption plan. Generally, this plan addresses alternate sources of supply for manufacturing operations, alternative office space, re-creation of the office environment and all associated equipment, etc.

As we will see later, good information security practices will put into place a disaster recovery plan to make sure that computer systems and data can be recovered within acceptable time frames. However, further plans of a wider scope are clearly needed to address all that must be done to get back into business after a disaster has occurred. Having computer systems without the support of offices, office equipment and sources of supply for goods or services is of little benefit.

STRATEGIES
FOR SUCCESS

A comprehensive business continuity plan should address the full restoration of the ability to serve customers as well as to protect assets after a catastrophe; this should be coordinated with the information security plan which addresses the ongoing availability and recovery of computer systems and data.

In summary, taken as a group, the four pillars – compliance, controls, privacy and confidentiality and business continuity – could be looked at as a framework for corporate governance that each department needs to implement. Of course, the pillars could be drawn and described in a variety of ways; however, the point remains that the role that information security plays in any pillar and the need to integrate activities across all pillars must be understood.

STRATEGIES
FOR SUCCESS

Each department needs to understand the relationships between information security and other risk management areas so that all risk management procedures can be designed and implemented in a coordinated and cost effective manner. This requires that all these policies be created in a logical and integrated manner in the first place.

THE THIRD PRINCIPLE

2.3 Careful consideration should be given to the formation of an information security committee to help ensure that the information security policies, standards and procedures continually meet the changing needs of the organization.

The point has already been made that information systems should be managed from an overall corporate perspective and that good information systems resources to support the company's critical success factors require the talents of the whole organization. This is also true of information security.

Under this principle, we want to draw together an appreciation of all the tasks that a corporate-wide committee needs to perform in regard to information security. You can then make a realistic appraisal within your company as to whether an existing overall information systems committee or IRM committee will have the time to address these matters directly, or whether some separate committee for information security should be formed to delve into these matters and then report back. In large measure, this decision will be based on the relative overall importance of information security to your organization.

First, as we have just reviewed, information security is inextricably bound up with the issue of overall internal controls. We need to manage the relationships between how information security is managed and how overall internal controls are managed. This by itself can be a difficult framework to manage and may require committee members who understand overall control concepts.

Also, in designing information security, as is the case for any internal controls, we have to achieve a proper balance between the cost of controls and administrative convenience and the appropriate management of risk and the losses we are willing to suffer. Where we invite customers to interact directly with our computer systems, we also need to balance the need to meet customer expectations of convenience with the organization's need to protect the company's assets and interests. We reviewed this important balancing act in *Chapter 1*. It is also true within the company; employees need efficient ways of accessing data but at the same time, the company must protect its information assets.

STRATEGIES
FOR SUCCESS

Information security is a complex balancing act. The organization must meet customer expectations and employee requirements for ease of access, while managing the costs of controls and restricting potential losses to an appropriately low level. Many different skill sets across the organization need to be brought together and coordinated to achieve these objectives.

Never think of information security and other controls in absolute terms to prevent any losses from occurring. The key to success is to minimize the sum of the cost of controls and the amount of loss that could occur.

To ensure our information security respects these balances, we should bring together expert knowledge of:

- business processes
- overall internal controls design, and
- information security.

Only in this way can we ensure that the information security policies, standards and procedures meet the balanced needs of the company.

The information security committee

One of the best ways to do this is to establish a company-wide committee to deal with information security and the related policies, standards and procedures. While it may be possible to give these responsibilities to the overall information systems steering committee (a committee with a wider mandate) that already exists, it may be more appropriate to establish a separate information security committee.

Wider committees are often comprised of very senior people who have a limited amount of time to meet and focus on information systems issues. To get their attention may be difficult, especially as regards information security which, of course, is only one aspect, albeit an important one, of the overall strategic management of information technology. If this is the case, then a separate information security committee may be required.

It is absolutely true that committees by themselves do not accomplish a lot and too many of them merely add to costs and create administrative delays. Thus, there is a proper resistance in many companies to the creation of too many committees. On the other hand, committees can be very effective in making sure that policies and standards are appropriately tuned to the overall needs of the organization. The chance for success rises when we put people on the committee that are concerned on a daily basis with the subject that the committee is focused on. A focused committee can help ensure that the information security policies and standards are developed in the first place on a consultative basis, so that they have the greatest chance of being moulded to the true needs of the organization.

So if we create an information security committee comprised of those responsible for owning major systems as well as those responsible for information security on a day-to-day basis, there is a good chance that they will see the relevance of the committee's work and will contribute enthusiastically. We can also make sure that we set reasonable expectations for the committee; their role is to review and approve and to provide overall advice and direction.

STRATEGIES
FOR SUCCESS

Where an information security committee is created, the chair should be a line executive who is a member of the overall information systems committee. Committee members should include major systems owners as well as information security specialists who have an ongoing and daily interest in information security matters.

Against this broader background, let us now recall the specific activities regarding information security that should be addressed at the committee level. The information security committee usually:

- reviews any information security policies or changes and amendments thereto, and recommends their adoption to top management
- approves changes to standards and procedures as recommended by the information security group
- if the following ownership responsibilities are not managed and allocated by some more senior committee, allocates responsibility for:
  - ownership of all systems
  - ownership of all computer sites
- reviews and approves any requested exemptions or exceptions to the information security policies or standards[4]
- receives reports and information on developments relating to information security from the information security officer, and assists that officer in deciding on the impact of such developments on the company
- receives reports from the information security group on emerging technologies and their associated risks from a security perspective and helps disseminate this knowledge to senior management, and
- promotes the development of security awareness programs and act as a focal point for the implementation of such programs.

There are some companies where the importance of information security is much higher, or one might say at even a greater level of magnitude than in other companies. In companies such as banks, trust companies and mutual funds, data is truly money. The same is true for stock brokers and insurance companies. Companies where the product itself includes their information systems and where widespread computer to computer exchanges with third parties exist may also fall into this very high category. For such companies, an ongoing information security committee is usually essential.

---

4 Managing exemptions and exceptions is discussed in *Chapter 4.*

Other companies may decide to form an information security committee on a temporary basis at the time that they are creating or revising their information security policies and standards or when there are huge and fundamental changes going on concerning the role of and dependency on their information systems. Once this task is completed, then the committee can be disbanded, with ongoing information security issues then being brought to the attention of the senior IRM or information systems committee.

STRATEGIES
FOR SUCCESS

At all times, an organization must have a corporate-wide committee that is charged with oversight and overall direction of information security policies, issues and management.

A separate information committee may be required when information security policies and standards are being fundamentally revised.

A standing, separate information security committee is often needed by organizations that are highly dependent on information security as a critical success factor. Financial institutions and companies that transact business with others by electronic means usually fall into this category.

THE FOURTH PRINCIPLE

2.4 Regardless of where and by whom information is created, stored or processed, information security must be managed.

The information security framework should cover all of the company's operations and risks. There must be accountability for the sufficiency of information security when we make use of outside service bureaus and facilities managers either to run our systems or to run their application packages on our behalf.

The need for security does not change when we make use of outside third parties, and its importance is in no way diminished. In fact, the inherent risk of obtaining appropriate information security goes up as some of the controls needed are performed by third parties who are not under our watchful eye from day-to-day. Furthermore, the design of overall controls is more complex, as we need to dovetail the procedures which we perform with those that are being performed by the outside facilities manager. We should also make sure there is a clear division and communication of the split of responsibilities between ourselves and this outside third party so that information security does not fall between the cracks.

We will take a look at how we do all of this in *Chapter 5* when we discuss standards. At this time, the important point is that the need to manage information security has not gone away when we use a third party; responsibility for it must be assigned. Our security policies should make this very clear.

STRATEGIES
FOR SUCCESS

The use of packages or of third party software being executed on the company's behalf or the use of outside service bureaus for computer processing does not change the need for information security.

Systems owners must be assigned for all packages or outside applications and these systems owners have the same responsibility as they have for applications that are run within the company itself.

Whenever an outside facilities management company is used as a computer site by the organization, responsibility as the computer site owner for such activities must be assigned within the company. The computer site owner has the same responsibilities as exist for company owned and operated computer sites.

Customer accesses

Our information security coverage and controls should extend to the access rights of customers and their ability to initiate transactions and or to make enquiries from our computer systems. We need to design access rights for such customers and see that they remain appropriate and are properly administered. We need also to make sure that the abilities of customers to access data or to directly submit transactions to us are properly controlled, with the company's interests being adequately protected by the overall systems of internal control.

To achieve all of this, systems owners and data owners need to be designated to take responsibility for customer access and for the transactions they initiate. Thus we see once again that the need for information security does not change and the responsibility to manage it remains the same; the only thing that has changed is the way in which it is done. Once again, later chapters will explain who should do this and how it should be done.

To ensure that our information security policies cover all activities, the following strategy for success is of value.

STRATEGIES
FOR SUCCESS

Responsibility for all customer accesses, whether to record transactions or to read data and information, should be properly controlled. Systems owners should accept responsibility for customer activities as they do for employees and need to work in the same manner with data owners to discharge these responsibilities.

Overview

Chapter 2 – Putting information security in its place

2.1 Before addressing information security policy, senior management should first develop and implement a corporate-wide Information Resources Management (IRM) policy to provide an overall framework for all of the organization's information technology activities, including information security.

2.2 Information security policies should reflect the relationships between information security and overall internal controls, privacy and confidentiality and business continuity planning.

2.3 Careful consideration should be given to the formation of an information security committee to help ensure that the information security policies, standards and procedures continually meet the changing needs of the organization.

2.4 Regardless of where and by whom information is created, stored or processed, information security must be managed.

STRATEGIES
FOR SUCCESS

The information resources management (IRM) policy serves to communicate senior management's view that information systems are too important and too costly to be left solely in the hands of the information systems department.

Because the IRM policy will affect the whole organization, it should be developed by a group representing all major departments of the organization and then issued by and actively supported by senior management.

Overall responsibility for reviewing and amending IRM policies and practices should be fixed. Often, this is assigned to a top corporate management committee as part of a portfolio of responsibilities or to a separate IRM committee with senior cross-departmental representation.

The IRM policy should set out the policies and standards that will ensure information security is dealt with in an integrated manner with all other activities in the acquisition and management of information technology. Through defining the responsibilities of systems owners, data owners, systems developers and computer site owners on all matters, it establishes the framework for cooperation on information security matters across departmental boundaries.

There should be appropriate liaison between those who are creating any information security policies and those responsible for adherence to external laws and regulations policies on corporate conduct.

Internal control procedures and activities should be designed to help ensure adherence to internal policies and standards, regarding the nature of business to be accepted and how business is to be conducted.

A broad set of internal control procedures and activities, including information security procedures, is needed to protect assets and ensure information integrity.

The organization's internal control policies and supporting standards must clearly fix accountability for and guide the development, implementation and monitoring of effective adherence to overall internal control processes for each business process.

Senior management must ensure each individual and every department throughout the organization understands that information security is only part of an overall internal control process that should exist over each business process.

The information security policy should include appropriate references to the relationships between overall internal controls and information security.

Separate policies and codes of conduct are needed to manage the organization's privacy and confidentiality responsibilities. These policies need to be integrated with information security policies. Also, processes are needed to deal with paper-based information.

A comprehensive business continuity plan should address the full restoration of the ability to serve customers as well as to protect assets after a catastrophe; this should be coordinated with the information security plan which addresses the ongoing availability and recovery of computer systems and data.

Each department needs to understand the relationships between information security and other risk management areas so that all risk management procedures can be designed and implemented in a coordinated and cost effective manner. This requires that all these policies be created in a logical and integrated manner in the first place.

Information security is a complex balancing act. The organization must meet customer expectations and employee requirements for ease of access, while managing the costs of controls and restricting potential losses to an appropriately low level. Many different skill sets across the organization need to be brought together and coordinated to achieve these objectives.

Never think of information security and other controls in absolute terms to prevent any losses from occurring. The key to success is to minimize the sum of the cost of controls and the amount of loss that could occur.

Where an information security committee is created, the chair should be a line executive who is a member of the overall information systems committee. Committee members should include major systems owners as well as information security specialists who have an ongoing and daily interest in information security matters.

At all times, an organization must have a corporate-wide committee that is charged with oversight and overall direction of information security policies, issues and management.

A separate information committee may be required when information security policies and standards are being fundamentally revised.

A standing, separate information security committee is often needed by organizations that are highly dependent on information security as a critical success factor. Financial institutions and companies that transact business with others by electronic means usually fall into this category.

The use of packages or of third party software being executed on the company's behalf or the use of outside service bureaus for computer processing does not change the need for information security.

Systems owners must be assigned for all packages or outside applications and these systems owners have the same responsibility as they have for applications that are run within the company itself.

Whenever an outside facilities management company is used as a computer site by the organization, responsibility as the computer site owner for such activities must be assigned within the company. The computer site owner has the same responsibilities as exist for company owned and operated computer sites.

Responsibility for all customer accesses, whether to record transactions or to read data and information, should be properly controlled. Systems owners should accept responsibility for customer activities as they do for employees and need to work in the same manner with data owners to discharge these responsibilities.

Chapter 3

Mobilizing the organization for information security success

In the previous chapter, we saw how information security should be addressed as part of the strategic management of information technology. Ideally, the company has an overall Information Resources Management policy which sets the scene for policies on information security.

We also saw how information security was part of larger processes of internal control and needed to be designed and implemented as part of the overall systems of internal control. Once again, it is desirable to have an overall policy on the management of internal control into which we can dovetail the information security policy.

In this chapter, we will directly explore information security as a separate subject. *Chapter 4* will provide and discuss a sample information security policy. Afterwards, the final chapter will describe the nature and purpose of information security standards which will serve to underpin and to put the goals and objectives of the information security policy into practice through specific activities.

Most of this chapter is devoted to the roles and responsibilities of various groups in the information security process. This is appropriate as a major responsibility of senior management is to clearly set forth the roles and responsibilities of various groups and departments within a company in respect of any policy which they promulgate.

However, before looking at the roles and responsibilities, it is useful to take a moment and discuss the overall information security process which the policy and its roles and responsibility assignments should mobilize.

The overall information security process

Information security starts with top management. Executive management must create an appropriate control environment and be involved in the creation, approval, and issuance of the information security policy. Indeed, executive management must communicate in word and deed their desire for appropriate information security which properly balances the need to protect information assets, the cost of controls and the relative ease of use which customers and employees need.

As part of the policy, executive management would normally create an information security committee, responsible for keeping the policy up to date and then creating and maintaining the detailed standards which underpin it. This committee also plays an ongoing role in ensuring that information security is being properly complied with throughout the organization.

Ownership and accountability must be established for all systems and all computer sites. This is true, regardless of where and how information is processed, including the use of outside service bureaus to process the company's information and systems. It is also true for all information and data. Accountability must be assigned for the integrity of all data, be it supplied by employees, entered by customers or received from third parties. The assignment of such all encompassing accountabilities is extremely important. The company must ensure that its information assets are properly protected and maintained, regardless of where the data comes from, where it is located or where and how it is processed.

Once ownership responsibilities have been established, the next step in the process is to determine the information security requirements for each system and the information it contains. For each system and its information, responsibility should be assigned to the owner of the business process (referred to as the systems owner throughout this book) that is the primary user of the system and that supplies the majority of data which it contains. In this way, we are best assured that information security requirements are defined in an integrated manner with the overall internal control systems and genuinely meet business needs. In this book, these important responsibilities have been assigned to the "systems owner", who should be the same individual or group within the company that owns the related business process.

As the chapter evolves, we will see that the systems owner plays a key role in the information security process. Basically, systems owners coordinate the activities of all others responsible for helping design, implement, and comply with information security requirements. They act as the orchestra conductor, with the other groups or departments, called information service providers, being the members of the orchestra. These interrelationships are illustrated in Exhibit 3.2 which follows.

As illustrated in the last chapter, information security addresses:

- integrity
- privacy and confidentiality, and
- the continuity and availability of information systems and the information they contain.

A key element in defining security requirements is the systems owners' classification of information in relation to the above three dimensions, a topic which is thoroughly discussed in this chapter.

Once the systems owners have determined information security requirements, it is the responsibility of systems developers, computer site owners and other information service providers to put in place and adhere to the necessary activities and controls to achieve the level of information security required. These controls should be responsive to and effectively manage the level and nature of risks defined above. Otherwise, we take too much risk which threatens information assets, or we have cumbersome, unnecessarily expensive security procedures.

In other words, the systems owner, being the party responsible for the business process in question, defines and communicates the level and nature of risks and the information security requirements to contain them. All other parties, working under the co-ordination of the systems owners, respond with appropriate controls drawn from information security standards. The nature of these overall control activities, defined in supporting standards, will be addressed in *Chapter 5*. However, this chapter will provide a solid, overall appreciation of what they are.

We must also remember information security is not a static process; it requires constant attention, updating and maintenance. As new systems are acquired or existing systems maintained the information security requirements must be revisited and redetermined. As we change our computer hardware and networks, the detailed control activities must be modified so that the defined information security requirements are still achieved. As new and better ways and technologies to achieve information security become available, we need to adopt them. In other words, information security is a dynamic process and the policies must assign accountabilities for everything to be kept up-to-date.

Against this overall description of the information security process, we can now discuss in detail the responsibilities of various groups and departments within the company for this process. As we go through this discussion, we will deepen our understanding of the process itself.

This chapter focuses on the following key principle.

3.1 Senior management should clearly define and communicate the roles and responsibilities of all employees and departments for information security.

The following two exhibits present the players and their interrelationships; the role of each is then discussed.

Exhibit 3.1

Information security is everyone's responsibility

- Executive management
- The information security committee
- The head of each department
- Systems owners
- Data owners
- Secondary data users
- Systems developers
- Computer site owners
- The information systems department
- Information security group
- All employees

As we discuss the role of each of these players, we'll see that information security success depends not only on what each group or individual does, but to a large degree on how they interact and support each other. The exhibit below illustrates the interrelationships of all of the information security players within the organization and illustrates activities in the order in which they are generally performed. You may find it useful to refer to this exhibit as we progress through this chapter.

Exhibit 3.2

Relationships of information security players

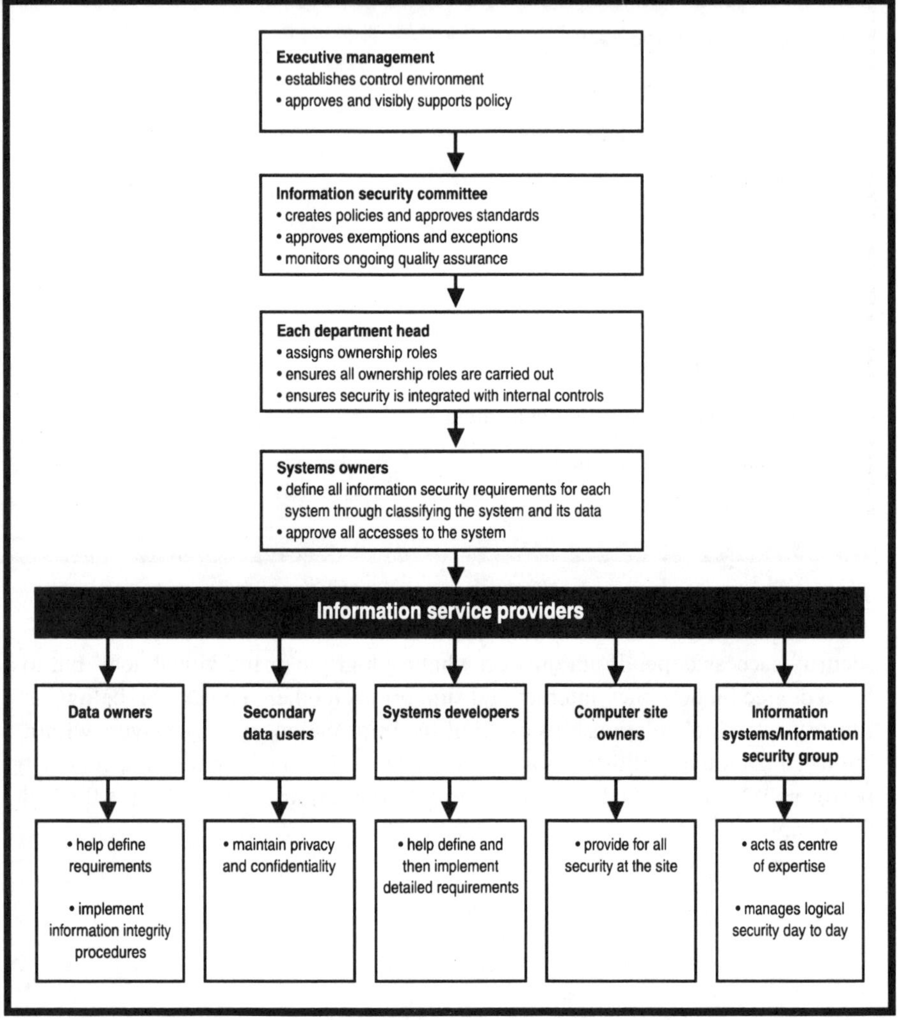

Executive management

The role of executive management is to cultivate an appropriate information security environment and attitude and to ensure all departments work together in a coordinated fashion. They accomplish this through establishing an appropriate set of information security policies, standards and procedures and by clearly communicating their desire and indeed expectation that all departments and employees adhere to them.

Executive management also has to ensure that an appropriate organizational structure is in place to deal with information security from a broad corporate viewpoint. Normally, they will discharge these responsibilities through a few key actions as set out in the exhibit below.

Exhibit 3.3

Information security – responsibilities of executive management

Executive management is responsible for:

- establishing an appropriate control environment to manage all risks, including information security
- defining the need for an information security policy
- approving the information security policy and being proactive in its issuance, ensuring the company understands it has top level support
- fixing responsibility for the initial creation and ongoing maintenance of the information security policy and its supporting standards and procedures, and
- creating a steering committee so that information security can be viewed, directed and quality assured on an ongoing basis from a corporate viewpoint that will effectively meet the needs of all departments.

The information systems steering committee

We have already discussed the importance of an IRM policy and the major role it plays in the overall management of information technology. We have also reviewed how the IRM policy would address information security matters and how information security policies would have to be broadened to ensure interfaces with other facets of information technology and internal controls in its absence.

Our major focus now is to review the nature of steering committees that should be in place to deal with information security policies and standards in an integrated manner.

The first decision is to determine whether the existing IRM Committee (or otherwise named top level information systems steering committee) can effectively address information security issues on an ongoing basis or whether the time commitment will require forming a subcommittee or a separate committee to address security policies and standards.

The creation of an effective committee with sufficient time and interest to mould information security to the overall needs of the corporation is vital. The topic of committee structures for information security was discussed in the previous chapter under Principle 2.3. At this point, we will focus on what a corporate-wide committee should *do* to strategically direct information security, regardless of whether these responsibilities are carried out by a separate committee or by an overall information systems committee.

Keep in mind that the management of information security is an ongoing issue. Policies, standards and procedures need to be continuously updated to reflect fast-paced information technology changes and new ways the organization is using information technology.

Also, we need an ongoing quality assurance process to approve exemptions from policy and exceptions to standards, to maintain the security awareness programs, to assign security ownership responsibilities for new systems and computer sites, etc. Like the establishment of initial policy and standards, these issues need to be managed and addressed from an overall corporate viewpoint.

STRATEGIES
FOR SUCCESS

A committee with corporate-wide representation should be charged with the responsibility of creating and maintaining information security policies and standards. This can be an existing information systems committee or a subcommittee or separate committee that is dedicated to information security issues.

Regardless of the committee to whom ongoing information security responsibilities are assigned, the accountabilities and related activities remain the same. Thus, the discussion below, on the shape and nature of an information security committee, is relevant whether a separate committee is formed or these duties are carried out as part of a broader information systems mandate by some other committee.

The information security committee

The composition of and the nature of the duties of any information security committee are very much the same, regardless of whether its mandate spans across all information systems issues or focuses solely on information security. While we will review how such a committee should be formed and illustrate its mandate with an information security focus, these responsibilities can be incorporated within a committee having a broader mandate.

Senior management should address who should be the chairperson of the committee and who its members shall be. As the day-to-day management of information security will come from the information systems department and the information security group located therein, it is often best to create a counterbalance and appoint a chairperson from some operational department. In this way, senior management can clearly demonstrate that information security is a corporate-wide concern and as such, must be addressed from an overall corporate perspective.

The ideal chairperson will come from a department that is one of the larger users of information systems. As an individual, the chairperson will most likely be someone who has demonstrated an interest in information systems and security and is knowledgable concerning the principles of information systems management. However, a technical knowledge of information security or information systems in general is not a necessary prerequisite for this role. Ideally, the chairperson will be an opinion shaper within the company who has a proven track record in building consensus across departmental boundaries in the organization.

Where the information security steering committee reports to a higher committee concerned with all information systems matters, ideally the chairperson will also be a member of this higher committee, fulfilling a useful liaison role between the two groups.

The composition of the information security committee is illustrated in the exhibit below.

Exhibit 3.4

The information security committee – composition

Chairperson

- a member of senior management from an operating department, and
- ideally also a member of the top committee that deals with all information systems issues.

Representatives

- represent their departments on the committee
- responsible for informing their department heads of major decisions and consulting with them as required
- ideally assume departmental responsibilities regarding information security on a day-to-day basis, and
- serve as liaisons between the departments and the specialists in the information security group.

The department will probably already have an individual generally responsible for liaison with the information systems department on all matters, especially the development of new systems. The above role regarding information security can either be added to the responsibilities of this individual, or assigned to someone else if a separate information security committee is formed.

STRATEGIES
FOR SUCCESS

The chairperson for the Information Security Committee should be a member of senior management from an operating department, and ideally also a member of the top committee that deals with all information systems issues.

Each major department within the organization should appoint a representative to the Information Security Committee. The person so appointed should be sufficiently senior to represent the views and needs of his or her department and have the confidence of the department head. Like the chairperson, a representative should have an interest in and overall understanding of information security issues, but need not be a technical expert.

The representatives on the committee should also be the persons responsible within their respective departments for all departmental activities regarding information security (or have overall responsibilities for liaising on information security issues) on a day-to-day basis. Put another way, ideally the department's committee representative is the person that the department head turns to for confirmation that information security objectives are being achieved.

Now that we have completed our discussion of the composition and chairmanship of such a committee, we can turn our attention to its roles and responsibilities as regards information security.

This committee is fundamentally the coordination point between top management, all departments in the company, and the information security group who work in the information systems department. The role of the committee is one of coordination, ongoing quality assurance, education and policy approval from a corporate-wide perspective.

Often, this committee is given responsibility to carefully review any new information security policies and then pass them on to the most senior management for approval. The more detailed underlying standards are approved directly by the committee, without need for further reference to higher authority.

In this way, top management can ensure that policies are consistent and cross supportive throughout the organization, but they do not have to have a hands-on involvement in the specific details of the standards.

Another important role the committee can perform is to ensure that systems ownership roles are always clearly allocated to a particular department. With today's integrated systems, determining the systems owner requires careful consideration and in some instances, may be difficult. For example, an order entry and sales system could be the responsibility of the order entry department *or* the sales department. An accounts payable system could belong to the purchasing department *or* the accounts payable department located in the finance group.

Where it is unclear which department should undertake overall responsibility for a system, this committee must make a decision and assign responsibility to a department head. Then as always, that department head will assign the system ownership responsibility to an individual or group within his or her department.

The same delegation of ownership responsibilities may be needed for computer sites, when these sites serve several departments or it is not otherwise evident which department should accept responsibility.

As we shall see in just a few pages, systems ownership brings with it a wide range of responsibilities, including, but by no means limited to, information security. Put another way, ownership of systems needs to be established and allocated for a variety of reasons. These include the responsibility for detailed requirements for the system, for business cases to replace or amend systems and for many other matters that extend beyond but certainly incorporate security issues.

Traditionally, committees are not responsible for performing tasks but rather serve to focus on the overview and subsequently on approving and coordinating the tasks that are to be performed. As discussed later in this chapter, the detailed work gets done principally by the information security officer and his or her information security group.

Against this background, we can now list the typical areas of responsibility for the Information Security Committee. Once again, we should keep in mind that these are ongoing responsibilities that need to be continuously addressed.

Exhibit 3.5

Information security – ongoing responsibilities of the information security committee

The Information Security Committee, whether part of an existing information systems, a subcommittee of it or a separate committee, is responsible for:

- reviewing information security policies or changes and amendments thereto, and recommending their adoption to top management
- approving supporting standards and changes thereto as recommended by the information security group
- if the following ownership responsibilities are not managed and allocated by some more senior committee, allocating responsibility for them:
  - ownership of all systems
  - ownership of all computer sites
- reviewing and approving any requested exemptions or exceptions to the information security policies or standards[1]
- receiving reports and information on developments relating to information security from the information security officer, and assisting that officer in deciding on the impact of such developments on the company
- receiving reports from the information security group of the information systems department on emerging technologies and their associated risks from a security perspective and ensuring this knowledge is clearly communicated to senior management, and
- promoting the development of security awareness programs and acting as a focal point for the implementation of such programs.

---

1 Exemptions and exceptions are discussed in *Chapter 4*.

STRATEGIES
FOR SUCCESS

A committee with representation from across the organization should be assigned ongoing responsibility for the continuing quality of all information security policies and standards and the related tasks of assigning ownership responsibilities, approving exemptions and exceptions, and addressing information security education and related matters.

The head of each department

The design and implementation of effective information security is a corporate-wide responsibility. It logically follows from this that each department head has several important roles to play in the information security area. The typical responsibilities are listed in the exhibit below.

Exhibit 3.6

Information security – responsibilities of department heads

Each department head is responsible for:

- appointing a representative for the department to the company-wide committee that deals with information security
- assigning people within the department to discharge duties as systems owners, and computer site owners for all the systems, data and sites owned by the department
- ensuring that effective systems of internal control are in place over all business processes within the department, and that information security is integrated within this overall internal control process
- communicating policy requirements and related standards to systems and computer site owners within the department and monitoring adherence to all policies
- taking appropriate action when weaknesses in internal controls or information security come to light, including the investigation of any internal control or security breaches
- making appropriate requests to top management for any exemptions to information security policies or exceptions from standards
- ensuring all staff receive appropriate security awareness training and support materials
- ensuring all vendors or subcontractors used by the department adhere to all internal control and information security practices and procedures, and
- obtaining annual confirmation of adherence to the policy from all departmental employees.

As these duties are onerous and important, in some companies the department heads may be reluctant to assume such a wide range of responsibilities. Later in our discussion, we will see there are several ways of providing the necessary help to these department heads to alleviate these valid concerns. In a few pages, we will discuss how the information security group works as an internal consultant to help department heads on security matters. *Chapter 4* also develops this support further in the setting of policy that permits department heads to contract out the performance of specific information security activities to the information systems or other departments, providing the other party accepts this responsibility in writing.

STRATEGIES
FOR SUCCESS

Department heads should be responsible for ensuring effective information security within the departments that they manage.

Computer site ownership

Most of the above roles and the managerial responsibilities for department heads are fairly obvious and easy to understand. However, one item needs further discussion from a departmental perspective: the responsibility for computer site ownership.

Fundamentally, a computer site is a shared resource that supports company or department wide information systems. Today, computer sites located in an individual departments are typically local area networks or LANs, although of course they can be midframe or even mainframe computers. These departmental computer sites may or may not be connected to other local area networks to form wide area networks (WANs) and may or may not be connected to the organization's mainframe computer.

Every computer site needs to have a computer site owner so that responsibility is clearly assigned for managing physical security and logical security, doing file backups, and developing and maintaining disaster recovery plans. However, the site ownership responsibilities do not have to reside in the same department as the physical hardware itself. It is both possible and effective to have the company's information systems department act as the site owner for remote computer sites located in other departments, even where these sites are in another city or possibly another country.

Today, virtually all computer site activities can be managed remotely except for the responsibility to mount tapes and to remove backup tapes to an off site storage site.

It is a major decision for departmental management to decide whether they want to take on all the technical tasks of being computer site owner for their own computer sites or delegate these responsibilities to the information systems department. These decisions do not have to be made on an all or nothing basis.

While the department remains responsible as overall computer site owner, the central information systems department could take responsibility for certain activities and areas, provided that responsibilities are clearly delineated and agreed to in writing. For example, the information systems department might agree to be responsible for all changes to the systems software and manage the logical security on a remote basis, while the department remains responsible for all other computer site controls.

If departmental management decides to act as computer site owner, then they will have to hire, supervise and review the activities of technical personnel. Departmental management will also have to design and implement an effective system of internal control over all computer site personnel and activities, which by itself requires considerable technical knowledge and practical experience in the control and management of computer sites.

Another deciding factor is the nature of the systems, data and information that is maintained on the computer site in question. Sometimes departmental computer sites only contain office automation software and copies of data obtained from mainframe systems for information creation purposes. However, if the computer site supports mission critical applications or is the primary and originating source for data used to conduct business, these are indicators that the computer site should be under the control of the information systems department, even if these functions have to be performed remotely.

Many companies have policies included in their IRM policy that define when computer sites can be owned by departmental personnel and when they need to be owned by the information systems department. If such policies exist, these, of course, should be followed; if not, they should be developed.

Most certainly, departmental management should exercise caution before they undertake responsibility for computer sites. They need to make sure that they have the requisite knowledge and employees with the necessary technical skills to undertake these responsibilities.

It is possible to transfer some computer site management responsibilities to the central information systems department without losing the benefits of end user computing and departmental systems. The department in question can still make its own decisions as to the nature of office automation and other packages it wishes to place on its local area network, and data and information can still reside there for local decision support purposes.

The above discussion supports the following strategies for success.

STRATEGIES
FOR SUCCESS

Effective information security is not possible without effective internal controls over all the employees and activities at a computer site. Thus the owner of a computer site must take responsibility for all internal control activities at the site.

The department owning a computer site can contract out certain computer site activities to the information systems department, provided that responsibilities of all parties are clearly defined and assigned and the information systems department formally accepts the responsibilities that are contracted out to it.

It is highly desirable that the overall Information Resources Management policies set out a framework for assigning computer site ownership responsibilities and the conditions and circumstances under which any or all of these can be assigned outside the information systems department.

In making computer site ownership decisions, management should consider that most of these functions can be conducted remotely by the central information systems department.

The nature and importance of data and systems located on a computer site should be reviewed and considered when deciding on who should be the designated computer site owner.

Before accepting computer site ownership responsibilities, departmental management should carefully review their ability to manage technical personnel and the nature of technical skill sets at their command to discharge computer site ownership responsibilities.

Systems owners

The role of the systems owners is much broader than information security issues. Basically systems owners are responsible for the initial proposal to develop the system, are the primary users or beneficiaries of the system, and take the lead in its definition and development from a user point of view. Most significantly, the systems owners also take the lead in defining the overall systems of internal control to control the overall business processes touched by the applications.

Succinctly, each systems owner is the owner or major owner of the business process that the system in question supports. For this reason, we place other players in a support or "information service provider" role to the systems owner. On a very broad basis, the systems owner is the conductor of the orchestra, defining and shaping systems and their security aspects as part of the overall business process and the overall system of internal control. Other players such as data owners, systems developers and computer site owners follow the conductor's lead but are nonetheless essential to the performance.

As part of and in coordination with these other responsibilities, the systems owners have very important roles to play as regards information security. These important responsibilities are listed in the exhibit below.

Exhibit 3.7

Information security – key responsibilities of systems owners

Systems owners are responsible for ensuring there is an effective system of internal control for the related business process and that information security is an integral part of this larger control process. Specifically, they are responsible for:

- assessing the level of information security required
- defining the division of duties and thus access rights for all who use the system
- working with the information security specialists and systems analysts to define the detailed information security procedures that are required for the system
- documenting the people performed (manual) procedures for the new system in procedures manuals, and
- identifying all data owners and ensuring that they are appropriately involved and consulted as information classification decisions are made and the security requirements of the systems are defined.

Assessing the level of information security required

Assessing the level of information security required is very important. It is the key to ensuring that we design information security and indeed other internal controls in a cost effective manner, tailored to the nature and degree of risks which exist. This process starts and is shaped in an overall sense by the classification of information and systems by the systems owner. Because information classification is so important to obtaining risk responsive information security, we will spend a considerable time discussing this subject. Specifically, we will look at how classification decisions are made and, of equal importance, how they are then used to obtain information security that is responsive to risk.

As we go through the following discussion, keep the following key points in mind:

- Classification of information and systems is a way of determining and communicating the overall nature and degree of risks which have to be managed through information security activities.
- Systems owners are the best people to make information classification decisions. They best understand the business process and its related risks. They are also in the best position to integrate information security and other internal control procedures.
- Information classification is not just an academic exercise. Once classification categories are determined, they are used as follows:
    - the systems owner and system developers work together to design detailed security requirements to effectively deal with the level of risk indicated by the classification category
    - computer site owners design and implement internal controls at the computer site that are capable of responding to the most demanding classification for all systems and information resident on the site.

Thus, information classification decisions drive the determination of detailed security requirements to be built into individual computer applications as well as the people performed procedures that surround their use. They also drive the internal controls implemented at a particular computer site.

The above discussion leads naturally to the following strategies for success:

STRATEGIES
FOR SUCCESS

When systems owners lead the process of classifying data, the classifications will more accurately reflect the manner in which business is being conducted and the related inherent risks.

The classification of data and systems is a means for ensuring systems owners communicate their information security requirements to technical information systems personnel clearly and completely.

The primary purpose of information classification is to define the level of risk that exists so that appropriate and cost effective information security controls can be designed and implemented.

Against this overall background, we will now review the nature of information classification categories and how they should be determined by systems owners, with the assistance of others.

We will then discuss how these classification decisions should be used by systems owners as they work with others to design detailed information security requirements for new or changing application systems.

As said earlier, information classification decisions are also used by computer site owners. This use of classification decisions will be discussed a little later in the chapter when we discuss the roles and responsibilities of computer site owners.

The nature and purpose of information classification categories

Separate classifications are needed from the viewpoints of integrity, privacy and confidentiality, and availability and continuity because each area presents different risks that must be mitigated by different standards.

Classification is a way of defining and communicating inherent risk. The higher the inherent risk, the higher the classification category. We can think of inherent risk as having two components:

- the likelihood of the risk or problem occurring, and
- the amount of damage or loss that might occur if problems arise.

Thus a problem with a low chance of occurring but having severe consequences can be as big an inherent risk as a problem which is more likely to arise but which would result in lesser loss.

Inherent risk is the chance or likelihood of an event occurring due to the innate manner in which business is conducted. We assess inherent risk so that we may determine the nature and level of controls that are required to reduce the remaining or residual risk to an acceptable level. For example, we may wish to allow third parties to connect to the application in question through dial up telephone lines. While this easy access benefits customers, it increases inherent risk. The application may contain monetary values such as in a payroll or an accounts payable system. Inherent risk is increased when monetary values are present and increases as the total value goes up. Individual transactions of significant value increase inherent risk, as a very low error rate can result in significant loss. In all these cases, the presence of the inherent risk factor should cause us to strengthen information security over what it otherwise would be.

If a means to reduce inherent risk at an acceptable cost to an acceptable level cannot be found, this is a clear indication that we should reconsider if we want to do business in this particular manner.

A good risk ranking (or classification) system will result in our knowing not only the degree of risk but from where it arises, or from where it flows.

Many efforts have been made over the years to develop fulsome methodologies to do information classification in a "scientific manner", giving a numerical value to each risk, a probability of occurrence and calculating the resulting overall risk values using probability theory. Generally, these methodologies do not provide any better risk ranking than the simpler approach of listing possible risks and asking the user to indicate whether the risk is higher, medium, lower or absent for a particular system.

By reviewing the overall nature and level of individual risks, we can then judgmentally risk rank the entire application system as being of high, average or low inherent risk. Guidance as to how to evaluate high, average and low inherent risk can be incorporated into the descriptions and definitions of these categories as part of the overall information security policies and standards. An example set of definitions follows.

Classifications for information integrity

The following are example categories to classify data from an integrity point of view. As previously discussed, integrity refers to the completeness, accuracy, authorization, authenticity and timeliness of data. The category descriptions given below focus on integrity from an information security point of view.

Exhibit 3.8

Evaluating inherent risks – integrity of data

Category	Description
High	• A number of significant information security risks have been identified[2]. • The application contains significant monetary values which if wrong, could result in significant financial loss. • The application can be accessed by a number of people, including those outside the organization. • Individual monetary values can be significant.
Average	• One or two significant information security risks have been identified. • The application contains monetary values which individually are small or keeps a record of the assets or liabilities of the organization. • The number of people and variety of means by which the application can be accessed is less than for the higher category. Customer access does not exist.
Low	• No information security risks of consequence have been identified when evaluating potential risks. • The application does not hold any monetary values nor does it record the assets and liabilities of the organization.

---

2 These might be identified from a checklist of potential information security risk factors.

STRATEGIES
FOR SUCCESS

Keep all data classification schemes and guidance material simple so that the user can focus on the source and degree of risk and not get lost in complex methodology. Classifying data integrity into the simple categories of "high, average or low" will almost always suffice and should be arrived at by assessing the likelihood and impact of individual risks that exist.

Classifying for privacy and confidentiality

As privacy and confidentiality are different from integrity, we need to use somewhat different control techniques to control these risks. For example, in a financial institution, data concerning our clients' incomes would not be highly rated from an integrity point of view, but would receive a very high rating from a privacy viewpoint.

In theory, there is a difference between privacy and confidentiality and companies who have very major challenges in these regards may need to make this distinction in their policies and standards. However, the means by which we manage privacy and confidentiality matters are much the same from an information security perspective. For most companies and for the purposes of this book, these two items can be addressed as one category.

Privacy

Privacy refers to the respect for employee and customer rights concerning information we obtain from them. Policies should address the sharing of this information with other parties as well as its use within the organization. The basic concept is that information supplied by customers and employees should be used only by the organization for the purposes for which it was supplied. Privacy procedures should be sufficient to address both legal responsibilities as well as the additional policies that the company wishes to follow. They should also address how such information is used and shared within the company itself, especially when the company conducts many different kinds of business and thus is at risk in using customer information gathered for one purpose to do "something else".

Privacy issues will continue to grow in importance in our society and over the years, will consume more and more corporate resources to meet legal requirements and customer expectations.

Confidentiality

Confidentiality refers to information that the company needs to keep to itself to guard its competitive position. It can range all the way from secret formulas and manufacturing processes and methods through to customer lists, financial information, strategic plans and reports prepared for senior management and the board of directors.

As we discussed earlier, information security can only make a minor contribution to privacy and confidentiality. Thus the classifications here will also be of use to departmental management as they adopt and apply the organization's privacy and confidentiality requirements to the entire business process, including paper-based information.

Once again, the purpose of the classification process is to determine the degree and nature of risk. We would use guidance or checklist material to locate the nature and degree of different risks that exist and then review each risk area to classify the data.

However in this case, we would use different terms to indicate we are focused here on risks to privacy and confidentiality. The names and descriptions of the risk categories could be as follows.

Exhibit 3.9

Evaluating risks – privacy and confidentiality of data

Category	Description
Very High	• Strictly private and confidential • Loss could seriously impair competitive advantage or breach laws and regulations concerning privacy. Thus access should be strictly limited and those having access should be fully aware of all restrictions regarding its availability and use. • Loss of confidentiality could directly lead to financial loss, e.g., passwords and encryption keys.
High	• Private and confidential • Information would be of benefit to competitors and third parties or customers and employees would reasonably expect this information to remain private.
Average	• Company confidential • This information should normally only be available to employees.
Low	• Public • This is information the company is willing to share with the public.

STRATEGIES
FOR SUCCESS

The risks identified and the classifications made for information security purposes will be of considerable help in designing overall privacy and confidentially practices.

Classifying for continuity and availability

To this point, we have been separately classifying each type of data within a system. For continuity and availability, we only need to classify the system in its entirety.

As explained in *Chapter 1*, continuity relates to the recovery in a number of days of information processing capability after a disaster such as a fire or flood to a computer site. Availability refers to how long we can tolerate minor disruptions in service due to routine problems that will inevitably occur during one particular business day. As the nature of the risks and controls to mitigate them have considerable overlaps, we can usually classify for continuity and availability together.

As we have already discussed, information security deals only with the continuity and availability of information systems and is only a part of business resumption planning. The assessment of risk done for disaster recovery planning purposes will be very useful in addressing plans for overall resumption of business.

When information systems are not available, a company can suffer a variety of consequences. It will not be able for a time to conduct business in the sense of receiving and processing customer orders, in making payroll payments or in scheduling or perhaps even making shipments. Where the information system is part and parcel of the product, it will not be able to deliver services. A bank will not be able to provide services through its ATMs, an airline company will be unable to accept reservations and a just-in-time manufacturing company will not be able to receive orders and manage shipments to its customers. It also means the company will be without the information that senior management needs to manage the business. If our company deals in foreign exchange, we will not know what our currency position is or be able to manage it. We will not have receivables records available to manage collections and inward cash flow, etc.

Put succinctly, when a company's computer systems are unavailable, it is unable to meet customer expectations. Downtime could result in a loss of customers and market share. The corporate image in the market place will suffer. Relations with employees may also deteriorate. And as time passes, additional financial losses will be incurred because we will be unable to access the information we need to manage the affairs of the corporation.

Thus our systems' continuity and availability requirements centre around balancing the costs we will suffer *if* a disaster does occur with the costs of a disaster recovery plan. As always, we are trying to balance the sum total of the costs of losses with the costs of control. As we demand a speedy recovery of our computing resources, the cost of the disaster recovery plan mounts exponentially. As we try to prevent the disaster from occurring in the first place, the costs of this "insurance" also increases exponentially.

The following examples illustrate how quickly these costs can multiply.

Company A is in the business of manufacturing huge concrete pipes. It knows its production schedule for the next month, which is not complex. As it only has a few customers, it can make shipments without reference to computer systems and can manage collections based on a receivables print out of a few pages. The payroll is prepared by an outside service bureau.

Company A may conclude that it could go without its computer systems for a month and does not need any elaborate precautions to safeguard it against damage. It uses a LAN based on microcomputers that could be quickly replaced.

The cost of the disaster recovery plan for Company A would be very small. There would be no need to spend money for a hot site[3]; environmental controls to prevent large scale damage to the computer hardware could be simple and inexpensive.

Company B operates an airline reservation service and has decided that it cannot be without its computer system for more than 48 hours. As a result, it has contracted for a hot site at a cost of $15,000 a month. A great deal of money is spent on reducing the chance of a disaster occurring in the first place. The primary data centre has guard stations, is protected by electronic monitoring and

[3] Hot sites are pre-existing computer sites that have all the equipment necessary to process a subscribing company's critical business applications in the event of a computer disaster. Hot site providers sell these services to many companies on a first come, first served basis. The fees per month for this considerable resource and facility are very expensive indeed.

entry systems and has diesel generators installed should there be an interruption in the electrical supply. The costs of disaster recovery and physical and environmental protection are huge.

From the above examples, it is apparent that we need to rank our applications in terms of how quickly we need to recover after a disaster. We create time categories that reflect that as time shortens, costs escalate rapidly.

In other words, disaster recovery costs are semi fixed costs, and as we move from one time category to another, the costs jump quickly and viciously. So do the related costs of reducing a chance of the disaster occurring in the first place, as we move from some prevention to doing everything we can. The time boundaries vary a great deal from company to company and should be determined by each company's information systems department so that the categories reflect real differences in physical safeguards and disaster arrangements costs.

STRATEGIES
FOR SUCCESS

The classification of applications for disaster recovery are valuable when creating overall business resumption plans for all facilities needed to get back into business after a disaster.

Application systems should be categorized in accordance with the maximum time the company can go without them before incurring unacceptable costs or loss of customer confidence.

The maximum times should be slotted into categories that reflect the time frames that have widely differing disaster recovery costs.

Thus a typical set of categories might be as illustrated below. Once again, the time frames are illustrative only; actual time frames should be determined for each company by their technical information systems staff.

Exhibit 3.10

Classifying applications for disaster recovery

Category	Description
High	• Recovery time must be less than 48 hours • The system is needed to provide vital product or service to customers and customers are entitled to be able to transact with the company during each business day.
Average	• Seven days or less • Same as above but it is acceptable to restore service within five days. • The company needs access within this time frame to keep up-to-date accounting records to manage its cash flows and the business.
Low	• Two to three weeks • The system is not used to directly support service to customers or alternate sources of accounting and management information such as last week's hard copy print-outs can be used to manage the company for this time frame without unacceptable loss.

The big jump from 48 hours to a time period of two to three weeks reflects whether or not hot site costs will be incurred. Generally, without a hot site, restoration times are quite long, unless the system is built around readily available microcomputer equipment.

Note once again that the creation of the time frame categories is a demanding technical task and will vary from company to company and from systems configuration to configuration.

Now that we have discussed classification responsibilities, we can now return to the remaining responsibilities of systems owners. For reference, return to Exhibit 3.7, responsibilities of systems owners, which appears earlier in this section.

Defining the division of duties for users

An appropriate division of duties is a fundamental building block in an overall system of internal control. At the same time, the enforcement of the division of duties is the primary reason that information security exists.

Information security will do us little good unless it is used to enforce a proper and appropriate division of duties. As the systems owners also own the business process, it is only right that the overall responsibility for this task is fixed on them.

As we have already discussed, once a division of duties has been designed, it should be translated into a set of access profiles, with one profile being created for every type of job. This task provides for the proper administration of access rights. Everyone is given access in accordance with his or her job profile, and any exceptions (e.g., additional access privileges) that an individual requires are dealt with on an exception basis, subject to careful review and approval procedures[4].

Internal controls and the division of duties usually bring to mind the ability to record transactions or alter information that already exists. For maintaining data integrity and protecting assets and information, this holds true. The mere ability to read data, without being able to add to it or alter it poses no threat to data integrity.

However, protecting privacy and confidentiality, also requires restricting who can read data, and if so, how much of it. Thus in creating our divisions of duty, we also have to define what data each employee category should be able to only read. (Remember that in almost all security systems, if I have a right to create or change certain data, I also have the right to read that type of data.) In making these decisions, keep in mind that as a general rule the ability to read data also gives the person the right to copy and to print that data.

---

4 For further information on the ways duties should be divided to support a strong system of internal control, refer to the book *Managing and Controlling Small Computer Systems Including LANs*. The matters related to internal controls are presented in this publication so as to be applicable to all computer systems and internal control systems of any size.

STRATEGIES
FOR SUCCESS

In creating access profiles for each job category, carefully consider the types of data that each job category should be able to read, and thus copy or print.

Pay special attention to the rights to create or alter data. These duties, unless properly segregated, can be a threat to the integrity of a company's data and the protection of its assets.

How systems owners use classification categories

As mentioned earlier, the primary purpose of classifying information and systems is to provide an overall indication of the level of risks which exist from an information security perspective. In performing the classification, we should have a detailed checklist or some guidance material which lists possible risks and their sources for each major type of business process. Thus, at the end of this exercise we not only know the overall level of inherent risk that information security should be responsive to, but have a good indication of the source and causes of these risks.

Systems owners should now make use of this information as they design their detailed information security requirements, both for new systems or for systems changes that have security implications. In carrying out this work, systems owners will ask systems developers to help them define their detailed requirements. They will also want to take counsel from information security specialists, who can help confirm classification decisions and risk analysis, as well as provide help in finding cost effective information security methods to counter the nature and level of risks identified.

The following discussion is designed to highlight some of the key concerns that systems owners should keep in mind when defining their detailed information security requirements. As always, some of these controls will be embedded in and performed by application software, whereas others will be performed through people performed procedures.

Controls over the completeness and correctness of data

Controls over the completeness and correctness of data should include the concept that transactions over a certain dollar value or of an unusual nature require the participation of another employee to authorize the transaction before it is accepted by the system. For example, a second employee may be required to write off accounts receivable, to issue a credit note of over say $10,000, etc. This type of supervisory control can take many forms. For transactions that are being entered by company employees, we can create within the application the need for a second employee to enter his or her password at the time the transaction is being submitted and indicate agreement with it. Alternatively, transactions requiring secondary approval could be placed in a suspense file which the supervisor separately accesses with his or her password, approving and then releasing the transactions for processing from time to time.

The same approach should be taken for transactions entered or submitted directly by customers, for example, sales orders received as electronic data interchange or EDI transactions. The software can be programmed to accept routine transactions under a certain dollar value where customers' credit limits are not exceeded and only standard stock-keeping items are involved; all other transactions would be referred to a supervisor for review and approval or rejection using his or her password.

Detective security controls

The above procedures deal with the initial approval of transactions being recorded. However, other procedures are usually required to ensure that all and only authorized transactions have been completely and correctly entered. These procedures require the existence of batch control totals, exceptions reports and transaction lists or some combination of such reports so that the work of those entering transactions can be supervised, controlled and verified. Collectively, such reports are referred to as control reports and may also include reports to show that daily processing and end of day routines have occurred and that detailed records are in balance with summary totals and records.

Consequently, systems owners have to work with the systems analysts and security specialists to define the supervisory approvals that are required and the nature of the control reports that must be created. It will be the job of the technical information systems staff to write these capabilities into the software; the users will be responsible for documenting in procedures manuals how transactions are to be recorded and balanced, how control reports are to be used and how customer initiated transactions are to be reviewed for approval either in total or individually.

STRATEGIES
FOR SUCCESS

Users must specify their requirements for supervisory approval of higher risk transactions and for control reports to monitor and control the completeness, accuracy and authenticity of transactions being recorded by employees or by customers. Manual procedures that are necessary to complete these control activities should be documented in procedures manuals.

The above detective controls are critical for protecting the company's assets. Without them, there are no effective ways to catch errors that inevitably arise from time to time and to ensure that employees authorized to record certain kinds of transactions are not entering additional ones by accident or for fraudulent purposes.

Authentication controls

When we discuss security standards, we will look at authentication controls in greater detail. However, as these controls are an important safeguard, the means of authentication needs to be defined at the time that the systems owners address all detailed systems requirements.

The purpose of authentication controls is to ensure that we are dealing with the person we intend to deal with. The most frequently used means of doing this is, of course, a unique logon ID and associated password that is the unique property of one individual.

The quality of our password structures should be defined in information security policies and procedures; we will explore these considerations in greater detail later in the book. For the moment, recall that the value of passwords depends on their structure and length. The more complex and lengthy they are, the harder they are to guess. In addition, passwords should be encrypted within the security system and operating system so that they are harder to steal if our system is penetrated.

For very high dollar transactions, access to confidential information or the provision to customers of the ability to directly enter transactions into our systems, passwords by themselves may not be enough. For these transactions, many new techniques can be used *in addition to passwords* to more fully authenticate a user. These include:

- one time password systems
- cryptographic techniques providing for non repudiation signatures
- smart cards
- biometrics, and
- pass phrases.

All of these will be reviewed in *Chapter 5* when we discuss standards.

The main point here is that the method a person uses to request access and to authenticate his or her identity must be incorporated into the detailed design of the system.

STRATEGIES
FOR SUCCESS

The minimum standards for passwords and the other ways that users request systems access and identify themselves should be included in the detailed systems requirements.

Administrative controls

Systems owners also have to work with the systems analysts and security specialists to determine the procedures needed to administer access rights and to review how these rights are being used.

Administrative controls are needed to control *all* access rights, including:

- providing access to new employees in accordance with their job responsibilities and the profile that has been created for that job
- requesting, reviewing and approving additional access rights for anyone beyond that which has been defined for their job profile
- cancelling an employee's access rights when he or she transfers to a new department and providing them with new profiles in keeping with their new job in the other department
- deleting all access rights of employees when they leave the company, and
- monitoring how access rights have been used and noting and investigating any attempted violations.

Normally, the monitoring and investigation of access is performed by the security officer who reports to the head of the department any attempts by an employee to obtain access beyond the capabilities of the password provided. We will also want to monitor the use of exceptionally powerful passwords issued for use in unusual circumstances to take special actions that are normally not required. Once again, the security officer will usually be responsible for generating these reports and passing them on to the department head or his or her designate for follow up.

In addition, we should define periodic reports listing all the access rights to the systems. This is needed as additional rights or administrative errors can creep in over time and require corrective action. Usually, we provide systems owners with a list of total access rights to the system and provide the head of each department with a list of access rights for all employees within that department.

STRATEGIES
FOR SUCCESS

The methods for administering access rights, including their issuance, cancellation and review, should be defined at the same time as all other systems requirements.

Procedures are also required to review access rights from time to time and to correct any excessive access rights that may have developed over time.

The security walk-through

Once the systems owners have defined all security controls, they should perform a "security walk-through" to confirm the design of all controls of a security nature. The risks that were originally identified can be compared to the control procedures which will either be built into the system or performed by people and the controls assessed to see that they are appropriate for managing each source of risk identified.

The purpose of the walk-through is to ensure that we have created a proper balance of preventative and detective controls, all in keeping with the classification category defined for the system and its data. Both these types of controls are needed to ensure a sound system of internal controls, including security controls. If we rely solely on preventative controls, then any breakdowns that occur in the control structure will go undetected for a considerable length of time. Damage and losses can stretch far beyond the level that the company can tolerate.

Detective controls serve to detect and correct losses and problems before they reach an unacceptable level. It is detective controls that allow us to balance the overall cost of controls on the one hand with an acceptable level of losses on the other so that the sum of controls costs and losses together is minimized.

The restriction of access, the primary purpose of security software, is only preventative in nature. However, many of the controls reviewed above are detective in nature.

STRATEGIES
FOR SUCCESS

Systems owners, systems analysts and security specialists should work together in carrying out the security walk-through in order to fully assess the sufficiency of all security controls, including the appropriateness of the balance between preventative and detective controls.

Data owners

So far the discussion on user responsibilities has focused on the role of the systems owners. Each systems owner must take the lead in coordinating all other activities. However, there are important roles for all these other information service providers. The first of these is data owners.

Data owners are those, other than the systems owners, who are responsible for entering a particular type of data into the system. Thus, like systems owners, they capture data, but do so from within other departments in which they reside. The following exhibit summarizes their responsibilities.

Exhibit 3.11

Information security – responsibilities of data owners

Data owners are responsible for:

- capturing the initial transactions
- ensuring the data is sufficiently complete, accurate and timely to meet the needs of all those who will use this data
- assisting systems owners in classifying data for integrity, confidentiality and privacy and continuity and availability
- defining access controls
- assisting systems owners in defining required control reports
- defining security requirements for that data
- helping design the user manuals and training required for the proper use of the system, and
- performing the necessary control activities for the data they capture on a day-to-day basis.

The primary responsibility of data owners is to ensure that data is complete, accurate, authorized, authentic and recorded on a timely basis. In other words, data owners *need to design a system of internal control* to ensure data integrity. They may also assist systems owners in determining confidentiality, privacy and business continuity requirements.

As is always the case, the internal controls, including information security controls, will be a mixture of people performed and software performed procedures.

The activities of the data owner will be very similar to those already described for the systems owner. The only difference is that the systems owner as the overall owner of the system acts as the overall coordinator of all user activities, including those of all data owners.

Data owners are responsible for the integrity of data, ensuring that it is sufficiently complete, accurate and timely to meet the needs of all those who will use this data. Usually data ownership responsibilities are assigned to the department or group who would normally record the data in the first place as a logical part of their overall responsibilities, as they are the ones who first "encounter" the data. For example, the sales department will normally be the owners of sales order data, the credit department will be the owner of credit limits, the shipping department will be the owner of shipping data, etc.

Often, most of the data for the system will be captured by the systems owner. For example, in a sales system, the systems owner will be the sales department and logically the sales department will also be the data owners for sales orders, sales invoices, and credit notes. In other words, systems owners act as data owners for much of the data.

But there are other data types or elements in a sales system such as shipment data and sales tax rates. These other types of data may also be recorded by many departments – for example, customer names and addresses may be changed by the customer service desk or by any other department that becomes aware of any changes.

It is important to recognize the many data owners in other departments and the important roles they play in security matters. Indeed, as these data owners will be the ones to capture the transactions initially, they should be involved in:

- designing controls for the capture of this data
- creating the access profiles for the employees who will perform these functions
- using the control reports that the system will produce to control and balance the data that has been recorded
- contributing to the process of classifying data, and
- determining the nature of risks that exist.

The systems owner should take responsibility for identifying all the data owners that exist and ensuring that they are appropriately involved and consulted during information classification and in defining the security requirements of the systems. It may also be useful to ask data owners to attend security walk-throughs.

STRATEGIES
FOR SUCCESS

Systems owners should coordinate with all data owners to ensure they are properly involved in classifying the data they are responsible for and in defining security requirements for that data.

Secondary data users

Secondary data and information users interact with data in a much different way than systems and data owners; they have no responsibility to record or create the data; instead they only want access to it or copies of it for informational or other purposes.

Financial analysts who summarize data to create financial statements or to support decisions are secondary data users. So are those who analyze and summarize sales data for various management reports, or anyone who is using an information warehouse for analysis purposes.

As a result, their primary responsibility relates to privacy and confidentiality, rather than having to concern themselves with integrity, continuity or availability. If the copies of the data they are using in local area networks or on personal computers are destroyed or altered by accident, they can always be replaced or refreshed from the primary data source.

Thus all secondary data users are responsible for protecting the privacy and confidentiality of data and information in keeping with the classifications established by the systems owner.

Exhibit 3.12

Information security – responsibilities of secondary data users

Secondary data users are responsible for:

- protecting the privacy and confidentiality of data and information in keeping with classifications established by the systems owner.

There are three ways for secondary data users to store or have access to data, each of which may merit separate consideration when considering privacy and confidentiality. Secondary data users may:

- use data on mainframe systems and gather their information and prepare their reports from that source
- use copies of relevant data on a departmental local area network or LAN that has already been transferred there from the mainframe, or
- use data that they have transferred to their own personal computers.

In the first two cases, information security will be the primary responsibility of the person who owns the computer site, be that a mainframe or LAN. We will discuss the responsibilities of computer site owners shortly.

In the last case where secondary data users use personal microcomputers, in effect the owner of the personal computer has to carry most of this responsibility. Policies for personal computing are discussed as a separate principle in *Chapter 4*.

Secondary data users need to understand the classification of data established by the systems owner and should put procedures into place to appropriately protect its privacy and confidentiality in accordance with its classification. They will need to design people performed procedures in this regard, including supporting procedures of an information security and administrative nature.

Secondary data owners should not pass on data to others because, if this were the case, we would rapidly lose track of who has access to what and access would become far too wide spread for privacy and confidentiality to be properly managed.

STRATEGIES
FOR SUCCESS

Access to data and information by secondary data users should be approved by the systems owner.

Requests for access to data should be passed back to the systems owner, rather than being acted on by each secondary data user.

Systems developers

In this section, we will primarily refer to the controls that are built into and surround access to data within a particular application. As discussed in *Chapter 1*, this is different from the overall logical security controlling overall access to the computer environment. If systems developers find that there are requirements for security that cannot be addressed within the application layer itself, then the response to this need should be assigned to security specialists and those responsible for systems software. These factors should come to light in any event if we conduct well structured systems walk-throughs as already discussed.

Within the application itself, we want to control the functions that different categories of users can perform so as to reinforce a proper division of duties, designed as part of overall internal controls. We also want to produce the control reports that are needed to control the integrity of data that has been recorded.

At the application level, we usually implement logical security in part by designing a set of menus, reflecting a grouping of functions within each menu that might be logical for a particular job function to perform.

Exhibit 3.13

Information security – responsibilities of systems developers

Systems developers are responsible for:

- assisting systems owners as they classify their data and systems
- assessing requirements for security and referring those that cannot be addressed within the application layer itself to security specialists and those responsible for systems software and the computer site
- helping users define and document all their internal control requirements, including those related to information security
- coordinating with the information security group to ensure that information security specialists and systems owners work together with them to define the security procedures and other internal controls that will mitigate the risks identified in the classification exercise, and
- leading the security walk-through session for documenting the detailed systems requirements.

Fundamentally, systems developers have the same responsibilities as regards information security as they have regarding any other user requirements and needs. Thus they should make use of their skills to help users define and document all their internal control requirements, including those related to information security. In doing this, as previously stated, they will work with the systems owners and data owners. The responsibilities are the same, whether the company is creating its own custom applications or acquiring and amending software packages.

Systems developers should also coordinate with the information security group and ensure that information security specialists and systems owners work together with them to define the security procedures and other internal controls that will mitigate the risks identified in the classification exercise. The talents and skills of information security specialists are usually required to help design a cost effective security solution.

Guidance materials

A word of caution is appropriate here. When developing systems or installing packages, the information systems department makes use of a systems development methodology to determine user needs, create the code, test and implement it. The methodologies are usually very rich in providing guidance on the tasks to be performed by information systems personnel, but usually have only very skimpy information on the tasks that the users should perform.

For this reason, your company should consider producing a handbook or guidance material on user responsibilities during systems development and acquisition of packages. This handbook will prove useful when designing overall systems of internal control, including information systems requirements.[5]

---

5 Further information on this subject is available in the book *Getting the Right Systems at the Right Price – Strategies for Senior Management.*

STRATEGIES
FOR SUCCESS

Guidance should be available to systems owners and others to help them discharge all their responsibilities in acquiring, defining, testing and implementing systems. This guidance should be integrated with the framework the company has established to define and implement overall systems of internal control. If this information and guidance is not available within the systems development methodologies used by the information systems department, it should be separately created and then cross referenced.

The security walk-through

As previously discussed, the final step in the design of information security procedures is to perform a security walk-through. The purpose of this walk-through is to combine all the talents available to confirm that an appropriate and effective set of information security procedures has been defined that is responsive to the risk classification and deals with the risks and threats that have been identified.

This session is usually led by the systems analyst responsible for documenting the detailed systems requirements. It is attended by the systems owner, data owners and information security specialists, who after the walk-through has been conducted, should formally accept the security design and procedures. This is also a good time to re-confirm the appropriateness of information classification decisions.

STRATEGIES
FOR SUCCESS

A security walk-through should be conducted for any new application or major enhancement, whether this be a purchased package or custom designed code. The walk-through should be attended by systems analysts, systems and data owners and information security specialists who as a team should, formally accept the sufficiency of all defined security procedures.

The need to define detailed internal control and related security requirements and confirm them in a walk-through is independent of the approach used to develop systems. The basic steps and procedures described above can easily be amended to work within an approach focused around a prototyping approach and is independent of whether or not case tools are used to help define systems requirements and generate code. It is also equally relevant when we buy and install packages, as we choose amongst the features and choices the package provides and design the people performed procedures which are an important part of information security.

The approach we have discussed so far should address the integrity, privacy and confidentiality of information security as regards a particular business process. However, we have not addressed continuity requirements, or from a security perspective, disaster recovery requirements and plans.

Revisiting disaster recovery requirements

As we enhance existing systems and acquire new ones, we increase our dependency on computer processes and their ongoing availability. For this reason, the process of developing a new system or acquiring major enhancements to an existing system must include revisiting disaster recovery requirements.

We have already seen that these requirements should be expressed in terms of the amount of time within which computer resources need to be recovered in the event of a disaster.

In turn, this review may require the computer site owner to re-plan the disaster recovery arrangements for the computer site on which the application and its data resides. This review is necessary because disaster recovery plans have to address the recovery of all applications on a site in priority sequence within stated time frames.

STRATEGIES
FOR SUCCESS

The systems development and enhancement process should include revisiting and determining the disaster recovery requirements for the application.

Dealing with routine changes

So far we have been discussing how systems developers and others deal with information security requirements for new systems or major enhancements to existing systems. But how do we manage security for the large number of routine changes to existing systems that take place every year? These could be changes to custom applications, or minor updates or fixes provided by package suppliers.

The key here is to find those changes that have security implications and then apply the same steps to the degree necessary as we have just discussed for new systems.

Identifying changes which have security implications

Many of the changes made each year will not have security implications. They will be focused on amending or adding new reports, revising the basis for routine computations, fixing minor problems, etc. We must pick out of this mass of routine changes those that have security implications.

Usually, if a change involves one or more of the following it has security implications:

- adding new types of data to the system

- adding new types of access points to the system, such as enquiry terminals for customers, telephone access, remote access, etc.
- allowing customer access for the first time, and
- making changes for the purpose of strengthening information security in particular or internal controls in general.

Systems owners and systems developers as a team should be responsible for reviewing all changes to locate those that have security implications. It is best if the organization provides some methodology or guidance material to assist in making these determinations.

STRATEGIES
FOR SUCCESS

Using guidance material provided, systems developers and systems owners should review all routine changes and note those that have security implications. Where such implications exist, they should apply the same steps used for designing detailed security requirements for new systems, but only to the degree required.

Thus, systems owners with the help of systems developers, data owners and information security specialists, to the extent necessary, may need to:

- revisit, review and amend classification decisions
- define the information security requirements as part of the definition of the change
- alter people performed procedures and related manuals, and request changes to the related control reports
- expand access matrices and profiles to include capabilities to read or alter new types of data, and
- re-consider disaster recovery arrangements.

Computer site owners

Basically, a computer site is a shared environment where there are programs and data that are used by a number of people. For example, the mainframes in the information systems department, and departmental local area networks are all computer sites. These are distinguished from personal computing where an individual is using his or her own microcomputer and programs and data that may reside on it to perform individual tasks using individual resources. While the results of personal computing may be shared with others, the programs and individual data items are not shared.

We saw in *Chapter 1* that the responsibilities of the computer site owners centre on ensuring the integrity of data and applications and maintaining continuous availability of data through a disaster recovery plan as detailed below.

Exhibit 3.14

Information security – responsibilities of computer site owners

Computer site owners are responsible for:

- ensuring that data can only be read, written on or altered by those who are authorized by the systems owner to do so
- ensuring application programs can only be changed or added if approved by the systems owner, and
- ensuring data and programs are otherwise maintained unchanged and the information systems resources are continuously available for use as called for in the disaster recovery plan.

We have also seen that computer site management accomplishes these objectives by using the logical security capabilities of the operating system and security software to ensure that:

- only authorized users can access data, and then only through authorized programs, and
- the ability to change or add computer programs is tightly controlled as well as enforced through logical security.

But the whole concept of information security is intimately tied to the overall internal controls used to run the computer site. Thus controls over all of the following inextricably contribute to the achievement of information security:

- physical security and environmental protection against fire and power failure
- changes to the operating system and related systems software
- operations to ensure that the right programs are run at the right time against the right files
- procedures to ensure that all changes made to application software are authorized and genuine
- procedures for emergency changes and fixes to restart computer operations when the system halts or "crashes"
- the integrity of databases
- back up and recovery arrangements for files, and
- disaster recovery plans.

And like any other system of internal control, there should be detective procedures in place so that errors are discovered and corrected. In a computer site, these include:

- the use of audit trails to keep track of how passwords have been used
- procedures to detect and then investigate attempted security violations
- reports for systems owners and department heads to periodically review all access rights to the system, and
- the use of problem management systems to log problems arising in any phase of computer programming or operations and a process to reduce or eliminate errors of this type in the future.

There must be a proper division of duties over activities within the computer site itself as well as laid down procedures and processes which, when followed, will result in the computer site's meeting its mandate and responsibilities through achieving *all* of the above control objectives. Many of the books that deal with internal controls and information security refer to these internal controls and procedures collectively as "general and environmental controls."

In *Chapter 5* of this book, we will look at the nature and basic contents of the standards that will support *all* of the above control objectives at a computer site.

General and environmental controls

The strength of general and environmental controls at a computer site directly affects security over all the applications that run on that site. Thus general and environmental controls have to be designed to meet the most demanding requirements of any systems and data that resides on the site. Unless the foundation infrastructure of general and environmental controls is strong, information security for all the applications and data at the site is imperilled.

While many well run companies have appropriately documented the controls and procedures in all other areas, it is quite amazing that many have not documented their general and environmental controls for the proper management and direction of computer sites. Perhaps this is indicative of a general feeling or attitude that the work of systems programmers, operators, database technicians and others is so technical that it cannot effectively be controlled. But this stance could be perilous.

The trend today is to set forth a set of control objectives, similar to the responsibility areas set forth above, and then create standards and procedures that should be followed to achieve them. This approach recognizes that it is both possible and important to have proper internal controls, including information security controls, over all the activities performed at a computer site. In fact, these controls have very considerable importance as they seek to compensate for the inherent risk that sites are run by employees with very powerful access privileges and the detailed technical knowledge to be able to accidentally or purposefully do great damage or commit large frauds.

On a positive note, strong general and environmental controls and supporting standards to shape this achievement make it possible for the organization to accept a dispersal of computer sites and distributed processing throughout the organization, if this appears to be desirable. The documentation of standards to achieve proper controls at each computer site will help to ensure security quality and can be the basis for clearly defining key functions for departmental management, in respect of their local area networks, to contract back certain responsibilities to the information systems department, if this is desirable.

All of these thoughts give rise to the following strategies for success.

STRATEGIES
FOR SUCCESS

The owner of a computer site is responsible to use all reasonable means to ensure that programs and data are only read or written on by authorized individuals in an authorized manner and that computer resources will be available as called for in the disaster recovery plan. These reasonable means should cover all computer site activities and can be referred to as general and environmental controls.

General and environmental controls are the foundation upon which all information security at a computer site rests. They must provide a strong and robust foundation and must be effectively designed and implemented, commensurate with risk, at every computer site.

Standards should exist to support the design and implementation of cost effective general and environmental controls at all computer sites. They can be the vehicle to ensure the necessary quality for information security should the company want to disperse or further disperse its EDP resources and sites.

The design of overall logical security and related general and environmental controls should be responsive to risk and meet the most demanding requirements of any application and data on the system.

Using classification decisions at the computer site

The last strategy above ensures that all controls at a computer site are designed and implemented to reflect that information classification decisions made by systems owners. As these general and environmental controls affect all systems and data at the site, they must be capable of meeting the most demanding classification needs of all systems and data located at that computer site.

Thus, systems owners need to quickly communicate new and amended classification decisions to the computer site owner as challenges will arise when, as a result, the computer site will require a higher level of protection than it is currently able to support.

Indeed, the strengthening of all general and environmental controls at a computer site to meet a new, higher classification requirement can be both expensive and time-consuming. The computer site owner may indeed respond by asking the systems owner to support a request for additional funding or directly bear the cost for this augmentation. Alternatively, the systems owner may be able to design and implement compensating controls for this demanding application so that overall risks can be managed even if the level of controls at the computer site are not generally raised or strengthened. It may even be possible to house this demanding application at another company site or at an outside service bureau that already has the stronger control processes in place.

STRATEGIES
FOR SUCCESS

When a new or changed application requires a higher level of controls than currently exist at its intended computer site, systems owners and computer site owners should work together to achieve the overall control required to meet these more demanding information security arrangements.

Managing a computer site

The management of a computer site is a complex, technical task that should be performed by employees with sufficient technical expertise and experience. Careful reflection is required when the ownership of a computer site is assigned to departmental management rather than having it remain the responsibility of the larger number of information systems professionals in the information systems department.

This is not to say that responsibilities should not be so assigned. There are many advantages to be gained through departmental or end user computing and these should not be lightly disregarded. However, if the computer site under consideration is the primary source of data for enterprise wide systems and contains the primary data necessary to manage the company's affairs, then caution should be exercised.

Many LANs or departmental computers are used as a base for information reporting and decision support systems and run using copies of data from the lifeblood or backbone systems of the organization-wide information systems department. Thus if the data on such systems is lost, it can be replaced, albeit sometimes with some disruption and delay.

Other LANs or departmental systems are used for office automation tools. Here we have to carefully reflect on the relative importance and value of the documents and information within such systems which could not be replaced from another system if irretrievably lost.

We also need to recognize that we can place LANs and departmental systems outside the information systems department and yet still ask the information systems department to be responsible for most and, in some cases, almost all of the procedures for general and environmental controls. In fact, almost everything can be done by remote access except the mounting of tapes that may be required to back up data for off site storage in case of a disaster and the transfer of these tapes off site.

Increasingly, the trend is to place responsibility for primary data and related transaction gathering systems within the information systems department. This recognizes the increasing dependency of most companies on their computer resources to be able to provide goods and services and to conduct business.

To a certain degree, de-centralization was driven by the costs of communications; these costs have now dropped to the point that this is often no longer a compelling economic argument.

While backbone systems and primary data systems are being re-centralized, there is a growing trend to de-centralize those systems that are information based, that is, those systems which are designed for decision support purposes. This allows information reporting systems to be tightly integrated at the departmental level with office automation tools. Thus users own and manage their own departmental systems for the information and office tools they require, while the lifeblood systems and the company's primary data are within and guarded by the central information systems department.

STRATEGIES
FOR SUCCESS

All computer sites should have a designated owner.

This strategy for success needs elaboration.

When outside service bureaus process data or provide external computer sites for the organization, we must still ensure that the requirements of our information security policies and standards are being fulfilled. This requires that we assign an *internal* computer site owner to see that our interests are addressed. We discussed this requirement in previous chapters and saw that, in these circumstances, the computer site owner would discharge his responsibilities by:

- ensuring that contracts with third parties clearly define in detail the responsibilities being performed by the outside third parties and their undertaking to adhere to our policies and standards
- ensuring that controls being performed by company personnel and by third parties integrate so as to provide for cost effective information security
- receiving and reviewing independent auditor's reports on controls at the outside service bureau, and
- conducting or arranging for internal audits from time to time to review and test internal controls at the outside service bureau.

The information systems department

The information systems department can be thought of as the department that is the owner of the company's principal computer site and the source of systems development or acquisition expertise for its backbone or lifeblood systems. However, while all of the previous discussions apply, the information systems department is more than just another computer site. Information systems departments are special because they have some special responsibilities for the company as a whole.

These additional, company-wide responsibilities include those listed on the chart below.

Exhibit 3.15

Information security – responsibilities of the information systems department

The information systems department is responsible for:

- being the source of expertise on all matters relating to information technology and providing help to other departments as requested
- being the "home" of the information security group which is responsible for quality assurance of information security policies and standards throughout the company
- carrying out research on emerging technologies and competitors' use of technology and sharing this information with the rest of the organization
- maintaining the strategic information systems plan of the organization and proposing changes or amendments to it as required
- maintaining an appropriate systems development methodology for the development or acquisition of new systems, including information security considerations, and
- developing standards for all operating systems and the information security management of all networks.

STRATEGIES
FOR SUCCESS

The responsibilities of the information systems department for overall strategic information systems planning, systems development methodologies and overall quality assurance of information security processes should be clearly spelled out and accepted throughout the organization.

There is one other major task that the information systems department should perform on behalf of the whole company, and that is to manage all activities related to the company's networks and ownership of the enterprise architecture. These important duties are pivotal to information security matters.

The overall enterprise architecture

The systems infrastructure of an organization consists of all the computer sites, the systems software that resides on them and the networks, both the private networks of the organization and the public networks, that interconnect them. It is important to have an overall process to manage this enterprise architecture. Without it, we will end up with a pantheon of different hardware and systems software that will impede the free flow of information and data. Our costs will also increase as we attempt to control and manage a large number of different environments requiring differing technical skill sets.

The enterprise architecture also has important information security implications. We must ensure that we do not use hardware and systems software that are incapable of providing the level of information security that we require. We must also ensure that our networks are reasonably secure in order to:

- protect the integrity of information and data during transmission
- protect its confidentiality and privacy during transmission, and
- ensure that there are disaster recovery arrangements in place for the networks themselves.

It is usually not feasible to distribute responsibility for these activities. For example, if we place this responsibility on the owners of each computer site, who is responsible, the sender of information or the receiver? Who will make sure that we do not send information requiring a high level of information security protection from a highly secure site to one that does not provide the required level of protection?

The analysis of operating systems from a technical information security perspective and the management of networks are highly technical tasks requiring skilled people who can command considerable salaries. It does not make sense to disperse responsibilities for these tasks and such highly skilled personnel throughout the organization.

The best approach is to centralize these resources within the information systems department and make them responsible for the management of all networks, including their information security aspects.

STRATEGIES
FOR SUCCESS

Except in unusual circumstances, the information systems department should be assigned responsibility for reviewing and approving the use of all operating systems used by the organization as well as responsibility for the security aspects of all networks.

The head of the information systems department should act as chief technology officer, managing the overall enterprise architecture of the organization and its overall related security architecture.

The information security group

We have already seen that information security responsibilities can and should be dispersed throughout the organization. We have seen that there are onerous security responsibilities placed on the shoulders of department heads, systems and data owners, systems developers and others. Also, it is highly likely that the organization has or will have computer sites located in various departments, with the management of that department assuming computer site owner responsibilities. Clearly, all these people will need help from time to time in discharging their information security responsibilities. And clearly, a quality assurance process is required to ensure that information security policies and standards have been properly designed and kept up-to-date. Finally, the Information Security Committee must be supported in all of its activities.

For all these reasons, we need a centre of expertise within the company on information security matters. As traditionally this centre of expertise has been called the information security group, we will use this label.

Exhibit 3.16

Information security – responsibilities of the information security group
The information security group is responsible for: • serving as the company-wide resource on information security, that is, acting as internal information security consultants to the organization • providing quality assurance that the information security policies and standards remain effective and appropriate • providing support to the Information Security Committee as it discharges its responsibilities, and • providing day-to-day information security management for the central or main computer site.

While the information security group may reside in the information systems department and perform line functions to manage security on a day-to-day basis at the central site, *it is important that they also be given a company-wide mandate for information security*. This mandate should be wide enough to allow this group to act as a company-wide resource on information security, that is, to carry out an internal consulting role. At the same time, by supporting the Information Security Committee, this group can provide the expertise we need for assessing whether the information security policies and procedures are being effectively applied and adhered to. Thus we can define below the company-wide responsibilities of the information security group in both a helping and quality assurance role.

In a helping role

Many people within the organization will require help from time to time in discharging their considerable information security responsibilities. These include department heads, systems owners and systems developers as well as computer site owners and information security officers resident in various departments of the company. Thus the central information security group should act as an internal consulting group to the organization, helping as requested with information security issues.

But there are also other internal consulting roles to play. Hopefully, the company has already devised a means for monitoring and reporting to top management developments in emerging technologies and the ways they might be used.

Reports and updates need to be given to senior management so that they can appreciate technology developments and can consider them in relation to the overall strategic plan and the supporting strategic information systems plan.

Emerging technologies not only have to be monitored for their possible benefits, but the risks associated with them should also be considered. In this regard, the information security group can play a major role in monitoring emerging technologies and their uses from a security perspective, advising the organization on how and with what effort newer technologies could be safely implemented from a security perspective. A wonderful example of this at the present time is the expanding use of the Internet, not only to provide information and marketing to the outside world but perhaps also to process business transactions.

Security awareness programs are an important part of effective information security. Programs are needed in the form of brochures, training sessions and information bulletins to ensure all levels of employees understand the company's information security policies and related standards. In addition, department heads, systems owners, data owners and others playing major roles may need security education to help them understand their responsibilities and how to discharge them.

It is usually the information security group that originally creates and then keeps these security awareness and education programs up-to-date.

In a quality assurance role

As discussed earlier, information security is a technical challenge and also an important part of the overall system of internal control. Thus we need measures and procedures to ensure its quality and its effective implementation in all new systems and at all new computer sites.

In addition to all of this, the ways that companies use information technology are constantly evolving. In turn, the overall manner in which information systems are managed on a day-to-day basis needs to change from time to time to accommodate new requirements and to reflect the ongoing search for further efficiencies and cost savings. All of this means that the information security policies and standards, together with their supporting standards, will need revision from time to time.

For these reasons, the information security group should normally be involved in quality assurance activities, discharging the responsibilities listed below.

Exhibit 3.17

Information security group – corporate-wide roles and responsibilities

The information security group's corporate-wide responsibilities include:

Helping role

- helping department heads, systems owners and systems developers discharge their information security responsibilities
- monitoring emerging technologies and their uses from a security perspective and advising the organization on how and with what effort newer technologies could be safely implemented from a security perspective
- providing security awareness programs such as brochures, training sessions and information bulletins, as well as security education for management.

Quality assurance role

- constantly reviewing information security policies, standards and procedures and propose amendments for approval
- reviewing information security controls in new computer sites at the time that such new sites are created in the company to ensure proper controls are in place to manage information security
- participating in classification decisions and in the defining of detailed requirements for new systems or major enhancements from an information security perspective, including significant end user and departmental systems
- reviewing information security controls and procedures at outside service bureaus and facilities management companies to ensure these controls meet the information security requirements of the organization and are being adhered to
- reviewing and commenting on any exemptions or exceptions from information security policies and standards that are requested.

STRATEGIES
FOR SUCCESS

The mandate of the information security group should include not only the performance of day-to-day tasks within the systems department but also an internal consulting and quality assurance role on information security matters throughout the organization.

The information security group should be involved from an information security perspective whenever the company acquires new applications or new computer sites or makes use of outside service bureaus and facilities managers to provide software or computer processing resources.

Exemptions and exceptions

This is the first time that we have discussed possible exceptions or exemptions from information security policy or standards. Any good policy and set of standards should provide these doors. To do otherwise would suggest that the policies and standards are so perfect that they can always be applied without change.

It's important to distinguish between exemptions and exceptions. For the purposes of this book:

- An *exemption* is permission to not adhere to a policy because it is not applicable in a rare and somewhat unusual circumstance. There should be a narrow and well controlled door for exemptions.

- An *exception* is the non application of a particular aspect or activity within a standard because there are other compensating procedures in the total system of internal controls that make the complete application of a particular standard unnecessary. The process for noting and approving exceptions can be far loss onerous than that required for exemptions.

We will look at the process for managing both these matters in the next chapter. However, this subject is mentioned here so that we can develop a complete list of all areas of responsibility for an information security group.

STRATEGIES
FOR SUCCESS

The information security group should be involved in evaluating all requests for exemptions from information security policies and exceptions from information security standards.

Reporting relationships

As shown above, in addition to its important day-to-day responsibilities to manage information security within the central or corporate computer site, the information security group has many responsibilities to the company as a whole. As the group is also a company-wide resource, the question naturally arises as to where it should report.

In the vast majority of companies, the information security function reports to management within the information systems department. In a large information systems department, it many not report directly to the chief information systems officer or vice president, but may be placed at the "third level" within the department.

However, there is a growing trend in many organizations towards other reporting relationships to reflect the company-wide impact of information security. These new reporting relationships reflect the concept that security is every department's responsibility.

Three alternatives include:

- *Report elsewhere*
  have the information security function report outside the information systems department, possibly directly to the Executive Vice-President of Finance and Administration.
- *Split the department*
  split the information security function in two, with those responsible for day-to-day activities remaining in the information systems department and those responsible for internal consulting and quality assurance reporting

elsewhere, either to the person responsible for overall internal control or to the head of the department that makes the greatest use of information technology within the company.

- *Create a dual reporting relationship*
  leave the information security group reporting within the information systems department in its day-to-day line responsibilities but create a dotted line reporting relationship to the chair of the committee that deals with information systems issues or to the chief information officer. Of course, the reporting would be to the information security steering committee, where this exists.

Given the importance of information security and the fact that it is both a concern and a function that crosses departmental boundaries, there is a good argument that one or more of the above approaches should be adopted, or at least some variant of them. Clearly, it is not appropriate to leave the information security group reporting to middle management within the information systems department.

Of course, the organization must choose the solution that best fits the overall organizational structure of the company and reflects the way that works best in the organization. The important thing is to put the best reporting structure in place so that:

- there is a clear message that information security is a company-wide concern and the responsibility of all department heads
- people will clearly know that help is available to support them in fulfilling their information security responsibilities, and
- the highly specialized and expensive people who are good at information security are kept together as a critical mass while at the same time their talents are deployed throughout the organization to provide quality assurance and internal consulting on information security.

STRATEGIES
FOR SUCCESS

The reporting relationships for the information security group should be carefully considered, including the need for some form of reporting relationship outside the information systems department.

The role of all employees

Adherence to the information security policy is the responsibility of all employees. In addition to clear statements in the policy itself, security awareness programs are needed to inform all employees that security is everyone's concern and to guide them on how to discharge their responsibilities.

Exhibit 3.18

Information security – responsibilities of all employees

The principal responsibilities of each employee are:

- keeping his or her password and other access methods private and confidential so that it cannot be known and improperly used by others
- respecting the parameters of their permitted accesses and not seeking to record data or to read information that is not required by their job responsibility or is beyond that provided by their password
- understanding and respecting the privacy of employee and customer data and the confidentiality of corporate information and to guard it accordingly
- reporting any breaches of information security or weaknesses in security that come to their attention, and
- managing their personal microcomputers in accordance with the organization's stated policies and procedures on personal computing.

In the next chapter, we will discuss the nature and content of policies and guidelines that should be created for personal computing and microcomputers.

In addition to the above, employees should understand that they will be held accountable as follows:

- they are personally responsible for actions taken with their passwords if they were negligent in guarding its confidentiality, and
- persistent attempts to gain access to computer files beyond the authorities granted can be grounds for dismissal.

It is also a good idea to ask each employee every year to confirm in writing that he or she has adhered to the information security policy over the past year and will continue to do so in the future. Of course, if the company already has a process in place asking employees to attest generally to their adherence to other policies, then information security can be included in this confirmation.

STRATEGIES
FOR SUCCESS

The information security policy should spell out the responsibilities of each employee as regards information security. A security awareness program should be put in place to reinforce this message.

On an annual basis, all employees should be asked to confirm their adherence to information security policies and their undertaking to continue to do so in the future.

The information security policy should be included in the orientation program for new employees and explained to them. They should then be asked to confirm that they will undertake to follow it.

Overview

Chapter 3 – Mobilizing the organization for information security success

3.1 Senior management should clearly define and communicate the roles and responsibilities of all employees and departments for information security.

STRATEGIES
FOR SUCCESS

A committee with corporate-wide representation should be charged with the responsibility of creating and maintaining information security policies and standards. This can be an existing information systems committee or a subcommittee or separate committee that is dedicated to information security issues.

The chairperson for the Information Security Committee should be a member of senior management from an operating department, and ideally also a member of the top committee that deals with all information systems issues.

Each major department within the organization should appoint a representative to the Information Security Committee. The person so appointed should be sufficiently senior to represent the views and needs of his or her department and have the confidence of the department head. Like the chairperson, a representative should have an interest in and overall understanding of information security issues, but need not be a technical expert.

The representatives on the committee should also be the persons responsible within their respective departments for all departmental activities regarding information security (or have overall responsibilities for liaising on information security issues) on a day-to-day basis. Put another way, ideally the department's committee representative is the person that the department head turns to for confirmation that information security objectives are being achieved.

A committee with representation from across the organization should be assigned ongoing responsibility for the continuing quality of all information security policies and standards and the related tasks of assigning ownership responsibilities, approving exemptions and exceptions, and addressing information security education and related matters.

Department heads should be responsible for ensuring effective information security within the departments that they manage.

Effective information security is not possible without effective internal controls over all the employees and activities at a computer site. Thus the owner of a computer site must take responsibility for all internal control activities at the site.

The department owning a computer site can contract out certain computer site activities to the information systems department, provided that responsibilities of all parties are clearly defined and assigned and the information systems department formally accepts the responsibilities that are contracted out to it.

It is highly desirable that the overall information resources management policies set out a framework for assigning computer site ownership responsibilities and the conditions and circumstances under which any or all of these can be assigned outside the information systems department.

In making computer site ownership decisions, management should consider that most of these functions can be conducted remotely by the central information systems department.

The nature and importance of data and systems located on a computer site should be reviewed and considered when deciding on who should be the designated computer site owner.

Before accepting computer site ownership responsibilities, departmental management should carefully review their ability to manage technical personnel and the nature of technical skill sets at their command to discharge computer site ownership responsibilities.

When systems owners lead the process of classifying data, the classifications will more accurately reflect the manner in which business is being conducted and the related inherent risks.

The classification of data and systems is a means for ensuring systems owners communicate their information security requirements to technical information systems personnel clearly and completely.

The primary purpose of information classification is to define the level of risk that exists so that appropriate and cost effective information security controls can be designed and implemented.

Keep all data classification schemes and guidance material simple so that the user can focus on the source and degree of risk and not get lost in complex methodology. Classifying data integrity into the simple categories of "high, average or low" will almost always suffice and should be arrived at by assessing the likelihood and impact of individual risks that exist.

The risks identified and the classifications made for information security purposes will be of considerable help in designing overall privacy and confidentially practices.

The classification of applications for disaster recovery are valuable when creating overall business resumption plans for all facilities needed to get back into business after a disaster.

Application systems should be categorized in accordance with the maximum time the company can go without them before incurring unacceptable costs or loss of customer confidence.

The maximum times should be slotted into categories that reflect the time frames that have widely differing disaster recovery costs.

In creating access profiles for each job category, carefully consider the types of data that each job category should be able to read, and thus copy or print.

Pay special attention to the rights to create or alter data. These duties, unless properly segregated, can be a threat to the integrity of a company's data and the protection of its assets.

Users must specify their requirements for supervisory approval of higher risk transactions and for control reports to monitor and control the completeness, accuracy and authenticity of transactions being recorded by employees or by customers. Manual procedures that are necessary to complete these control activities should be documented in procedures manuals.

The minimum standards for passwords and the other ways that users request systems access and identify themselves should be included in the detailed systems requirements.

The methods for administering access rights, including their issuance, cancellation and review, should be defined at the same time as all other systems requirements.

Procedures are also required to review access rights from time to time and to correct any excessive access rights that may have developed over time.

Systems owners, systems analysts and security specialists should work together in carrying out the security walk-through in order to fully assess the sufficiency of all security controls, including the appropriateness of the balance between preventative and detective controls.

Systems owners should coordinate with all data owners to ensure that their needs and requirements are taken into account in designing detailed systems requirements and the security procedures that should be an integral part of them.

Access to data and information by all data owners should be approved by the systems owner.

Requests for access to data should be passed back to the systems owner, rather than being acted on by each secondary data user.

Guidance should be available to systems owners and others to help them discharge all their responsibilities in acquiring, defining, testing and implementing systems. This guidance should be integrated with the framework the company has established to define and implement overall systems of internal control. If this information and guidance is not available within the systems development methodologies used by the information systems department, it should be separately created and then cross referenced.

A security walk-through should be conducted for any new application or major enhancement, whether this be a purchased package or custom designed code. The walk-through should be attended by systems analysts, systems and data owners and information security specialists who as a team should, formally accept the sufficiency of all defined security procedures.

The systems development and enhancement process should include revisiting and determining disaster recovery requirements for the application.

Using guidance material provided, systems developers and systems owners should review all routine changes and note those that have security implications. Where such implications exist, they should apply the same steps used for designing detailed security requirements for new systems, but only to the degree required.

The owner of a computer site is responsible to use all reasonable means to ensure that programs and data are only read or written on by authorized individuals in an authorized manner and that computer resources will be available as called for in the disaster recovery plan. These reasonable means should cover all computer site activities and can be referred to as general and environmental controls.

General and environmental controls are the foundation upon which all information security at a computer site rests. They must provide a strong and robust foundation and must be effectively designed and implemented, commensurate with risk, at every computer site.

Standards should exist to support the design and implementation of cost effective general and environmental controls at all computer sites. They can be the vehicle to ensure the necessary quality for information security should the company want to disperse or further disperse its EDP resources and sites.

The design of overall logical security and related general and environmental controls should be responsive to risk and meet the most demanding requirements of any application and data on the system.

When a new or changed application requires a higher level of controls than currently exist at its intended computer site, systems owners and computer site owners should work together to achieve the overall control required to meet these more demanding information security arrangements.

All computer sites should have a designated owner.

The responsibilities of the information systems department for overall strategic information systems planning, systems development methodologies and overall quality assurance of information security processes should be clearly spelled out and accepted throughout the organization.

Except in unusual circumstances, the information systems department should be assigned responsibility for reviewing and approving the use of all operating systems used by the organization as well as responsibility for the security aspects of all networks.

The head of the information systems department should act as chief technology officer, managing the overall enterprise architecture of the organization and its overall related security architecture.

The mandate of the information security group should include not only the performance of day-to-day tasks within the systems department but also an internal consulting and quality assurance role on information security matters throughout the organization.

The information security group should be involved from an information security perspective whenever the company acquires new applications or new computer sites or makes use of outside service bureaus and facilities managers to provide software or computer processing resources.

The information security group should be involved in evaluating all requests for exemptions from information security policies and exceptions from information security standards.

The reporting relationships for the information security group should be carefully considered, including the need for some form of reporting relationship outside the information systems department.

The information security policy should spell out the responsibilities of each employee as regards information security. A security awareness program should be put in place to reinforce this message.

On an annual basis, all employees should be asked to confirm their adherence to information security policies and their undertaking to continue to do so in the future.

The information security policy should be included in the orientation program for new employees and explained to them. They should then be asked to confirm that they will undertake to follow it.

Chapter 4

Creating the information security policy

In this chapter we will first discuss the importance of creating an overall information security strategy and then build a sample information security policy. The strategy document is a brief overview that defines the layers of policy, standards and procedures and how they support each other. It also serves to help the reader understand how our information security policies and standards are laid out and thus how to use them.

We will build a sample information security policy by drawing on the information and knowledge discussed in the previous chapters. This sample policy can be used as a starting point to create the organization's own policy or as a benchmark to upgrade an existing policy. Of course, the policy must be adapted to the organizational and information structures of the organization and be consistent with related policies that have already been established.

Policies are broad, guiding statements of goals to be achieved; significantly, they define and assign the responsibilities that various departments and individuals have in achieving policy goals. The activities necessary for realizing these goals are stated in supporting standards rather than in the policy document itself.

As this chapter and its sample policy unfolds, we will see that our sample policy does not contain any in depth description of the information security process. The information security policy should be short and easy to understand. The reader can then focus on the important objectives and each individual's role in achieving them. An effective policy does not have to be more than ten to twelve pages.

This approach enables us to write a policy that should serve the organization for a number of years before it requires amendment. The underlying standards and detailed procedures can and will be amended more frequently to reflect changes in business processes and the ways in which information systems are used as well as developments in security software and other changes that will inevitably occur.

Some companies like to include a brief overview of the security process in the policy, somewhat along the lines of the brief overview that was provided at the start of *Chapter 3*. This of course is fine as long as one is willing to accept that the policy will be 30 to 40% longer if this is done.

Regardless of the approach taken, we should not try to use policy as a vehicle for education or to explain or teach. No matter how well our policy is written or how much explanation it may contain, good introductory seminars to management on information security concepts, goals and roles are essential to the successful launch of the policy. These seminars should be provided to those members of management that are most affected by the policy and who have key roles to play in the information security process.

Throughout this chapter, each part of a sample information security policy is presented in its logical order followed by a discussion of its important features. An appendix to this chapter contains the entire sample policy as well as a glossary of terms for reference. The underlying standards, which are the means to implement the policy, are discussed in *Chapter 5*.

The last section of this chapter discusses the use of microcomputers and personal computing and provides a sample microcomputer policy. This document is best presented as an appendix to the information security policy. Having all policies with regards to microcomputers together in one place makes it easier for the many affected employees to understand their responsibilities.

This chapter discusses the principles:

4.1 An overall security strategy that describes and links all information security policies, standards, procedures and practices should be developed and distributed throughout the organization.

4.2 Senior management should involve as many departments as possible in the development or revision of the information security policy; this full and active participation is critical to the successful acceptance and implementation of the policy.

4.3 The information security policy should begin with a statement of the principles on which it is based.

4.4 The interrelationships of the information security policy and other corporate policies should be clearly described.

4.5 The scope of and the authority for the information security policy and supporting standards and the means by which exemptions from policy and exceptions from standards are to be requested and approved should be set forth in the policy itself.

4.6 The information security policy should clearly state the need to classify information and systems so that information security is responsive to risk.

4.7 The roles and responsibilities for information security should be clearly defined in the information security policy.

4.8 A separate microcomputer policy, usually set out as an appendix to the information security policy, should address the responsibilities of all those who use microcomputers or perform personal computing.

THE FIRST PRINCIPLE

4.1 An overall security strategy that describes and links all information security policies, standards, procedures and practices should be developed and distributed throughout the organization.

Many companies produce an information security strategy document as an overview of the total contents of all materials that relate to information security. This document briefly defines and illustrates the layers of policy, standards and procedures in the materials and how they support each other. It enables readers to navigate through the various layers of policies, standards and procedures. When such an information security overview strategy document is created, it is yet another good place to stress the importance of information security and why it exists. The strategy should be issued as an introductory or companion document to the information security policy.

The sample document below illustrates the possible content of the information security strategy overview document.

Sample information security strategy

Background

Information security is concerned with obtaining and retaining the integrity of data and information in machine readable form, making adequate provision to guard its privacy and confidentiality and ensuring that the information systems resources and data are available as required to allow business to be conducted on a continuous basis to meet customer expectations and protect the interests of the company.

Thus, information security is of vital interest to all of us. Without proper information security, we are unable to safeguard our assets or reasonably assure the integrity of our data and information. We would not be able to discharge our responsibilities to customers and employees regarding the privacy of the information they entrust to us nor would we be able to safeguard the confidentiality of vital data and information which provides us with competitive advantage. Furthermore, information security is vital to ensuring that we have the information and resources necessary to be able to continuously conduct business. Any inability to conduct business for an unacceptable length of time could lead to severe and unacceptable financial losses as well as erosion of our customers' perception of our ability to serve them and their needs.

Today, information security is more than an internal matter. It is part and parcel of the products and services which we offer to our customers and is vital to meeting their valid expectations of complete, accurate and secure data and information concerning the transactions between us or those which we perform on the customer's behalf.

As information security is part and parcel of all we do, it is everyone's responsibility. Thus, all officers and employees are expected to obtain and maintain their knowledge of our information security policies and standards to the extent this is necessary to fulfil their particular job responsibilities.

Scope

The information security strategy and its supporting policies and standards is to be applied by all locations of the company and all of its subsidiary companies, once these subsidiary companies have formally adopted it. The strategy defines the protection and means of protection to be applied to all information and programs stored in electronic form and also provides for the effective protection of computer sites and networks. While the policy does not specifically address printed information or data, the concepts and principles set forth in this strategy will be useful in designing processes and procedures to appropriately safeguard printed material.

Information is to be protected throughout its life cycle including its generation, capture, the accuracy and logicality of programs which manipulate and store it, its ongoing use and its final destruction when no longer required.

The strategy applies to all of the information, data, programs and facilities used in the conduct of business, including the activities of third parties that process or store information and data on our behalf.

Our information security strategy consists of a policy layer providing for corporate governance, underneath which are a set of standards setting forth how information security should be implemented. In addition, various manuals have been developed to provide further guidance as to administrative practices and detailed procedures which are produced on an "as needed" basis. These components of our information security strategy are illustrated in the graphic below.

The information security strategy

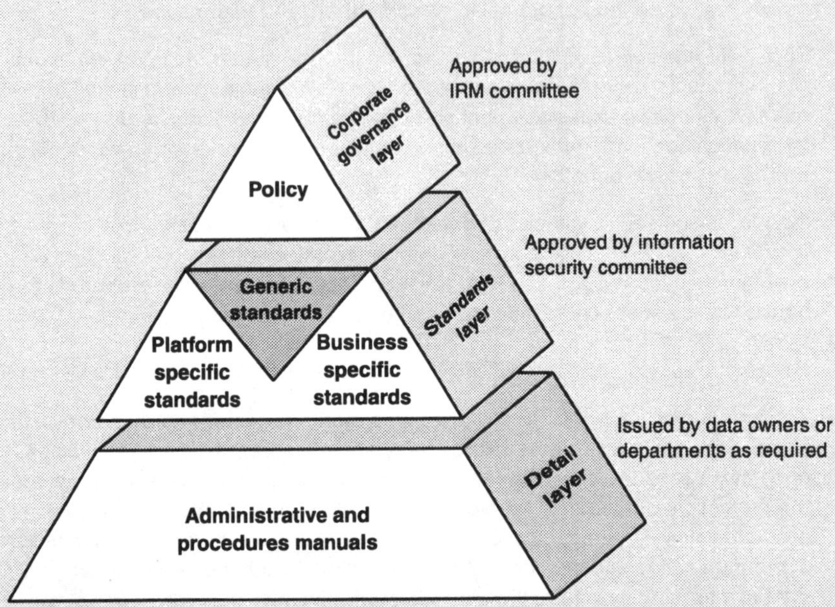

Corporate governance or policy layer

This is the highest statement of requirements in the policy and has been issued under authority of the Information Resources Management Committee. Its purpose is to define the scope of our information security policies and to fix responsibilities of various departments, groups and all employees in respect thereto. It also requires that information be classified as to the nature and degree of risks which need to be protected against, so that our information security standards and procedures can be designed and applied in a cost effective manner responsive to risk.

Our overall goal is to design and implement information security which uses all reasonable means in the circumstances to protect the integrity, privacy and confidentiality, continuity and availability of our EDP resources and the systems and data which they contain.

It is important to recognize that information security is a means to an end and not an end in itself. Most importantly, information security should be viewed as a major element of overall systems of internal control designed to properly risk manage each business process. Accordingly, those responsible for designing and implementing information security should ensure that this is done as an integral part of an overall system of internal control.

The standards layer

The purpose of standards is to define the particular security processes and methods which need to be employed in order to provide effective information security for various categories and classes of information and data. The basic common standards are written in a generic format, designed for use by all business processes and in the presence of all types of computer frames and operating systems.

From time to time, it may be useful and efficient to redefine these common standards to take into account a particular hardware and operating system environment or the exigencies of a particular business process. Accordingly, this strategy provides for the development of platform specific standards in the first case and business specific standards in the latter case. These platform specific or business specific standards should be reflective of and maintain the same overall level of information security as is contained in the generic standards from which they are derived.

The detail layer

From time to time, various departments or computer site owners may find it useful and effective to develop detailed manuals, stating administrative procedures and detailed practices which should be followed as regards particular detailed aspects of information security. These administrative practices are to be developed on an "as needed" basis and will be shared throughout the company and its subsidiaries so that other departments and computer site owners can take advantage of them as appropriate.

STRATEGIES

FOR SUCCESS

The information security strategy is a brief overview document which describes the purpose and importance of information security and the policies, standards and procedures which support it. Its purpose is to help everyone navigate through and understand all security practices; it can also be a valuable resource for the development of a security awareness training program.

THE SECOND PRINCIPLE

4.2 Senior management should involve as many departments as possible in the development or revision of the information security policy; this full and active participation is critical to the successful acceptance and implementation of the policy.

The previous chapters have clearly shown that information security is everyone's responsibility and that everyone in the company has a role to play in achieving effective information security. The mere creation of a policy on paper will not change anything; the accomplishment of goals requires goodwill and active support across the organization.

Thus the method by which we create our new information security policy (as well as the standards supporting it) should be considered as the first of many steps leading to its successful and enthusiastic adoption throughout the organization. We should involve as many people as we logically can in the development of the policies and standards. These people will in turn not only support and appreciate our information policy and security goals but also impart this support to others in the organization.

It is important to create a steering committee to provide oversight for the development and ongoing revision of these policies and standards. This committee should include representation from the major operating departments in the company. Those areas or departments not directly represented on the committee should be interviewed to determine their needs and to seek their comments on the draft policy.

Of course, the various major operating departments who own the major systems and who may manage computer sites will be heavily involved in the development of the policies and standards. However, we should also consider how the following groups or departments will be involved:

- systems developers
- the legal department, as the polices may have legal ramifications
- human resources, as we will need their help in security awareness programs and in obtaining annual confirmations of adherence

- those responsible for overall internal control systems, as information security is only part of overall internal controls[1]
- those responsible for privacy and confidentiality and codes of employee conduct, as these interrelate with information security
- those responsible for any compliance department we may have
- those responsible for business resumption planning, as disaster recovery is a part of this larger whole, and
- any other group in our organization who may be specially affected by the policy.

The previous chapter discussed whether an organization should have a standing committee on information security. If such a group exists, then it would be the logical group to manage the creation of the new information security policy. If not, a working group should be created. To demonstrate that information security is a corporate-wide challenge and not just the responsibility of the information systems department, we should, if possible, appoint a member of an operating department to be chair of this group.

1 This is often the finance department or the controller's office.

STRATEGIES
FOR SUCCESS

The plan for the development of the information security policy is the first step in gaining widespread support for the new policy. It should include the formation of a working committee to reflect the advice of all groups and departments within the organization that will be significantly affected by the policy. Ideally this working group will be an information security committee that will coordinate information security matters on an ongoing basis.

The information security policy should focus on overall goals and objectives and the roles and responsibilities of various groups or departments in achieving them. It should provide broad statements of principle that will endure over a number of years. The more detailed means by which information security should be obtained should be placed in supporting standards. In this way the policy can be a short, succinct and relatively constant statement while the supporting materials can be amended more frequently to reflect changes in processes to meet changing conditions.

The following illustrates the table of contents for the information security policy that we will create throughout this chapter (the complete sample information security policy is included in the *Appendix* of this chapter). Against this background, we can now create our sample information security policy.

A sample information security policy

I Principles

II Relationship to other policies

III Scope, authority and exemptions

IV Information classification

V Assignment of ownership

VI Roles and responsibilities

- i) IRM committee
- ii) Information security committee
- iii) Department heads
- iv) Systems owners
- v) Data owners
- vi) Secondary data users
- vii) All employees
- viii) Computer site owners
- ix) Information systems department
- x) Systems developers
- xi) Information security group

VII Authority of the vice president of information systems

VIII The internet

IX Security awareness programs

THE THIRD PRINCIPLE

4.3 The information security policy should begin with a statement of the principles on which it is based.

We will begin with the contents of a principles section for the information security policy and then discuss it.

I Principles

Information is a major asset of THE COMPANY and thus needs to be protected and safeguarded. In this policy, the term "information" includes the data from which it is derived. This information security policy has been designed to ensure that:

- data has the integrity required to support its many uses in conducting and managing the business
- the privacy of our customers and employees is respected
- the confidentiality of our information, which gives us competitive advantage, is preserved, and
- our information systems and data are available as required to meet valid customer expectations for ongoing delivery of goods and services and protect our hard-earned reputation for reliability and service.

The quality of our information systems and the information they contain is part of the goods and services that we sell to our customers and plays a major role in meeting customer expectations. We need complete, accurate and timely data to fulfil customer commitments and support the electronic data interchanges and other electronic interfaces that customers have with us. We need to respect the privacy of customers and employees who give us data and fully meet their valid expectations in these regards. The information derived from our systems plays a key part in managing our business in these competitive times; we need to safeguard both its integrity and its confidentiality. In other words, information security is part of our competitive advantage.

Thus, in designing and implementing information security, we seek to balance the cost of security, the losses that occur and the ease of access for customers and employees.

As information security is part of a larger overall system of internal controls, it should be designed and implemented in an integrated manner with other control procedures.

Information security is everyone's responsibility. All employees must only access company systems for valid business purposes within the limits of their granted authority and protect the confidentiality of their passwords and other means of gaining access to the company's systems. Our information security procedures are designed to give all employees the access that they require to discharge their responsibilities, while at the same time protecting the interests of the company and providing for individual accountability. In keeping with this principle, the password or other means of authentication used by each employee to gain access shall be unique. The nature of passwords, the requirement for their uniqueness and their frequent change are all addressed in the supporting standards to this policy.

Note: A separate microcomputer policy addresses the responsibilities of all those who use microcomputers or perform personal computing.

Starting the information security policy with a clear statement of the principles on which it is based will help readers understand the purpose of the policy. In this way, they will be in a better position to actively support the goals of senior management in issuing it.

Note also that the principles state that information security is a critical success factor for the organization. We have pointed out that data must have integrity so that we can serve customers and also have the base for information that is needed to manage the company. We have reminded the reader that ongoing availability of our information systems and data are critical success factors for the organization, as customers expect us to be in business and have the ability to provide goods and services on a continuous and prompt basis.

The principles also reinforce the important concept that information security is everyone's concern and that all employees have a role to play in achieving and maintaining the information security that is required.

Of course, each company will have to alter the words used in the principles to reflect its own culture and organizational structures. But overall, the principles should clearly illustrate the importance of information security in the context of how the organization conducts business. If your organization has a corporate motto or slogan encapsulating your service strategy or corporate goals, then the principles should show how information security contributes to this.

STRATEGIES
FOR SUCCESS

The statement of principles in the information security policy should clearly describe how information security plays a major role in achieving the organization's critical success factors. It should illustrate that information security is part and parcel of customer service and that the ongoing availability of reliable data, information and systems resources is essential for meeting customer service expectations and effectively managing the company. If the company has a motto or slogan expressing its corporate values, this should be incorporated into the principles statement and the ways in which information security serves to achieve these shared values clearly illustrated.

THE FOURTH PRINCIPLE

4.4 The interrelationships of the information security policy and other corporate policies should be clearly described.

The sample policy should link information security with the overall framework for corporate governance and information risk management. Once again, the words actually used will, of course, have to be adapted to suit the particular polices and terms used within your company.

II Relationship to other policies

Information security is an important part of the company's overall policies and procedures for corporate governance and risk management. Accordingly, this information security policy should be read in conjunction with the following:

- the information resources management policy which describes the overall strategic management of all aspects of information systems
- the internal control framework, which describes responsibilities for the overall design and implementation of systems of internal controls for overall business processes
- polices for compliance with laws and regulations
- the company's code of privacy and confidentiality
- policies for business resumption planning, and
- principles for the use of our systems development methodologies, which set forth the steps normally required for the development of new systems and assigns responsibility for them.

The importance of these interrelationships was reinforced in previous chapters. These should be communicated in the policy itself so that the reader will see that information security is only part of the overall web of policies for corporate governance and understand that information security contributes to many other objectives.

Where a company does not have any of the policies referred to above, it may be necessary to expand the information security policy to provide at least some guidance in the missing area until the required related policy is developed. The is especially true regarding the information resources or IRM Policy.

We are building the sample information security policy in this chapter on the assumption that all of these other related policies already exist. If your organization needs to supplement the sample policy for any other policies that are temporarily missing, revisit *Chapters 1* through *3* for a detailed discussion of the relationships between information security and these other policy areas.

STRATEGIES
FOR SUCCESS

The information security policy should refer to all other related policies that are part of the overall framework within the company for corporate governance and information risk management. Such other policies may include those related to overall information resources management, compliance policies, internal control frameworks, privacy and confidentiality codes, business resumption planning and principles for the use of systems development methodologies.

THE FIFTH PRINCIPLE

4.5 The scope of and the authority for the information security policy and supporting standards and the means by which exemptions from policy and exceptions from standards are to be requested and approved should be set forth in the policy itself.

The sample policy deals with this area as follows:

III Scope, authority and exemptions

Scope

This policy covers all of the company's locations, branches and operations and is intended to apply to all of its subsidiaries, once it has been approved by them. It should be applied to all of the company's computer sites and networks, including local area networks and all of the systems and the data that they contain. This policy also applies to fax transmissions and electronic mail systems and messages. A separate appendix to this policy addresses the responsibility of those performing personal computing or using personal microcomputers.

While information and data in printed form is not specifically addressed by this policy, the protection of the confidentiality and privacy of printed material can be enhanced by applying the principles and concepts contained herein. Fax transmissions are inherently insecure and this should be borne in mind when deciding to send a document by fax or to act upon information received by fax.

Authority

This policy has been issued by the Information Resources Management Committee which is responsible for amending this policy from time to time as required. Reporting to this committee, an Information Security Committee has been formed to address information security matters on a regular basis and to develop and approve supporting standards for this policy, and to keep such standards up-to-date.

Exemptions and exceptions

On rare occasions, there may be circumstances where this policy is not appropriate and those assigned ownership responsibilities below may wish to request an exemption to the policy. Such exemptions should be requested in writing by the department head and forwarded to the chair of the Information Security Committee. The committee will review such requests and forward them with their comments to the Information Resources Management Committee for final decision.

The supporting standards to this policy document the activities and minimum requirements for information security commensurate with varying levels of risk. As information security is only part of an overall system of internal control, some of these standards may not be applicable due to the existence of other compensating controls in the overall system of internal controls. In such circumstances, systems owners or computer site owners should, after obtaining the approval of their department head, document exceptions in employing the standards and the related compensating controls that make this appropriate and provide this information to the chair of the Information Security Committee for review and approval.

Breadth of scope

The sample policy is very broad in scope, applying to all branches, locations and computer sites of the company. We have also stated that the policy should apply to all subsidiaries after the formality of its adoption by each of them. Such a broad policy is normally required for integrated systems where much data and information is passed back and forth between locations and entities within a large corporate group. Like a chain, security is only as strong as its weakest link and thus information security policies and standards should be the same throughout the organization.

This raises a logical concern: How can policies and standards be created that can be applicable across a wide variety of businesses and operations? The key to doing so lies in the creation of standards that are responsive to risk and which take into account the various types of computer hardware and software that may be employed. In other words, the standards should be written in a way that provides the needed flexibility so that they can be adapted for varying business circumstances and computer environments, while at the same time providing an overall framework for appropriate consistency and quality assurance for information security. We set the scene for this earlier when we developed the information security strategy.

The formation of a broadly-based team to create the policies, as recommended in Principle 1 above, will be instrumental to ensuring that the policies and standards can be effectively used in all the business units and for all activities of the organization.

STRATEGIES
FOR SUCCESS

Information security strategies and policies should be designed for use throughout the company and all of its subsidiaries. In large part, this broad applicability depends upon creating underlying standards that can respond to different levels of risk and that can be adapted to the varying business circumstances and computer environments throughout the organization.

Printed material

The scope of the information security policy does not include printed material, except to suggest that: "the protection of the confidentiality and privacy of printed material can be enhanced by applying the principles and concepts contained herein". Printed material is a contentious issue. Some companies do not include it in the information security policy; others try to write a comprehensive policy that covers all information and documents, including printed material.

The inclusion of printed material significantly complicates the creation of an information security policy, and especially its underlying standards. Inclusion requires making many decisions regarding the classification and safeguarding of printed information such as letters, printed reports, contracts, board minutes and other elements of a huge variety of printed information. Other decisions must be made as to the ways in which such paper should be classified and by whom, whether all pieces of paper should bear their classification on their face, and how and where important contracts and legal documents should be stored to prevent their loss and destruction. The issues are many and complex.

Furthermore, while the vast majority of organizations need and have policies that deal with electronic information and data, many organizations address their concerns about printed material in less formal ways. Written rules for the classification of and access to printed material can be quite bureaucratic and time-consuming to both create and follow; thus only the largest of organizations and those with a very high need for confidentiality develop formal policies for security of printed material.

To the extent it may be required, it is usually better to address printed material in a separate policy or within an overall policy on business ethics or privacy and confidentiality. If the organization tries to address all of the security matters related to printed material in the policy and standards designed for information systems, there is a danger that the focus on electronic information and data will be lost. In addition, the document and its underlying standards will be long and complex, difficult to understand and unwieldy to work with.

For all these reasons, printed material is excluded in both this sample policy and this book. However, as shown in the sample policy, the organization can point out that printed material can be protected and safeguarded by intelligently applying the principles set forth in the information security policy.

STRATEGIES
FOR SUCCESS

While the information security policy should point out that printed material can be protected by applying the principles set forth for electronic data and information, the policy should focus on information systems and data. The many and complicated issues surrounding printed material should be addressed as a separate policy or within the organization's overall policy on business ethics or privacy and confidentiality.

Faxes

While some may view faxes as printed material, today's software allows for the conversion of documents directly into faxes and vice versa. Because of this and their widespread use, faxes are directly covered in the sample information security policy.

The fax is an vulnerable medium. Faxes exist in plain text. They can be easily intercepted or forged so that the receiver thinks the fax is from A when really it has been sent by B. They can be intercepted within the office of the person they are addressed to or accidentally sent to the wrong telephone number. Faxes make it difficult to positively identify the sender, guard confidentiality or know that the message received has not been altered en route. For all these reasons, the policy states that we should consider faxes as insecure and cautiously use them and rely on them accordingly.

The limitation of faxes as a secure form of business communication, and how and when they might be used are fit subjects for any information security awareness course.

STRATEGIES
FOR SUCCESS

Faxes are an inherently insecure medium, both for guarding the privacy and confidentiality of communications and ensuring the identity of the sender and the integrity of the information. The information security policy should highlight their vulnerability and caution the reader to use or accept them accordingly.

Electronic mail

Electronic mail is included in the sample policy for obvious reasons – its widespread use and the fact that sometimes we also attach documents containing very confidential data to electronic messages.

STRATEGIES
FOR SUCCESS

Electronic mail should be included in the scope of the information security policy and such systems and their information should be classified and secured in the same manner as any other system and its data.

Authority – ownership and approval of policy and standards

The most senior level committee within the company that has responsibility for broad matters affecting information systems should also be responsible for the information security policy and for keeping it up-to-date. In this way there is a greater chance that information security will be seen as a corporate-wide responsibility and the cooperation and participation needed to successfully implement information security will be fostered.

The sample policy fixes these responsibilities on the Information Resources Management committee, consistent with the concept that the company should have an IRM Policy and that information security should be addressed within the context established by it. If your organization does not have an IRM policy, then the information security policy should be approved (and kept up-to-date) by the most senior committee in the company that has overall responsibility for information systems matters.

Note that the policy should *not* be created and approved by the head of information systems. Information security is a company-wide responsibility and thus the policy should be approved and actively supported by a committee that has a corporate-wide mandate and includes representatives from many key departments.

STRATEGIES
FOR SUCCESS

The most senior committee in the company that deals with information systems matters should be responsible for the information security policy. Ideally, this should be the Information Resources Management Committee, having senior management representation from major departments as well as the information systems department.

Any information security committee that may be formed would receive its mandate from the IRM Committee and report to it. We have already discussed the useful role that an information security committee can play in many companies: where it exists, it would be responsible for the approval of standards underlying the policy and would review requested exemptions from the policy and exceptions from the standards.

Management of exemptions and exceptions

Throughout this book, the terms exemption and exception are defined as follows:

- exemption refers to a narrow and controlled dispensation from following a particular aspect of policy

- exception refers to the non adherence to a particular standard as other compensating procedures in the total system of internal control make the application of a particular standard unnecessary.

Providing for exemptions and exceptions is a key part of any policy. We have all been frustrated by a bureaucratic approach to policies and standards at some time in our lives. In fact, it is almost impossible to write policies and standards to fit all occasions and all business operations. So clearly there needs to be a well-controlled route to obtaining exemptions and exceptions which provides the flexibility that will allow these policies and standards to be applied intelligently.

Exemptions to the policy should be very rare. Often, exemptions are granted at the time when a new policy is first put into place so that a business unit or responsible party can have the time required to make the necessary changes in existing systems and processes to conform with the new policy. For example, the policy may require that security access matrices be in place to define the access rights for each job function. Some departments may not have such matrices at the time the policy is promulgated and thus need an exemption for a period of time while they are being created. Such exemptions are usually given for a limited period of time, appropriate to the amount of time and effort that will be required to make the necessary adjustments.

Other exemptions may be requested on the more permanent grounds that adherence to policy is just too expensive for a particular business unit or operation. Thus the requester of an exemption will argue that more risk than the policy would permit should be accepted in order to better balance risks and costs of control. For example, the policy might require that audit trails be built into all systems so that we can always determine who has initiated a particular transaction. A business unit may have a system where the dollar value of individual transactions is low and for which it would be very expensive to program for the creation of audit trails and then store details on who had initiated the thousands of individually small transactions. In this case, the small increase in risk could be argued as being acceptable. The additional losses, if any, which might arise would be less than the administrative costs of creating, maintaining and then following up on audit trails.

Of course, all exemptions should be reviewed on an annual basis to ensure that they are still appropriate. In the latter example given above, the costs of data storage may continue to drop and the company may decide to buy a new application package which may provide for audit trails in any event. Thus the need for the exemption may be resolved with the passage of time.

Exemption procedures

The following details would normally be included in a request for an exemption from policy:

- the underlying reasons for the request
- the cost savings if the exemption were approved
- indications of the nature of the risk that would be increased, and
- the monitoring processes that will be put in place to prevent unacceptable losses.

Depending on its nature, an exemption should only be requested and then granted for a given period of time.

The sample policy illustrates that exemption requests might go first to the Information Security Committee, who, if they support them, would pass them along to the IRM Committee for final approval. The key points here are:

- exemptions should be tightly controlled and approved at a very senior level
- they should be documented and agreed to explicitly within the organization, and
- they should be infrequent.

If there is an internal audit department, the approving level within the organization may indeed wish to solicit its advice before deciding upon an exemption request. They may also wish to have the advice of the information security group.

STRATEGIES
FOR SUCCESS

Exemptions from policies should be rare and carefully controlled through review and approval procedures at a senior level within the organization. All requests for exemptions should be supported by a statement of the related risks, costs savings and monitoring procedures against unacceptable losses. In certain cases, exemptions should only be requested and granted for a limited period of time. In the case of longer term exemptions, responsibility should be fixed for a periodic review to determine if they are still required.

Exception procedures

Exceptions are very different from exemptions. They refer to the inapplicability of standards rather that policies, and thus have a less pervasive impact on the overall risk management of information security. Secondly, they will be more numerous, as they relate to the inapplicability of a particular standard or an activity it contains due to other compensating procedures in the overall systems of internal control.

Indeed, exceptions will often not increase risk; the standard becomes inappropriate as the risk is already being effectively contained by other procedures in the broader, overall system of internal control.

For all these reasons, the approval mechanisms for exceptions can be less rigorous. However, an approach that is too cavalier could foster an overall disrespect for standards.

Our sample policy requires that exceptions be documented, both as regards the standard or standards that are inappropriate and the compensating controls which make up for their absence. This documentation would be forwarded to the Information Security Committee for approval. This is, of course, only one way to ensure a quality assurance review over exceptions. Another way is to involve the internal audit department, either by having them review all exceptions at the time that they are first put into play or by having them review all exceptions at the time they carry out their audit work in the various departments. Once again, in deciding on exceptions, the Information Security Committee may request the advice of the internal audit department and information security group.

Note that we have not involved the more senior IRM Committee in these decisions due to the lesser importance of exceptions. However, they may want to receive overall summaries of approved exceptions from time to time.

STRATEGIES
FOR SUCCESS

Exceptions to standards may be more frequently encountered as certain activities within a standard may not be appropriate or required due to other compensating procedures in the overall system of internal control. Exceptions should be documented, including details concerning the compensating controls. They should also be subject to independent review and approval to help ensure that risks are being properly managed. If an Information Security Committee exists, it could be assigned this task.

THE SIXTH PRINCIPLE

4.6 The information security policy should clearly state the need to classify information and systems so that information security is responsive to risk.

The sample policy contains the following:

IV Information classification

Making classification decisions

Effective information risk management requires that information security be designed and implemented in a manner that is responsive to the nature and degree of risks involved. The goal is to achieve reasonable, but not absolute assurance as regards the effectiveness of information security, recognizing the balance between the risks to be contained, the costs of doing so, the relative ease of access required by customers and employees and the losses which may occur.

Risks will vary from business process to business process and will also vary with the type of data or information under consideration. The assessment of risk must not only consider the protection of the company's assets and information, but also reflect our responsibility to customers and employees to protect confidentiality and to have processes in place so that our systems will be available to help us provide timely goods and services in accordance with reasonable customer expectations.

Thus, the responsibility to classify information rests with the systems owners.

All information should be classified from three points of view:

- data integrity
- privacy and confidentiality, and
- continuity and availability.

The classifications should be determined by applying the company's standard on information and data classification.

Using classification decisions

The classification categories shall be used by the systems owner when working with others to define the detailed security requirements for new systems or changes to existing systems.

Computer site owners shall ensure that their computer site is capable of fulfilling the requirements of the supporting standards as regards the most demanding classification category for all information and systems on the site.

The supporting standards to this policy set forth the activities and internal controls systems owners and computer site owners should follow in these regards.

The above policy statement is in keeping with the detailed discussion of information classification in *Chapter 3*.

Classification is a vitally important activity as it helps achieve three important goals:

- *Information security is responsive to risk*
  Through classification, we are in a much better position to ensure that information security is responsive to risk and that there is a correct balance between management of risks and the costs of information security.
- *There is one set of consistent, corporate-wide policies which are applicable across varying circumstances*
  Because information is classified and standards are flexible and can respond to the results of this classification process, we can have one set of policies that can be used throughout the company and all the different types of business we conduct.
- *Security needs are fully defined*
  Classification is the major way in which the users define their information security needs and communicate them to computer site owners and systems developers.

As discussed, risks should be classified from three points of view (integrity of data, confidentiality and privacy, and availability and continuity) as each of these risk areas are fundamentally responded to by different standards or procedures. In this way we can fine-tune our information security as best as possible.

We have fixed responsibility for classification onto the systems owner. Determining the nature of risk and its degree or severity requires a strong knowledge of the business process to which the data and information relates; thus it is only logical that the systems owner, who is the most knowledgeable person concerning the business process, be responsible for classification.

STRATEGIES
FOR SUCCESS

Information and data should be classified by the systems owner to which that data and information relates. The classification should be done separately from the points of view of integrity, privacy and confidentiality, and continuity and availability so as to produce as comprehensive a view of the nature and degree of risk as possible. Classification decisions should be used by systems owners and computer site owners when designing detailed security controls.

We will illustrate in some detail in *Chapter 5* how this classification is done and how activities can be adjusted to be responsive to risk.

THE SEVENTH PRINCIPLE

4.7 The roles and responsibilities for information security should be clearly defined in the information security policy.

Before examining each role individually in the sample policy, we will focus on why a definition of responsibilities is so important and what we are trying to achieve by it.

The whole purpose of a policy is to fix accountability and delegate authority across an organization. Thus it is not surprising that the largest part of our information security policy focuses on roles and responsibilities.

While responsibilities are assigned to specific departments or groups, on most occasions the active cooperation of others and their skills will be required to do a good job. Thus the start of this section in the development of the sample policy underscores this reality and calls for the needed cooperation across departmental boundaries to be provided.

Most of the sample policy is stated in terms of what the responsibilities of each business unit or department are. However, for greater clarity, there are a few sections where we have defined areas and then stated the responsibility for it. This approach can be useful where we want to centralize or focus responsibility in one place for a goal for which two or more departments may feel responsible. By naming the activity as a sub heading and then allocating the responsibility, we can highlight how that activity is to be managed and by whom.

If a company has an information resources management (IRM) policy, then many of the roles and responsibilities discussed below will have already been defined and will have been communicated. Thus our information security policy can make reference to the IRM policy, its terms, roles and responsibilities and then define only those responsibilities that relate specifically to information security.

The sample policy is written with the assumption that an IRM policy does not exist; this provides for a fuller discussion and explanation of roles and responsibilities.

The first part of our sample policy on roles and responsibilities is as follows:

V Assignment of ownership

As set forth below, various departments and areas of the company and all employees are responsible for important information security activities. Often, those who carry primary responsibilities will require assistance from others and this should be provided on request.

As information security must be managed on a total basis:

- All systems must have a systems owner who is responsible for the information and data contained by that system. The system will normally be owned by the business department that owns the related business process. In case of any doubt as to who owns the system, the ownership responsibilities will be delegated to a department by the IRM Committee.
- All computer sites[2] must have a designated computer site owner. In case of any doubt as to who owns a computer site, the ownership responsibilities will be delegated by the IRM Committee.

Contracting with third parties

From time to time the company may use a software package supplied by or maintained and operated by an outside third party. These systems must also have a designated systems owner who carries the same responsibility as if the system were created or run within the company.

If the company makes use of an outside service bureau or facilities manager to provide a computer site, there must be a designated computer site owner within the company who has the same responsibility as if the computer site resided within the organization.

The supporting standards to this policy set forth the manner in which arrangements with third parties shall be managed.

---

2 A computer site is any computer that contains systems, information or data that is shared by two or more individuals. Thus all mainframes as well as file servers on local area networks are computer sites, with the exception of personal microcomputers used for personal computing. Microcomputer and personal computing policies are discussed later on in this chapter.

Internal contracting

Where it is appropriate and efficient to do so, a party having a responsibility under this policy may, while retaining overall responsibility, contract out to someone else within the company the responsibility to carry out certain activities or apply certain standards. In such a case, the other party must acknowledge acceptance of this responsibility in writing.

Where third parties are used to provide any computer site or information systems services, the contractual arrangements with them shall be approved by the systems owner and the vice president of information systems.

Determining systems ownership

With large, complex and integrated systems, systems ownership may not be clear. For example, if an organization has a fully integrated system that manages sales order entry, sales, billing, cash receipts, accounts receivable and relieves inventory for shipments made, it may not be clear which department should be the owner of this system. In these instances, an "authority" must be appointed to delegate ownership responsibilities. This "authority" should also ensure that all systems have designated owners.

In the example just given, we might delegate the sales department as the owner of the system. But in designing and managing security, the sales department will require the help and cooperation of many other departments that use the system. This is why we stated in the sample policy that other departments should provide help and cooperation when required and requested.

Some might argue that two or more departments could be named co-owners of such systems. While this approach can, of course, be followed, joint ownership often leads to problems falling between the cracks. Thus the sample policy in this book uses the approach of defining one systems owner and then introduces (in a few pages!) the concept of data owners who are also involved on a daily basis in using the system and entering data into it. In the example given above, the shipping, billing and accounts receivable department as well as the cash receipts area would be data owners. As we will see, such data owners have important roles to play in information security but perform these under the coordinating umbrella of the systems owner.

Determining ownership of a computer site

Determining ownership of a computer site may also cause some confusion. For example, an organization may have an important local area network in the finance department or a sales and billing system at another geographical location where the departmental management of these two areas has hired employees to run the computer site on a day-to-day basis. However, the central information systems department supplies all of the operating systems and application programs and is responsible for making any changes to them. Clearly, there are two groups which have important computer site responsibilities.

But again, it is more effective to have only one responsible owner. In the example, the computer site ownership could be assigned to either local management or the central information systems department. The owner can then contract internally for the other party to manage certain activities and fulfil the requirements of certain standards. This example illustrates why an information security policy should provide for internal contracting within the company of defined responsibilities.

Note that the sample policy assigns responsibility to the IRM Committee for delegating ownership responsibility for computer sites and ensuring all systems are owned. The key thought is that such allocations should be made by a senior group, having representatives from major areas within the company. After all, the assignment of ownership responsibilities for activities that cross departmental boundaries is important and involves a fair element of politics.

STRATEGIES
FOR SUCCESS

Each computer system and computer site must have a designated owner. A senior management committee should see that such responsibility is assigned in all cases and when necessary, make the determination of ownership. Where responsibilities are shared within the company on a day to day basis, the owner should formally contract with the other department as to the activities they will support on behalf of the owner.

In the earlier example, a department assigned a responsibility role under the policy may want to contract out responsibility, such as managing certain tasks or applying certain standards, to another internal department. A "contracting out" clause can be very beneficial both in gaining support for the policy and in helping to contain costs.

Today's technology makes such contracting out possible and effective. A computer site can be managed remotely (i.e., at a distance) in almost every respect, except for physical security, including the off site storage of backup copies of files.

Some executives in the company may be concerned with the ability of their departments to fulfil all aspects of a responsibility role or indeed with their own ability to manage the activities in question. In this situation, the contracting out clause can be very helpful as it allows this department to contract with another department and thus transfer a particular set of activities for which they lack the necessary skill sets. For example, a department that was assigned computer site ownership responsibilities for its local area network could contract out to the central information systems department the responsibility for all changes to applications and the operating system and management of the logical security software. However, the department might retain responsibility for less technical activities such as physical security and backup procedures.

Another benefit of providing the flexibility to contract out is that it can save money. In a company where small departments may each have their own LAN, it is not economically sound for each to have trained personnel to run them. To a very great extent, LANs can be managed remotely by the central information systems department with a fraction of the personnel that would otherwise be required. Furthermore, the centralized LAN support specialist group will develop real expertise and consequently do this work with greater economy and efficiency.

STRATEGIES
FOR SUCCESS

Departments should make appropriate use of the right under the information security policy to contract out certain activities and responsibilities for certain standards to another department, while still retaining overall responsibility. This allows each task within the organization to be done in the most cost effective manner by personnel who have the necessary knowledge and training.

Third party computer systems, sites and standards

Clearly all systems, information, data and the computer sites regardless of where they reside should be properly secured in accordance with the company's policies. The transfer of systems development and maintenance or management of computer processing to a third party does not change this reality, even though it will have a major impact on the methods used to achieve these policy goals.

When third parties operate computer sites for us, and perhaps also the applications which are executed there, we should ensure that our information security policies and standards are still being effectively met.

Outside service bureaus or facilities managers may supply us a wide variety of services. On the one hand, they may only supply computer hardware and a physical environment which our employees operate remotely. On the other hand, they may supply all computer site services and may even provide the application software which processes the data. Of course, any variant between these two limits is possible. Thus often there will be a division of responsibilities, with some information security activities being managed by our employees and others being managed by the service bureau. While we will manage our own activities in the normal way, the ways in which we ensure that the service bureau has defined and continues to follow information security procedures to meet our policy requirements will be quite different. These procedures include:

- a review of the controls followed by the outside service bureau
- proper contractual arrangements with them, and

- a method for ensuring that the outside service bureau is continuing to apply the information security procedures as required and agreed to.

At the policy level, we need to ensure that these responsibilities are allocated. Thus our sample policy requires that systems owners and computer site owners be designated within the company for all systems and computer sites operated by outside third parties. As the contracts establish the required controls and these arrangements are complex and technical, the information security policy should require that all contracts with third parties be approved by the systems owner (if applications are involved) and by the vice president of information systems, as regards a third party supplying a computer site.

STRATEGIES
FOR SUCCESS

Ownership responsibilities should be fixed within the company for systems and computer sites even when these systems or sites are managed in whole or in part by third parties. Contracts with third parties for information systems services should be approved by the systems owner and the vice president of information systems.

The sample policy continues on and lists the various responsibilities of departments and groups within the company.

VI Roles and responsibilities

i) IRM committee

The IRM Committee owns the information security policy; its responsibilities as regards information security are to:

- ensure this policy is kept up-to-date and approve all changes to this policy
- assign ownership responsibilities for systems and computer sites to individual departments, and
- approve all exemptions from this policy.

Note that we have used bullet points to define the role of the IRM Committee. Keeping the information security policy short, user-friendly, and to the point will encourage others to read and use it.

VI Roles and responsibilities

ii) Information security committee

The mandate of the Information Security Committee is defined by the IRM Committee. As a minimum, the Committee shall:

- assist the Information Resources Management (IRM) committee in keeping this policy up-to-date and suggesting amendments to it
- review and approve the underlying standards that support this policy and ensure they are kept up to date
- provide advice to the IRM Committee as requested
- receive, review and make recommendations to the IRM Committee on any request for exemption from this policy
- receive, review and approve requests from all departments for exceptions to the supporting information security standards, and
- provide advice to the information security group as to the needs and priorities of the company with regard to information security.

Other activities that the Information Security Committee might perform were discussed in previous chapters.

VI Roles and responsibilities

iii) Department heads

The responsibilities of department heads are to:

- assign responsibilities for all systems and computer sites owned by the department
- ensure that systems owners, data owners, secondary data users and computer site owners within their department discharge their responsibilities
- ensure that information security is properly designed as part of an effective system of internal control for all business processes owned by their department, including the definition of a proper division of duties to be reinforced by information security processes
- establish an appropriate procedure to grant, amend and cancel access rights for all employees within the department
- establish procedures to monitor adherence to laws and regulations, including the requirements of any organization to which the company may belong, and take steps to ensure that information security procedures are designed as required to meet such requirements
- review and approve all requests for exemptions from the information security policy and forward requests to the Information Security Committee and through them to the IRM Committee for approval
- review and approve all exceptions to standards and forward them to the Information Security Committee for approval
- provide appropriate information security awareness training to all employees within the department
- obtain annual confirmations of adherence to information security polices from all employees in the department, and
- appoint an individual to be responsible for all matters within the department related to information security and to represent the department on the Information Security Committee.

This whole area of responsibility for department heads is extremely important as it is through these responsibility assignments that we ensure that information security becomes a company-wide concern.

Of course, the department heads are not expected to do all these things personally. Rather, the expectation for many of the responsibilities is that the department head will set up the necessary supervisory and management internal controls processes so that he or she can determine that all of the activities named above are being properly carried out on a regular basis.

STRATEGIES
FOR SUCCESS

The responsibilities of all department heads should be defined so as to make it clear that all departments have important information security responsibilities. In response, all department heads should establish supervisory or management controls to ensure information security procedures and controls, like any other internal controls, are being respected on a day-to-day basis.

While most of the responsibilities of department heads are obvious from previous chapters, one or two areas require some further discussion.

Division of duties

A key interface between information security and the rest of the system of internal control is the division of duties. Good internal control requires that duties be divided in such a manner that no individual has complete control over any business activity and the related recording of the transactions and maintenance of accounting records. Good internal control also requires that limits be placed on the authority of various individuals, either in the sense of the nature of the transaction they can authorize and or the dollar values of such transactions.

Thus we need to create an appropriate division of duties which can then be reinforced by information security processes. No matter how well we carry out information security by itself, it cannot be effective if it is reinforcing an ineffectively defined division of duties and authorities in the first place. Accordingly, department heads should ensure that all the following processes are in place within their department.

One of the best ways to do this is by designing an access matrix for each application. The importance of access rights has been emphasized throughout *Chapters 1* and 2. As discussed in these chapters, an access matrix is a means for defining the access rights for each job. When the jobs involve the entry or approval of transactions, the matrix will also define dollar limits for each particular job description. This access matrix is used both to assist in the design of a proper division of duties and authority limits as well as to design the access rights themselves. When a particular employee may require special, additional access rights not required by others holding the same job function, this would, of course, be documented, approved and created on an exception basis.

The following is an excerpt from an access matrix for the sales and accounts receivable system which shows some transactions and jobs. Note that "release" in this chart implies that transactions would be held in a separate suspense file of transactions and released by the system for processing only after a supervisor has so released them using a separate password.

"Alter" implies the ability to cancel a previously recorded transaction which in incorrect and replace it with a corrected transaction.

Note also other internal controls are required to ensure the completeness, accuracy, and other attributes of data as discussed in *Chapter 1*. These are not illustrated in the access matrix chart, which is focused on the rights to create, alter, or read data.

Exhibit 4.1

Sample access matrix

	Sales orders				Shipping reports			Cash receipts			Credit notes				Receivable balances
	Read	Create	Alter	Release	Read	Create	Alter	Read	Create	Alter	Read	Create	Alter	Release	Read*
Sales order clerk	X	X			X										X
Sales order supervisor			X												X
Shippers	X				X	X	X								
Cash receipts clerk	X				X			X	X						X
Salespeople	X	X									X	X			X
Sales supervisor			X	X over $10,000									X	X over $1,000	X

*Balances are created by the application logic; thus balances are changed by cancelling.

Departmental management should also establish procedures to request access rights for new employees, change them when the employees change jobs and delete them when an employee leaves the company. Because errors can creep into even well-controlled systems, procedures for ensuring periodical reviews of the access rights of all employees should also be established.

Overall, establishing effective divisions of duties and granting and managing the access rights that respect these divisions includes the following:

- the creation and approval of access matrices, showing the access rights and authority limits for each job description
- the definition of procedures to add, change and delete access rights of individual employees and the communication of these changes to the person who will create or amend the access by issuing commands to the logical security software
- the means by which additional access rights over and above those called for by job descriptions shall be determined and approved
- a process to review and approve the access rights of all employees on a periodic basis, and
- where the ability to create or alter access rights using security software has been delegated to an employee within the department by the information security staff, procedures to review and approve the activities of that departmental information security officer.[3]

[3] The actual implementation of access rights or changes thereto can be done either on a centralized or decentralized basis. Where a decentralized approach is used, the information security group creates abilities for departmental information security officers to create or amend access rights of certain types to a limited number of sets of data, all related to a particular department and its applications.

STRATEGIES
FOR SUCCESS

Each department head should establish an appropriate set of internal controls to grant, amend and cancel access rights of employees within the department and, on a periodic basis, review the access rights that do exist. Access rights should be based on an access matrix which sets forth the nature and scope of access rights that should be given to each job description.

Adherence to laws and regulations

Department heads should put a process in place to ensure adherence to any laws and regulations that affect their business processes, including information security considerations.

The recent surge of laws and regulations by governments and associations regarding privacy and confidentiality can have a serious impact on information security. Given the interest of society in these matters and our increasing reliance on computer processes generally, we can anticipate the proliferation of these laws and regulations to continue and should be prepared for the impact on our policies and practices generally and our information security processes in particular.

While sometimes these laws and regulations do not involve information security directly, they may require an information security response in order for companies to comply with them. For example, pharmaceutical companies are required to keep track of to whom each shipment of a particular lot of drugs has been shipped. Amongst other matters, this requires especially strong controls over the integrity of data on shipments by lot, as well as solid backup procedures and disaster recovery plans.

Some companies may also belong to organizations which impose information security requirements. For example, in order to belong to networks such as Interac, Plus and other groups that enable the transmission of ATM credit card and debit card transactions, banks, trust companies and credit unions must meet certain minimum information security standards. Many companies make use of value-added third party EDI networks that impose minimum internal control and information security procedures.

The best way to deal with these matters is to make the department head who is responsible for the related business process also responsible for knowing about and putting processes in place to ensure adherence to any laws and regulations that could affect information security. Of course, the legal department should assist the department heads on these matters. However, it may not be practical to rely on the central legal department to have a detailed knowledge of all laws and regulations, especially when the company may operate in many different business areas and jurisdictions.

STRATEGIES
FOR SUCCESS

Department heads should ensure that changes to laws and regulations, including those of any organizations the company may belong to, are noted and that information security procedures are adjusted to meet these requirements. The legal department may assist department heads in this regard.

VI Roles and responsibilities

iv) Systems owners

The responsibilities of systems owners are to:

- classify the information and data in their systems in accordance with the supporting standard on information classification
- as set forth in the supporting standards, define the information security requirements for the system as part of an effective overall system of internal control for the business process in question (including any data entered by or received from customers and other third parties)
- define a proper division of duties and document same in an access matrix chart for the system
- consider information security requirements when making requests for changes or enhancements to any existing system they own

- approve all requests for access to the system and periodically review the accesses to the system that exist
- identify data owners and ensure their proper involvement when systems are designed or amended
- coordinate the efforts of all other departments when new systems are required or changes or enhancements are made to existing systems, and
- report any requests for changes to policies or exceptions to standards to the head of the department.

Basically, it is the role of the systems owner to define and design the information security requirements for any systems they own, both at the time the system is acquired and whenever it is changed. In other words, they are in charge of defining what is required so that the information security group and the systems developers can ensure that these security requirements are delivered. There is also an interface with the computer site owner which we shall discuss in a few pages.

While the systems owners will own most of the data within the system, other departments may be responsible for entering certain data elements. Data owners will be entering data and therefore need to have an appropriate division of duties for those approving, entering and balancing such data built into the access matrices and reflected in the design of input screens for the system. Data owners will also need batch control reports, transaction lists and other controls reports to ensure the completeness, accuracy, authenticity, timeliness and completeness of the data for which they are responsible. They will also have a detailed knowledge of the data in question, and the related business operations that generate it.

Thus systems owners should coordinate with and receive assistance from other data owners and see that they define their requirements, which are then incorporated into the overall systems requirements. The systems owner acts as an orchestra conductor to see that all the needs of users for information security are properly defined and communicated. In this way, the systems owner becomes a focal point of contact between the users and the information systems department.

In fact, we can look at all the remaining roles which follow over the next few pages as being service providers to the systems owners as they define and obtain the necessary level of information security for their business processes, the applications they contain and the computer sites on which the applications and data reside.

This is illustrated in the exhibit below.

Exhibit 4.2

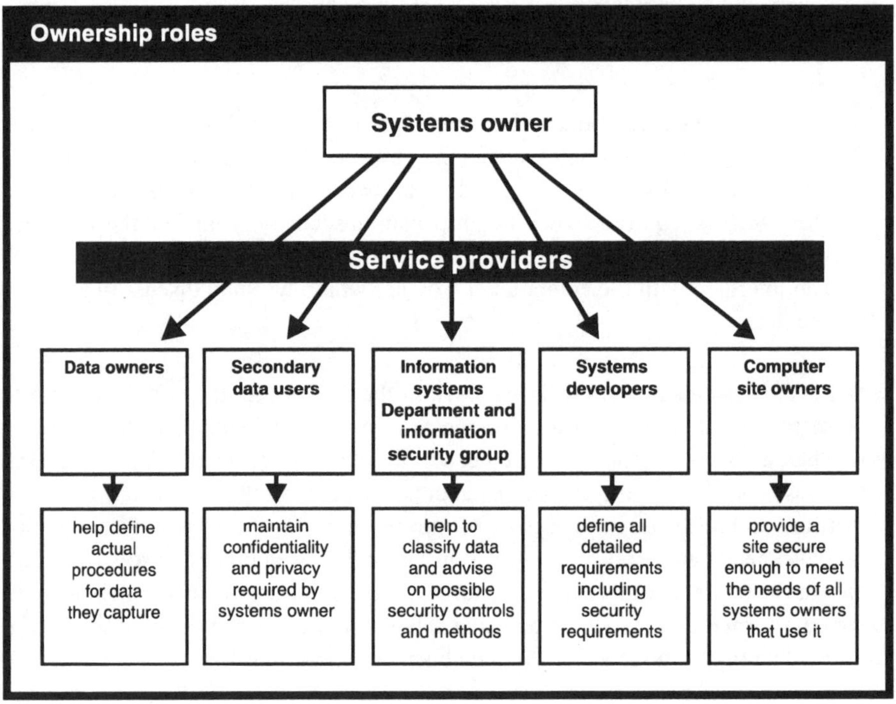

As we look at the roles of these service providers over the next few pages, we will see in more detail how they support the systems owner.

STRATEGIES
FOR SUCCESS

When new systems are designed or changes and enhancements are made to existing systems, the systems owners should be responsible for involving and coordinating the efforts of all other players.

Systems owners should work with data owners, systems developers and information security specialists to classify their data and define in detail the information security procedures that are needed to effectively respond to the level of security required as reflected by the classification. Secondary data users and computer site owners should ensure data is secured commensurate with the classification levels determined by the systems owner.

VI Roles and responsibilities

v) Data owners

The responsibilities of data owners are to:

- meet with systems owners and provide assistance in classifying the data which they own
- work with systems owners to define an appropriate system of internal controls concerning those data elements they are responsible for recording
- assist systems owners in creating access matrix charts for jobs that exist in their area of responsibility, and
- properly implement the standards supporting this policy in all their data capture and related activities.

A key role of the data owner is to design and implement an effective system of internal control, including its information security aspects, for those types of data and transactions that they own. Ownership of a transaction or data type implies that the owner will normally be responsible for creating or capturing that data. Thus data owners are most concerned with the integrity of data but, of course, will also contribute to privacy and confidentiality as well as continuity and availability decisions.

As already mentioned, data owners should always work in concert with and under the overall coordination of the systems owner. For a large, integrated system, there may be several departments with data ownership responsibilities, and unless they allow the systems owner, often with the help of the project manager from the information systems department, to coordinate and assign tasks and areas, there is a risk that matters will fall between the cracks or efforts will be duplicated.

STRATEGIES
FOR SUCCESS

Data owners need to be deeply involved in creating the controls and the access matrices for the data they own. However, these efforts need to be coordinated by the systems owner to ensure matters do not fall between the cracks or efforts are not duplicated.

VI Roles and responsibilities

vi) Secondary data users

The responsibilities of secondary data users are to:

- direct all requests for access to data to the systems owner
- decline to make copies of electronic data in their possession available to others and refer such requests to the systems owner
- safeguard data in their possession commensurate with its classification
- when data is copied on to another computer site, inform that computer site owner of its classification, and
- when data is stored on a microcomputer, refer to and follow the microcomputer and personal computing policy found in the appendix to this policy.

Secondary data users are in a different position than systems or data owners with regard to information security. A secondary data user is someone who requests access to data for information proposes. In other words, the person wants to be able to read the data and perhaps aggregate it, possibly with other data, into information. *Secondary data users do not create or alter data.* If a secondary data user incorrectly alters or accidentally or purposefully destroys data, this data can always be refreshed by obtaining new and correct data from the mainframe or other computer site that holds the "official data of record" owned by the systems owner.

Thus the responsibility of secondary data users centres around maintaining the privacy and the confidentiality of data and the information they derive from it. Generally, this presents no problems if the secondary data users access the same computer site as is used to store the original data, with privileges only to read that data. However, secondary data users often transfer or copy data to a local area network or to their own personal microcomputers.

Where data is copied to a LAN, the LAN must be sufficiently secure to protect data commensurate with its classification from a privacy and confidentiality perspective. Hence the requirement to inform the computer site owner. For example, if a LAN had previously been used for only office automation tools, this computer site might not be sufficiently secure to allow someone to copy confidential cost data to it.

When data is copied on to a personal microcomputer, then in effect that personal microcomputer becomes a computer site and the owner of the site must assume the responsibility to protect the confidentiality and privacy of the data. Microcomputers and personal computing require a separate policy section, as presented later in this chapter.

STRATEGIES
FOR SUCCESS

Secondary data users should protect electronic copies of data they make in accordance with the classification of that data, with special emphasis on privacy and confidentiality. They should inform owners of computer sites about the nature and classification of data they copy on to that site so the computer site owner can ensure that the site is able to provide appropriate security.

When copying data on to a microcomputer, secondary data users should adhere to the microcomputer security policy.

The policy states that secondary data users should not provide copies of data to others. Without this rule, electronic copies of data could proliferate throughout the company. A would give the data to B and C, and B and C in turn would give it to two others and so on. We would quickly lose track of all the places where the data is and the many copies would imperil our security efforts. To avert this risk, secondary data users must direct all requests for copies of electronic data files to the systems owner. In this way, the systems owner has a total knowledge of who has the data and can question any new requests.

STRATEGIES
FOR SUCCESS

All requests for access to electronic data files must be directed to the systems owner. This rule prevents widespread copying of electronic data and ensures the location of all copies of data is known and that security is sustained.

VI Roles and responsibilities

vii) All employees

The responsibilities of all employees are to:

- be familiar with this policy and its supporting standards to the extent necessary in relation to their job responsibilities
- make all reasonable efforts to maintain the secrecy of passwords assigned to them and guard access devices such as smart cards and one time passwords from loss or theft
- immediately inform the information security group if they have reason to believe their password has become known to others or if they have concerns that their other access methods have been compromised or lost
- attend security awareness sessions as required
- make no purposeful attempts to access electronic data over and above that for which access has been granted
- respect the privacy and confidentiality of customer and employee data that comes into their possession
- only use information systems and information resources of the company for authorized purposes, and
- annually re-confirm their adherence to this policy in writing.

Note: Any purposeful attempts to breach information security or any persistent actions taken in a manner contrary to the above are grounds for disciplinary action, including dismissal.

Generally, most employees will not have many responsibilities for information security above and beyond what is set out above. The small section above and the microcomputer section to come comprise all of the security information that most of the company's employees need to read. In addition, these sections could form the basis of employee security awareness training.

STRATEGIES
FOR SUCCESS

The responsibilities common to all employees should be contained in one section of the information security policy. This focus will help the majority of employees, who do not have additional responsibilities, understand the policy as it applies to their job functions quickly and easily.

VI Roles and responsibilities

viii) Computer site owners

The responsibilities of computer site owners are to:

- provide information security capable of meeting the requirements of the highest level of classification of any system or data residing at the computer site
- design overall systems of internal controls for all activities at the computer site and make appropriate use of the standards supporting this policy in doing so
- create access matrices for all job functions within the computer site
- except for emergency changes which shall be approved after the fact, obtain the prior approval of systems owners for all changes to application programs and data
- assume responsibility for all disaster recovery plans and their periodic testing
- report and obtain approval for all exemptions from this policy related to computer site ownership to the Information Security Committee and through them from the IRM Committee, and
- document and forward to the Information Security Committee for approval all exceptions in applying the relevant standards.

Any piece of hardware that stores data and/or programs for general use by a group of employees is a computer site. Thus each mainframe or other computer in a major data centre is a separate computer site, and any local area network that supports a number of users is a separate computer site. Within a major data centre, management will usually establish common procedures to be used for all of the different pieces of hardware. Of course, some variations may be needed for situations if there are differences in the technical requirements of the hardware or if some hardware contains information that is classified at a higher level and thus requires more stringent controls.

Since all activities at a computer site have a significant impact on information security, controls for all activities at a computer site are part of information security. The next chapter deals with the majority of standards required for this purpose.

STRATEGIES
FOR SUCCESS

The information security policy and its underlying standards must address internal controls over all activities at a computer site.

The policy states that internal controls and information security at a computer site must be capable of meeting the most demanding classification for all of the data and programs which the computer site contains. Thus it is not a good idea for the sake of economy and efficiency to put applications with considerably different security requirements on one computer frame. Just as a chain is no stronger than its weakest link, information security is no stronger than its weakest area.

Mixing applications and data with varying requirements together can drive security up to a level which all the applications may not require.

Sometimes it makes sense to put systems and data having an unusually high classification on a separate piece of hardware. In this way, separate and more stringent information security can be constructed for them without burdening all other applications and data with more stringent procedures. The only elements of control in common would be physical security, as all other internal controls could be designed differently for the various hardware platforms.

Of course, having two pieces of hardware instead of just one with a larger capacity will cost more. But these incremental costs may be justified in view of the savings that would flow from reduced administrative efforts, plus the intangible benefit of being more flexible and able to respond more quickly to users with the lower risk systems and information.

STRATEGIES
FOR SUCCESS

As the information security for each computer site must be capable of addressing the most demanding classification for all the systems and data that it contains, avoid placing both high risk and low risk applications on the same piece of hardware whenever possible.

Note that the computer site management is responsible for creating access matrices just like everyone else. Managers of computer sites are sometimes reluctant to carry out this task, feeling that all their technical employees are special and that this approach, while good for others, is not required for computer site personnel. This is not true. Many weaknesses in internal control occur in all sizes of computer sites because management has not formally decided on an access matrix for all job functions, and then reviewed that matrix to see if certain employees have more powerful privileges than they need to do their jobs. Instead, they deal with divisions of duties at their site on an informal basis, making uncoordinated decisions on a person by person basis. To prevent this situation, the sample policy requires computer site owners to create access matrices just like everyone else.

STRATEGIES
FOR SUCCESS

Access matrices should be created for all job functions at a computer site.

VI Roles and responsibilities

ix) Information systems department

The responsibilities of the information systems department are to:

- provide a systems development methodology which addresses how information security needs are to be defined and systems then built in response to these requirements
- ensure that the information security group has the skills required to carry out its responsibilities under this policy
- provide advice and assistance to other computer site owners as requested
- be the designated owner of all computer networks and the methods used to communicate using them
- be the designated owner of the enterprise architecture, and
- review and approve all contracts with third parties for the provision of information systems services, including those that provide for processing being done by third parties.

From a policy point of view, the information systems department is just another department that happens to operate computer sites. Thus all the responsibilities of department heads apply to the head of information systems and all the responsibilities of computer site owners apply to the information systems department in respect of the computer sites which they own.

The responsibilities in this section focus on the additional duties of the central or major information systems department.

The above excerpt from the sample policy is merely pulling together in one place responsibilities we have already discussed.

STRATEGIES
FOR SUCCESS

The head of the information systems department has all the responsibilities of a department head and of a computer site owner for the sites that he or she owns. Thus the policy section on the information systems department need only spell out the additional, unique responsibilities which are assigned to it.

VI Roles and responsibilities

x) Systems developers

The responsibilities of systems developers, in accordance with the supporting standards to this policy, are to:

- assist systems owners in classifying or reclassifying their systems and data when systems are acquired or amended, and
- assist systems owners in defining in detail their security requirements for new or amended applications, at the same time all other requirements are defined.

We saw in *Chapter 1* that much of information security is implemented within an application. The operating system may only be able to control who can execute a particular application and then all other divisions of duties need to be created and enforced within the application.

Furthermore, the application needs to generate batch control lists, transaction lists, exception reports and other reports and information that are needed so that people performed procedures related to information security and overall internal controls can be carried out. Lastly but not least, an application can contain a host of programmed controls of an information security nature, such as reviewing the nature and value of transactions submitted by an employee or customer for suspicious patterns, maintaining audit trails to support accountability and enabling instances to be investigated, etc.

Thus the development of detailed requirements for security within an application, at the same time and in the same manner as all other requirements are defined and documented, is an important part of overall information security. As previously stressed, all this needs to be done in keep with the information classifications.

STRATEGIES
FOR SUCCESS

Systems developers should assist users in defining and documenting their detailed security requirements for new and amended systems at the same time and in the same manner as for all other detailed systems requirements.

VI Roles and responsibilities

xi) Information security group

The information security group or information security specialists in other departments or subsidiaries shall for all computer sites for which it is responsible:[4]

- manage and administer logical security and perform all information security administration functions to change access rights in accordance with the related standards
- participate in the acquisition of all new operating systems and application systems and determine whether these acquisitions provide for the required level of information security based on the related information classifications
- assist systems owners in classifying their data and systems

4 Normally the information security group would have direct responsibility for the central computer sites owned by the information systems department and would carry out quality assurance reviews or provide consulting advice for other computer sites as required.

- assist systems owners and data owners in formulating the detailed requirements for new systems from an information security perspective, and
- carry out reviews, where appropriate, of changes being made to application systems to determine whether such changes would adversely impact information security.

For other computer sites for which the central information security group does not have direct responsibility, it shall:

- review the classification of data and the detailed security requirements for major new systems
- provide assistance, as requested, by these other computer site owners, and
- carry out a quality assurance review of information security at that site, if so requested by the Information Security Committee.

For the entire company and all of its subsidiaries, the central information security group shall:

- be the designated owner of all cryptographic methods and keys
- provide virus detection software for local area networks and microcomputers
- provide support to the Information Security Committee and propose to that committee any additions or changes which are necessary either to this policy or its underlying standards to keep them up-to-date
- research new security methods, software and products and keep the Information Security Committee and through them, the IRM Committee, apprised of developments in information security, as well as sharing this knowledge with others as appropriate, and
- carry out independent reviews of third party data centres to help ensure that the policies and standards on information security are being met by them.

We can see from the above that the central information security group has four key roles to play:

- perform a day-to-day line function for all the computer sites for which it is directly responsible
- be a source of advice and counsel to all on information security matters and provide a quality assurance function for other computer sites

- provide support to the Information Security Committee, including the proposal of needed amendments to keep the policy and standards up-to-date, and
- perform certain key roles on a total corporate basis, such as the management of cryptography, virus detection software and research into new security methods and tools.

STRATEGIES
FOR SUCCESS

The central information security group should have responsibilities for the day-to-day management of information security at the major central computer site. They should also provide consulting help to others on information security, carry out quality assurance reviews of information security in other computer sites, and take responsibility for recommending changes needed from time to time to information security policies and standards. The information security group should also keep abreast of developments in information security methods and tools and, in turn, keep others informed as well as providing support to the Information Security Committee.

The ways in which these roles are defined will, of course, vary depending on the overall organizational structure of your company and the degree to which it operates on a centralized or a decentralized manner.

Your company may have all of is computer sites in one central department and thus be able to bypass this discussion as to how we manage information security when we have many sites and several computer site owners.

The additional roles of the central information security group have been distinguished above for those large companies where there may also be separate information systems departments, including information security specialists, in separate divisions and subsidiaries. As a minimum, in these large companies there will be LANs owned by other departments.

In these circumstances, overall corporate management at the centre would logically look to a central information technology function and its supporting central information security group to support its corporate governance structures for information security as well as providing overall quality assurance on the security aspects of major initiatives.

These matters of course need to be addressed in a consistent manner with the overall organizational structure and approaches taken generally to overall corporate governance.

The sample policy presumes a rather decentralized approach, including the assumption that other computer sites in other geographic locations and in subsidiaries have their own information systems management, including information security. The role of the central information security group is defined as advisory in nature, providing assistance and carrying out quality assurance reviews based on requests received. However, even in a decentralized company, there should be one centre of expertise for information security and there should be one group whose leader is the de facto head of information security from a policy and overall corporate governance viewpoint. It also usually makes sense that a central "mass of expertise" be responsible for shaping research into evolutions in information security, for maintaining the standards, for dealing with other complex technical issues such as virus detection software and cryptographic methods and for supporting the Information Security Committee.

Once again, these are areas where we have to shape the central role to conform with the overall organizational structure within the company.

VII Authority of the vice president of information systems[5]

The vice president of information systems owns both the enterprise architecture and all networks or use of public networks. Accordingly, his or her approval must be sought before undertaking to:

- acquire any hardware or operating system that is not currently part of the enterprise architecture
- connect any computer site with any other internal or external computer site, and
- make any new use of a network.

From an information security perspective, we do not want to be adding new hardware or operating systems to our enterprise architecture that would compromise our security. We also want to ensure that we understand each new piece of hardware or operating system and know the degree of protection it can provide, relating this to our various information classifications. From a business point of view, we want to avoid an unnecessary proliferation of hardware and operating systems that drive up costs.

Much the same is true of networks. Various networks have varying degrees of security, and networks are indeed part of the enterprise architecture. Furthermore, there are a variety of methods that can be used to help ensure the privacy and confidentiality and authenticity of messages sent or received over a network and to guard them against accidental or fraudulent change or the receipt of false messages. On top of all of this, we want to pause and reflect before we make a network connection between highly secure computer sites and computer sites that are not so secure. There are ways of doing this, including having the higher

5 Where there are subsidiaries or divisions with their own information systems departments, architectures and networks, it will probably be necessary at the overall parent company level to develop and approve overall enterprise architectures and provide for the management of needed network connections amongst the companies in the group. Each division or subsidiary would then act in harmony with these overall designs and plans.

security computer site directly authenticate, with its own separate password, users who want to gain access to it. However, all these things need to be carefully thought through.

STRATEGIES
FOR SUCCESS

The vice president of information systems should own the enterprise architecture, including the networks or the use of the networks that connect them. Thus the use of any new hardware or operating systems, the addition of any computer sites, the use of any new networks or new uses of existing networks should be approved by this vice president.

Note that the sample policy is somewhat liberal compared to those we would find in many companies. Companies that require a very high level of security would also include the following, more stringent requirements to the policy or its supporting standards:

- no one can add any device to the network without the permission of the vice president of information systems, and
- every computer site, unless otherwise authorized by the vice president of information systems, shall directly authenticate anyone seeking to gain access and not rely on the fact that the requester is making his or her request from another company computer site.

The first point is necessary to avoid having equipment such as printers or terminals being added without approval and proper security measures. In the sample policy, the owner of the particular computer site to which the new device is being attached assumes this responsibility.

The second point is an important one. Some computer systems are designed so that if I signed on to site A, then without any further checking, I will be permitted as a "guest" into one or more, and perhaps all, other company sites. Clearly this is a risk, because if I break into one site, I will have a route to all others. Company-wide access can be prevented by requiring that each site re-authenticate my identity by asking for a password that I have obtained from that site owner and which is stored in the logical security software at that site. This is only one way of addressing what is a complex problem.

The key point is that the company must carefully think through these situations; the sample policy takes a rather neutral position. Organizations requiring a higher level of protection, such as financial institutions, will need to investigate the use of these other procedures.

Cryptography

The information security group should own and control all cryptographic methods and hold the master keys.

The use of cryptography is growing along with the business use of the Internet. Cryptography already plays a large role in information security, and in the future, will play an even larger role. It is a good way to help ensure the privacy and confidentiality of data during transmission and to ensure that messages are not intercepted or altered during transmission. In addition, it can be used to ensure the integrity of stored data.

Cryptography is a very specialized area, difficult to design and providing a variety of methods ranging from somewhat effective through to more elaborate techniques that are virtually foolproof in nature. It only makes sense, given the specialized nature of the area, that all cryptography be the responsibility of one centralized group. In fact, it can be dangerous to rely on cryptography unless it is indeed effective and up to the task. If improperly implemented, cryptography can be broken. If our keys and algorithms are lost, then our messages and files can be read, and even worse, messages apparently coming from us can be forged and sent to others to act upon. The reverse is also true, and we may receive and act on messages that are forged or altered.

STRATEGIES
FOR SUCCESS

Cryptography should only be used and relied upon if the company has access to appropriate skills to design, implement and maintain it effectively. To help ensure this, the central information security group should own and control all cryptographic methods and hold the master keys.

VIII The internet

Any server which provides Internet services shall be owned by the vice president of information systems. All others who wish to make corporate information available, have a page on the Internet or transact business through the Internet shall do so through these designated sites.

The Internet is already widely used to distribute information, market products and services and conduct business transactions. While it offers tremendous opportunities, its very openness and flexibility present information security challenges of all types. The responses to the challenges are technical, often involving cryptography, the use of special computers and operating systems called firewalls, etc. We will see in the next chapter that special standards are required for Internet sites.

Even where the company is currently only using the Internet to provide marketing data, appropriate security is still a very important concern. The company needs to protect itself from a hacker finding access and maliciously changing the marketing data and price lists.

Thus the sample policy stipulates that all uses of the Internet be put through the vice president of information systems to ensure that the server or servers for the company's web sites are properly protected. In other words, to help manage risk, all Internet servers should be owned by the central information systems department.

At the time of publication of this book, the Internet is not secure and providing even a reasonable level of security is a very challenging technical task. Even as security capabilities increase over time, management of information security for the Internet will remain a daunting technical task. Thus, these kinds of measures are appropriate to ensure that the Internet is only used in those circumstances where sufficient security can be provided.

STRATEGIES
FOR SUCCESS

All Internet sites should be owned by the vice president of information systems and all information and data transmissions and business transactions through the Internet should be placed on these sites.

IX Security awareness programs

The personnel department is responsible for ensuring:

- appropriate security awareness programs are made available to all employees, and
- appropriate information concerning security and this policy is provided to all new employees.

The information security group is responsible for providing:

- additional security awareness training to department heads, systems owners, data owners and others who request this additional help.

THE EIGHTH PRINCIPLE

4.8 A separate microcomputer policy, usually set out as an appendix to the information security policy, should address the responsibilities of all those who use microcomputers or perform personal computing.

It is important that all of the policies regarding microcomputers and personal computing appear in one place so that those using them can go to one document and understand all their responsibilities. Thus the policy discussed and illustrated below goes somewhat beyond information security in a narrow sense and addresses all major responsibilities.

Personal computing means the use of a computer (almost always a microcomputer) to create or copy and store information for access and use by one individual. If computer programs are created, then once again they are for use by an individual rather than a group. While the results of personal computing may be shared, the programs and data are not.

This definition is very important as it implies that data which is corporate data or which is used by more than one person should not be stored on a microcomputer, but rather should be stored on a computer site.

It follows from this that if I use a microcomputer for personal computing, I am probably acting as a secondary data user. If I am working on copies of files and the data becomes corrupted, I can always refresh my data from the computer site where the "official copy" of it is maintained in a more secure environment. Thus my responsibilities as a microcomputer user are focused on privacy and confidentiality. However, if I am creating original data, then of course, I must see to its back up and recoverability.

As microcomputers are often attached to LANs as work stations and thus can be a source of viruses, the policy must also address virus protection measures and the use of virus detection software.

From examining these points, we can develop some basic principles that our policy should cover. These are summarized below.

STRATEGIES
FOR SUCCESS

The microcomputer and personal computing policy should require that:

- *copies of all original data and information, including word processing documents, should be backed up on a LAN from time to time*
- *data which is of a corporate nature should be created and stored on a computer site in the first instance, rather than on the local drive of a microcomputer*
- *data and information should not be stored on a local hard drive of a microcomputer if it has a classification higher than x; instead such data should be stored on a local area network or at least on a floppy disk or removable hard drive that is removed and stored in a safe place and manner commensurate with its classification*
- *the virus detection software supplied by the company should be executed (or allowed to execute if automatic execution has been provided for) periodically*
- *all programs, data and floppy disks received from others should be scanned for viruses before being used or copied onto local hard drives or to a LAN*
- *microcomputers which are the property of the company should not be directly connected to the Internet. Instead, Internet access should be through the company's Internet server and should be limited to the type of interactions provided for on that server*[6]*, and*
- *when a microcomputer is used to connect remotely to a company computer site, standards regarding remote access should be obtained and followed.*

---

6 As we have already discussed, the Internet is inherently insecure and among other things, a potential source of virus infections and of hackers accessing a local microcomputer and possibly from there getting into a LAN. Thus the Internet should only be accessed through a company server that can properly protect itself and thus other company resources.

The following sample policy reflects the above strategies and could be a useful starting point to create or revise your company's policy.

Sample microcomputer and personal computing policy

The purpose of this policy is to define the responsibilities of all employees who make use of microcomputers or perform personal computing. Microcomputers can either be desktop units or portable units such as laptops.

Personal computing can be thought of as the creation of a computer program or data or the download of data by one individual to meet his or her personal job responsibilities. It is distinct from the use of other information system resources, whereby data is created or stored on a computer site either for the use of several or more individuals or to create and store data and information which constitutes part of the "official records" of the company.

In personal computing, while the results of computer processing may be shared, the underlying programs and data are not shared.

Personal computing

Use of personal computers to create and store original data or information

When data is obtained from sources other than the Company's electronic records or is altered after it has been obtained, it is original data.

Every employee is responsible for appropriately backing up original data and information. The frequency with which these backups are performed should be reflective of the importance of the original data and information and the efforts that would be necessary to re-establish it. One good means of providing backup is to copy original data to a local area network. Between times, data could be backed up on a diskette.

Responsibility for data and information downloaded from company systems

Before downloading any data, the employee should have the consent of the systems owner as required by the information security policy.

Whenever possible, data should be downloaded to a local area network and accessed there rather than to a local hand drive or diskettes.

Data which has a classification of X or more sensitive as regards privacy and confidentiality may not be copied to the local hard drive of a microcomputer or transferred to diskettes.

When data is downloaded to a personal computer, employees are responsible for safeguarding the microcomputer, its hard drive, the removable hard drive and the floppy diskette as they would guard similar information were it printed out on paper, and all in accordance with its classification for privacy and confidentiality.

Employees authorized to download data shall not provide copies of this data or information in machine readable form to others. Others making requests of this nature should be referred to the systems owner.

Remote access

Employees using a microcomputer to remotely access data on the computer sites of the company shall follow all standards for such remote access. Specifically, they shall safeguard their passwords or other access identification methods carefully and shall follow and use the access identification methods specified for each computer site they choose to address. No one shall purposefully attempt to gain access to computer sites, programs or data they have not been authorized to access.

The internet

Direct connection of a company owned microcomputer to the Internet can expose both the individual microcomputer and any company computer sites to which it may be attached from time to time to a variety of information security risks, including but not limited to infection by computer viruses.

Accordingly, employees are prohibited from connecting to the Internet using microcomputers supplied by the company, unless that connection is made through the company's own Internet server and the employee has received specific authorization to make such a connection.

Virus protection

The company will from time to time install on all personal computers virus detection software packages and/or new versions thereof.

The virus detection software will be installed in such a manner that it will automatically execute on a periodic basis and scan all memory and files for possible viruses. No employee should interfere with the operation of such virus detection software. If a virus is detected then the employee must:

- immediately disconnect from any network and turn off his personal computer, and
- hand in the personal computer to the information centre for the virus to be removed and files to be repaired.

In addition, employees are discouraged from making use of any data or programs on their personal microcomputers that have not been supplied by the company or personally key entered. In the rare eventuality that such data or programs are used, the diskettes and/or files which have been received should be scanned by the virus detection software immediately as a first step.

Programs on individual microcomputers

As employees have been provided with microcomputers to conduct business of the company, these microcomputers shall not contain any application programs or executable files except those which have been supplied by or directly authorized by the company.

All employees are put on notice that the company takes seriously its responsibilities to only use authorized copies of software. Any employee found making use of an unauthorized copy of a software program or using software programs purposely in an unauthorized manner shall be subject to disciplinary action.

From time to time, employees using company supplied software may create spreadsheet templates, construct small databases or perform other activities to create models or do analysis which can be construed as computer programming. Employees undertaking such tasks will be held responsible for appropriately testing and ensuring the accuracy of such programs to produce logical results. If any doubt arises, employees are encouraged to refer their needs for the development of such templates or databases to professional information systems specialists employed by their department or the information systems department.

Overview

Chapter 4 – Creating the information security policy

4.1 An overall security strategy that describes and links all information security policies, standards, procedures and practices should be developed and distributed throughout the organization.

4.2 Senior management should involve as many departments as possible in the development or revision of the information security policy; this full and active participation is critical to the successful acceptance and implementation of the policy.

4.3 The information security policy should begin with a statement of the principles on which it is based.

4.4 The interrelationships of the information security policy and other corporate policies should be clearly described.

4.5 The scope of and the authority for the information security policy and supporting standards and the means by which exemptions from policy and exceptions from standards are to be requested and approved should be set forth in the policy itself.

4.6 The information security policy should clearly state the need to classify information and systems so that information security is responsive to risk.

4.7 The roles and responsibilities for information security should be clearly defined in the information security policy.

4.8 A separate microcomputer policy, usually set out as an appendix to the information security policy, should address the responsibilities of all those who use microcomputers or perform personal computing.

STRATEGIES
FOR SUCCESS

The information security strategy is a brief overview document which describes the purpose and importance of information security and the policies, standards and procedures which support it. Its purpose is to help everyone navigate through and understand all security practices; it can also be a valuable resource for the development of a security awareness training program.

The plan for the development of the information security policy is the first step in gaining widespread support for the new policy. It should include the formation of a working committee to reflect the advice of all groups and departments within the organization that will be significantly affected by the policy. Ideally this working group will be an information security committee that will coordinate information security matters on an ongoing basis.

The information security policy should focus on overall goals and objectives and the roles and responsibilities of various groups or departments in achieving them. It should provide broad statements of principle that will endure over a number of years. The more detailed means by which information security should be obtained should be placed in supporting standards. In this way the policy can be a short, succinct and relatively constant statement while the supporting materials can be amended more frequently to reflect changes in processes to meet changing conditions.

The statement of principles in the information security policy should clearly describe how information security plays a major role in achieving the organization's critical success factors. It should illustrate that information security is part and parcel of customer service and that the ongoing availability of reliable data, information and systems resources is essential for meeting customer service expectations and effectively managing the company. If the company has a motto or slogan expressing its corporate values, this should be incorporated into the principles statement and the ways in which information security serves to achieve these shared values clearly illustrated.

The information security policy should refer to all other related policies that are part of the overall framework within the company for corporate governance and information risk management. Such other policies may include those related to overall information resources management, compliance policies, internal control frameworks, privacy and confidentiality codes, business resumption planning and principles for the use of systems development methodologies.

Information security strategies and policies should be designed for use throughout the company and all of its subsidiaries. In large part, this broad applicability depends upon creating underlying standards that can respond to different levels of risk and that can be adapted to the varying business circumstances and computer environments throughout the organization.

While the information security policy should point out that printed material can be protected by applying the principles set forth for electronic data and information, the policy should focus on information systems and data. The many and complicated issues surrounding printed material should be addressed as a separate policy or within the organizations's overall policy on business ethics or privacy and confidentiality.

Faxes are an inherently insecure medium, both for guarding the privacy and confidentiality of communications and ensuring the identity of the sender and the integrity of the information. The information security policy should highlight their vulnerability and caution the reader to use or accept them accordingly.

Electronic mail should be included in the scope of the information security policy and such systems and their information should be classified and secured in the same manner as any other systems and its data.

The most senior committee in the company that deals with information systems matters should be responsible for the information security policy. Ideally, this should be the Information Resources Management Committee, having senior management representation from major departments as well as the information systems department.

Exemptions from policies should be rare and carefully controlled through review and approval procedures at a senior level within the organization. All requests for exemptions should be supported by a statement of the related risks, costs savings and monitoring procedures against unacceptable losses. In certain cases, exemptions should only be requested and granted for a limited period of time. In the case of longer term exemptions, responsibility should be fixed for a periodic review to determine if they are still required.

Exceptions to standards may be more frequently encountered as certain activities within a standard may not be appropriate or required due to other compensating procedures in the overall system of internal control. Exceptions should be documented, including details concerning the compensating controls. They should also be subject to independent review and approval to help ensure that risks are being properly managed. If an Information Security Committee exists, it could be assigned this task.

Information and data should be classified by the systems owner to which that data and information relates. The classification should be done separately from the points of view of integrity, privacy and confidentiality, and continuity and availability so as to produce as comprehensive a view of the nature and degree of risk as possible. Classification decisions should be used by systems owners and computer site owners when designing detailed security controls.

Each computer system and computer site must have a designated owner. A senior management committee should see that such responsibility is assigned in all cases and when necessary, make the determination of ownership. Where responsibilities are shared within the company on a day to day basis, the owner should formally contract with the other department as to the activities they will support on behalf of the owner.

Departments should make appropriate use of the right under the information security policy to contract out certain activities and responsibilities for certain standards to another department, while still retaining overall responsibility. This allows each task within the organization to be done in the most cost effective manner by personnel who have the necessary knowledge and training.

Ownership responsibilities should be fixed within the company for systems and computer sites even when these systems or sites are managed in whole or in part by third parties. Contracts with third parties for information systems services should be approved by the systems owner and the vice president of information systems.

The responsibilities of all department heads should be defined so as to make it clear that all departments have important information security responsibilities. In response, all department heads should establish supervisory or management controls to ensure information security procedures and controls, like any other internal controls, are being respected on a day-to-day basis.

Each department head should establish an appropriate set of internal controls to grant, amend and cancel access rights of employees within the department and, on a periodic basis, review the access rights that do exist. Access rights should be based on an access matrix which sets forth the nature and scope of access rights that should be given to each job description.

Department heads should ensure that changes to laws and regulations, including those of any organizations the company may belong to, are noted and that information security procedures are adjusted to meet these requirements. The legal department may assist department heads in this regard.

When new systems are designed or changes and enhancements are made to existing systems, the systems owners should be responsible for involving and coordinating the efforts of all other players.

Data owners need to be deeply involved in creating the controls and the access matrices for the data they own. However, these efforts need to be coordinated by the systems owner to ensure matters do not fall between the cracks and efforts are not duplicated.

Secondary data users should protect electronic copies of data they make in accordance with the classification of that data, with special emphasis on privacy and confidentiality. They should inform owners of computer sites about the nature and classification of data they copy on to that site so the computer site owner can ensure that the site is able to provide appropriate security.

When copying data on to a microcomputer, secondary data users should adhere to the microcomputer security policy.

All requests for access to electronic data files must be directed to the systems owner. This rule prevents widespread copying of electronic data and ensures the location of all copies of data is known and that security is sustained.

The responsibilities common to all employees should be contained in one section of the information security policy. This focus will help the majority of employees, who do not have additional responsibilities, understand the policy as it applies to their job functions quickly and easily.

The information security policy and its underlying standards must address internal controls over all activities at a computer site.

As the information security for each computer site must be capable of addressing the most demanding classification for all the systems and data that it contains, avoid placing both high risk and low risk applications on the same piece of hardware whenever possible.

Access matrices should be created for all job functions in a computer site.

The head of the information systems department has all the responsibilities of a department head and of a computer site owner for the sites that he or she owns. Thus the policy section on the information systems department need only spell out the additional, unique responsibilities which are assigned to it.

Systems developers should assist users in defining and documenting their detailed security requirements for new and amended systems at the same time and in the same manner as for all other detailed systems requirements.

The central information security group should have responsibilities for the day-to-day management of information security at the major or central computer site. They should also provide consulting help to others on information security, carry out quality assurance reviews of information security in other computer sites, and take responsibility for recommending changes needed from time to time to information security policies and standards. The information security group should also keep abreast of developments in information security methods and tools and, in turn, keep others informed as well as providing support to the Information Security Committee.

The vice president of information systems should own the enterprise architecture, including the networks or the use of the networks that connect them. Thus the use of any new hardware or operating systems, the addition of any computer sites, the use of any new networks or new uses of existing networks should be approved by this vice president.

Cryptography should only be used and relied upon if the company has access to appropriate skills to design, implement and maintain it effectively. To help ensure this, the central information security group should own and control all cryptographic methods and hold the master keys.

All Internet sites should be owned by the vice president of information systems and all information and data transmissions and business transactions through the Internet should be placed on these sites.

The microcomputer and personal computing policy should require that:

- copies of all original data and information, including word processing documents, should be backed up on a LAN from time to time
- data which is of a corporate nature should be created and stored on a computer site in the first instance, rather than on the local drive of a microcomputer
- data and information should not be stored on a local hard drive of a microcomputer if it has a classification higher than x; instead such data should be stored on a local area network or at least on a floppy disk or removable hard drive that is removed and stored in a safe place and manner commensurate with its classification
- the virus detection software supplied by the company should be executed (or allowed to execute if automatic execution has been provided for) periodically
- all programs, data and floppy disks received from others should be scanned for viruses before being used or copied onto local hard drives or to a LAN

- microcomputers which are the property of the company should not be directly connected to the Internet. Instead, Internet access should be through the company's Internet server and should be limited to the type of interactions provided for on that server, and
- when a microcomputer is used to connect remotely to a company computer site, standards regarding remote access should be obtained and followed.

Appendix

A sample information security policy

Table of contents

I Principles
II Relationship to other policies
III Scope, authority and exemptions
IV Information classification
V Assignment of ownership
VI Roles and responsibilities
- i) IRM committee
- ii) Information security committee
- iii) Department heads
- iv) Systems owners
- v) Data owners
- vi) Secondary data users
- vii) All employees
- viii) Computer site owners
- ix) Information systems department
- x) Systems developers
- xi) Information security group

VII Authority of the vice president of information systems
VIII The internet
IX Security awareness programs
Glossary

I Principles

Information is a major asset of THE COMPANY and thus needs to be protected and safeguarded. In this policy, the term "information" includes the data from which it is derived. This information security policy has been designed to ensure that:

- data has the integrity required to support its many uses in conducting and managing the business
- the privacy of our customers and employees is respected
- the confidentiality of our information, which gives us competitive advantage, is preserved, and
- our information systems and data are available as required to meet valid customer expectations for ongoing delivery of goods and services and protect our hard-earned reputation for reliability and service.

The quality of our information systems and the information they contain is part of the goods and services that we sell to our customers and plays a major role in meeting customer expectations. We need complete, accurate and timely data to fulfil customer commitments and support the electronic data interchanges and other electronic interfaces that customers have with us. We need to respect the privacy of customers and employees who give us data and fully meet their valid expectations in these regards. The information derived from our systems plays a key part in managing our business in these competitive times; we need to safeguard both its integrity and its confidentiality. In other words, information security is part of our competitive advantage.

Thus, in designing and implementing information security, we seek to balance the cost of security, the losses that occur and the ease of access for customers and employees.

As information security is part of a larger overall system of internal controls, it should be designed and implemented in an integrated manner with other control procedures.

Information security is everyone's responsibility. All employees must only access company systems for valid business purposes within the limits of their granted authority and protect the confidentiality of their passwords and other means of gaining access to the company's systems. Our information security procedures are designed to give all employees the access that they require to discharge their responsibilities, while at the same time protecting the interests of the company and providing for individual accountability. In keeping with this principle, the password or other means of authentication used by each employee to gain access shall be unique. The nature of passwords, the requirement for their uniqueness and their frequent change are all addressed in the supporting standards to this policy.

Note: A separate microcomputer policy addresses the responsibilities of all those who use microcomputers or perform personal computing.

II Relationship to other policies

Information security is an important part of the company's overall policies and procedures for corporate governance and risk management. Accordingly, this information security policy should be read in conjunction with the following:

- the information resources management policy which describes the overall strategic management of all aspects of information systems
- the internal control framework, which describes responsibilities for the overall design and implementation of systems of internal controls for overall business processes
- polices for compliance with laws and regulations
- the company's code of privacy and confidentiality
- policies for business resumption planning, and
- principles for the use of our systems development methodologies, which set forth the steps normally required for the development of new systems and assigns responsibility for them.

III Scope, authority and exemptions

Scope

This policy covers all of the company's locations, branches and operations and is intended to apply to all of its subsidiaries, once it has been approved by them. It should be applied to all of the company's computer sites and networks, including local area networks and all of the systems and the data that they contain. This policy also applies to fax transmissions and electronic mail systems and messages. A separate appendix to this policy addresses the responsibility of those performing personal computing or using personal microcomputers.

While information and data in printed form is not specifically addressed by this policy, the protection of the confidentiality and privacy of printed material can be enhanced by applying the principles and concepts contained herein. Fax transmissions are inherently insecure and this should be borne in mind when deciding to send a document by fax or to act upon information received by fax.

Authority

This policy has been issued by the Information Resources Management Committee which is responsible for amending this policy from time to time as required. Reporting to this committee, an Information Security Committee has been formed to address information security matters on a regular basis and to develop and approve supporting standards for this policy, and to keep such standards up-to-date.

Exemptions and exceptions

On rare occasions, there may be circumstances where this policy is not appropriate and those assigned ownership responsibilities below may wish to request an exemption to the policy. Such exemptions should be requested in writing by the department head and forwarded to the chair of the Information Security Committee. The committee will review such requests and forward them with their comments to the Information Resources Management Committee for final decision.

The supporting standards to this policy document the activities and minimum requirements for information security commensurate with varying levels of risk. As information security is only part of an overall system of internal control, some of these standards may not be applicable due to the existence of other compensating controls in the overall system of internal controls. In such circumstances, systems owners or computer site owners should, after obtaining the approval of their department head, document exceptions in employing the standards and the related compensating controls that make this appropriate and provide this information to the chair of the Information Security Committee for review and approval.

IV Information classification

Making classification decisions

Effective information risk management requires that information security be designed and implemented in a manner that is responsive to the nature and degree of risks involved. The goal is to achieve reasonable, but not absolute assurance as regards the effectiveness of information security, recognizing the balance between the risks to be contained, the costs of doing so, the relative ease of access required by customers and employees and the losses which may occur.

Risks will vary from business process to business process and will also vary with the type of data or information under consideration. The assessment of risk must not only consider the protection of the company's assets and information, but also reflect our responsibility to customers and employees to protect confidentiality and to have processes in place so that our systems will be available to help us provide timely goods and services in accordance with reasonable customer expectations.

Thus, the responsibility to classify information rests with the systems owners.

All information should be classified from three points of view:

- data integrity
- privacy and confidentiality, and
- continuity and availability.

The classifications should be determined by applying the company's standard on information and data classification.

Using classification decisions

The classification categories shall be used by the systems owner when working with others to define the detailed security requirements for new systems or changes to existing systems.

Computer site owners shall ensure that their computer site is capable of fulfilling the requirements of the supporting standards as regards the most demanding classification category for all information and systems on the site.

The supporting standards to this policy set forth the activities and internal controls systems owners and computer site owners should follow in these regards.

V Assignment of ownership

As set forth below, various departments and areas of the company and all employees are responsible for important information security activities. Often, those who carry primary responsibilities will require assistance from others and this should be provided on request.

As information security must be managed on a total basis:

- All systems must have a systems owner who is responsible for the information and data contained by that system. The system will normally be owned by the business department that owns the related business process. In case of any doubt as to who owns the system, the ownership responsibilities will be delegated to a department by the IRM Committee.
- All computer sites must have a designated computer site owner. In case of any doubt as to who owns a computer site, the ownership responsibilities will be delegated by the IRM Committee.

Contracting with third parties

From time to time the company may use a software package supplied by or maintained and operated by an outside third party. These systems must also have a designated systems owner who carries the same responsibility as if the system were created or run within the company.

If the company makes use of an outside service bureau or facilities manager to provide a computer site, there must be a designated computer site owner within the company who has the same responsibility as if the computer site resided within the organization.

The supporting standards to this policy set forth the manner in which arrangements with third parties shall be managed.

Internal contracting

Where it is appropriate and efficient to do so, a party having a responsibility under this policy may, while retaining overall responsibility, contract out to someone else within the company the responsibility to carry out certain activities or apply certain standards. In such a case, the other party must acknowledge acceptance of this responsibility in writing.

Where third parties are used to provide any computer site or information systems services, the contractual arrangements with them shall be approved by the systems owner and the vice president of information systems.

VI Roles and responsibilities

i) IRM committee

The IRM Committee owns the information security policy; its responsibilities as regards information security are to:

- ensure this policy is kept up-to-date and approve all changes to this policy
- assign ownership responsibilities for systems and computer sites to individual departments, and

- approve all exemptions from this policy.

ii) Information security committee

The mandate of the Information Security Committee is defined by the IRM Committee. As a minimum, the Committee shall:

- assist the Information Resources Management (IRM) committee in keeping this policy up-to-date and suggesting amendments to it
- review and approve the underlying standards that support this policy and ensure they are kept up to date
- provide advice to the IRM Committee as requested
- receive, review and make recommendations to the IRM Committee on any request for exemption from this policy
- receive, review and approve requests from all departments for exceptions to the supporting information security standards, and
- provide advice to the information security group as to the needs and priorities of the company with regard to information security.

iii) Department heads

The responsibilities of department heads are to:

- assign responsibilities for all systems and computer sites owned by the department
- ensure that systems owners, data owners, secondary data users and computer site owners within their department discharge their responsibilities
- ensure that information security is properly designed as part of an effective system of internal control for all business processes owned by their department, including the definition of a proper division of duties to be reinforced by information security processes
- establish an appropriate procedure to grant, amend and cancel access rights for all employees within the department

- establish procedures to monitor adherence to laws and regulations, including the requirements of any organization to which the company may belong, and take steps to ensure that information security procedures are designed as required to meet such requirements
- review and approve all requests for exemptions from the information security policy and forward requests to the Information Security Committee and through them to the IRM Committee for approval
- review and approve all exceptions to standards and forward them to the Information Security Committee for approval
- provide appropriate information security awareness training to all employees within the department
- obtain annual confirmations of adherence to information security polices from all employees in the department, and
- appoint an individual to be responsible for all matters within the department related to information security and to represent the department on the Information Security Committee.

iv) Systems owners

The responsibilities of systems owners are to:

- classify the information and data in their systems in accordance with the supporting standard on information classification
- as set forth in the supporting standards, define the information security requirements for the system as part of an effective overall system of internal control for the business process in question (including any data entered by or received from customers and other third parties)
- define a proper division of duties and document same in an access matrix chart for the system
- consider information security requirements when making requests for changes or enhancements to any existing system they own
- approve all requests for access to the system and periodically review the accesses to the system that exist
- identify data owners and ensure their proper involvement when systems are designed or amended

- coordinate the efforts of all other departments when new systems are required or changes or enhancements are made to existing systems, and
- report any requests for changes to policies or exceptions to standards to the head of the department.

v) Data owners

The responsibilities of data owners are to:

- meet with systems owners and provide assistance in classifying the data which they own
- work with systems owners to define an appropriate system of internal controls concerning those data elements they are responsible for recording
- assist systems owners in creating access matrix charts for jobs that exist in their area of responsibility, and
- properly implement the standards supporting this policy in all their data capture and related activities.

vi) Secondary data users

The responsibilities of secondary data users are to:

- direct all requests for access to data to the systems owner
- decline to make copies of electronic data in their possession available to others and refer such requests to the systems owner
- safeguard data in their possession commensurate with its classification
- when data is copied on to another computer site, inform that computer site owner of its classification, and
- when data is stored on a microcomputer, refer to and follow the microcomputer and personal computer policy found in the appendix to this policy.

vii) All employees

The responsibilities of all employees are to:

- be familiar with this policy and its supporting standards to the extent necessary in relation to their job responsibilities
- make all reasonable efforts to maintain the secrecy of passwords assigned to them and guard access devices such as smart cards and one time passwords from loss or theft
- immediately inform the information security group if they have reason to believe their password has become known to others or if they have concerns that their other access methods have been compromised or lost
- attend security awareness sessions as required
- make no purposeful attempts to access electronic data over and above that for which access has been granted
- respect the privacy and confidentiality of customer and employee data that comes into their possession
- only use information systems and information resources of the company for authorized purposes, and
- annually re-confirm their adherence to this policy in writing.

Note: Any purposeful attempts to breach information security or any persistent actions taken in a manner contrary to the above are grounds for disciplinary action, including dismissal.

viii) Computer site owners

The responsibilities of computer site owners are to:

- provide information security capable of meeting the requirements of the highest level of classification of any system or data residing at the computer site
- design overall systems of internal controls for all activities at the computer site and make appropriate use of the standards supporting this policy in doing so
- create access matrices for all job functions within the computer site

- except for emergency changes which shall be approved after the fact, obtain the prior approval of systems owners for all changes to application programs and data
- assume responsibility for all disaster recovery plans and their periodic testing
- report and obtain approval for all exemptions from this policy related to computer site ownership to the Information Security Committee and through them from the IRM Committee, and
- document and forward to the Information Security Committee for approval all exceptions in applying the relevant standards.

ix) Information systems department

The responsibilities of the information systems department are to:

- provide a systems development methodology which addresses how information security needs are to be defined and systems then built in response to these requirements
- ensure that the information security group has the skills required to carry out its responsibilities under this policy
- provide advice and assistance to other computer site owners as requested
- be the designated owner of all computer networks and the methods used to communicate using them
- be the designated owner of the enterprise architecture, and
- review and approve all contracts with third parties for the provision of information systems services, including those that provide for processing being done by third parties.

x) Systems developers

The responsibilities of systems developers are to:

- assist systems owners in classifying or reclassifying their systems and data when systems are acquired or amended, and
- assist systems owners in defining in detail their security requirements for new or amended applications, at the same time all other requirements are defined.

xi) Information security group

The information security group (or information security specialists in other departments or subsidiaries) shall for all computer sites for which it is responsible:

- manage and administer logical security and perform all information security administration functions to change access rights in accordance with the related standards
- participate in the acquisition of all new operating systems and application systems and determine whether these acquisitions provide for the required level of information security based on the related information classifications
- assist systems owners in classifying their data and systems
- assist systems owners and data owners in formulating the detailed requirements for new systems from an information security perspective, and
- carry out reviews, where appropriate, of changes being made to application systems to determine whether such changes would adversely impact information security.

For other computer sites for which the central information security group does not have direct responsibility, it shall:

- review the classification of data and the detailed security requirements for major new systems
- provide assistance, as requested, by these other computer site owners, and
- carry out a quality assurance review of information security at that site, if so requested by the Information Security Committee.

For the entire company and all of its subsidiaries, the central information security group shall:

- be the designated owner of all cryptographic methods and keys
- provide virus detection software for local area networks and microcomputers
- provide support to the Information Security Committee and propose to that committee any additions or changes which are necessary either to this policy or its underlying standards to keep them up-to-date

- research new security methods, software and products and keep the Information Security Committee and through them, the IRM Committee, apprised of developments in information security, as well as sharing this knowledge with others as appropriate, and
- carry out independent reviews of third party data centres to help ensure that the policies and standards on information security are being met by them.

VII Authority of the vice president of information systems

The vice president of information systems owns both the enterprise architecture and all networks or use of public networks. Accordingly, his or her approval must be sought before undertaking to:

- acquire any hardware or operating system that is not currently part of the enterprise architecture
- connect any computer site with any other internal or external computer site, and
- make any new use of a network.

VIII The internet

Any server which provides Internet services shall be owned by the vice president of information systems. All others who wish to make corporate information available, have a page on the Internet or transact business through the Internet shall do so through these designated sites.

IX Security awareness programs

The personnel department is responsible for ensuring:

- appropriate security awareness programs are made available to all employees, and
- appropriate information concerning security and this policy is provided to all new employees.

The information security group is responsible for providing:

- additional security awareness training to department heads, systems owners, data owners and others who request this additional help.

Glossary to the sample information security policy

The purpose of this glossary is to define certain terms in the context of the information security policy.

access The ability to connect with a computer to execute programs, or to read, copy, change, add or delete data and programs.

access matrix A chart showing on one axis, various job functions and on the other axis, the access rights of each job function. It is used to define all access rights of groups to a particular system in a manner that assists in a review to determine if a proper division of duties has been created. (see division of duties below)

access method The means by which a user identifies himself to gain access to a computer. Access methods include passwords, smart cards, one time passwords, biometrics such as finger prints and voice recognition or combinations thereof.

access rights The rights provided to a particular individual or groups of individuals as to what programs or data they may execute, read, copy, write upon, add or delete.

availability The ability to have available computer resources, programs and data throughout a typical business day and how minor interruptions to this ability are to be handled. (see continuity below for the longer term aspects)

business resumption planning The plans by which the company ensures that all the resources needed to conduct business, including its offices and plants, would be available again after damage or loss within a time period short enough that unacceptable damage to the company's interests and customer service would not occur. (contrast with disaster recovery planning below)

compliance The process by which a company becomes aware of the laws and regulations which it needs to obey and then puts processes in place to ensure adherence.

or

The adherence to the system of internal control in the performance of job responsibilities.

computer site Any group of computer resources (hardware, operating software and the applications and data it supports) which is used to create or store corporate data and programs or which is accessed and used by a group of people. (contrast with personal computing below)

computer site owner The department that owns a computer site and is responsible for all internal controls relating to the operation of the site.

confidentiality The safeguarding of corporate information so that its competitive advantage to the company is protected.

continuity The availability of computer resources, programs and data on an ongoing basis to serve the needs of the company and its customers. It includes the concept of determining how long the company may go without these resources before unacceptable damage occurs to the company's interests and customer service, and putting a disaster recovery plan in place to ensure these time limitations can be met in the event of a disaster. (also see disaster recovery planning)

data owner The department that is responsible for entering the data in question into computer systems. This is normally the department that first acquires or becomes aware of the type of data in question. Data owners work in harmony with systems owners described below.

disaster recovery planning The plans by which the company ensures that all the computer resources needed to conduct business would be available again after damage or loss within a time period short enough that unacceptable damage to the company's interests and customer service would not occur. (contrast with business resumption planning above)

division of duties The allocation of work to different job functions and individuals within a system of internal control so that responsibility for entering into business transactions and events, recording those events and custody of the related assets are segregated to better safeguard assets and ensure complete and accurate accounting records.

emergency change A change made to computer programs or data on an emergency basis so that computer processes, which are now halted, may continue to support the business on a timely basis. Emergency changes may initially be made with less control than normal, but then should be subjected to all normal review and approvals as soon as possible after the fact.

enterprise architecture The entirety of hardware, operating systems, peripheral devices and networks used by the company within and between all its computer sites.

exception A deviation or non-application of a particular requirement of an underlying standard to this policy, properly documented and approved.

exemption Formal approval by the IRM Committee for the non application of this policy in a particular, clearly defined circumstance.

integrity Data or information that is sufficiently complete, accurate, authentic, authorized and timely to meet all the uses to which it is put.

internal control A system of inter-related procedures and processes, performed by people or computer software, that provide reasonable assurance that business is conducted and accepted in accordance with policy and laws and regulations, that all economic events are accurately reflected in the records and that the assets and interests of the organization are protected against loss.

logical security The protection by special software of all stored data and programs against unauthorized access and the creation of trails and reports to allow the monitoring and reporting of accesses which have occurred. The special software may reside in the operating system, in special security software or both.

operating system The master system in computer hardware that allows the hardware to function, execute programs, store and retrieve data and communicate. Operating systems also have a role to play in logical security. (see above)

personal computing The use of a stand-alone computer (usually a microcomputer) by an individual employee to work on copies of data transferred from a computer site or to create programs and data used solely by that employee.

physical security The physical protection of a computer site or the building in which it resides against unauthorized physical access
and
the processes and equipment used to protect computer sites and their physical premises against destruction by fire, flood, etc.

privacy The protection of data or information supplied by customers and employees against disclosure or use for other than the valid purposes for which it was provided.

systems development methodology The methods used to define user requirements and then create or acquire, test and implement new computer applications or changes to existing ones.

systems owners The department that owns the computer system and has general overall responsibility for information security for the system from a user perspective. Usually, the systems owner is the department that owns the related business process. Systems owners may also act as data owners for much of the data entered, and for other data work with the other data owners. (see data owner)

Chapter 5

Tailoring security measures to the organization's needs

Standards are the means by which the information security policy is implemented. Without effective standards, an organization will *not* have effective information security, no matter how good its policy is. Thus standards are vital. To be effective, standards must be:

- developed by team of people having a technical knowledge of information security as well as a sound knowledge of the principles of internal controls and information risk management, and
- designed so they can be applied in a risk responsive manner, so that there is a proper balance between risk containment and the costs of controls, including information security.

But what is the role of senior management in the creation and ongoing evolution of standards to meet changing conditions? Clearly senior management should not have to write the standards and need not have the technical knowledge to review them in detail.

But this does not mean senior management does not have an important role to fulfil. Top management is always faced with the challenge of providing managerial oversight in areas in which they do not have technical or expert knowledge. These can range from pension plan costs where they direct the work of actuaries and human resources personnel through to the design of industrial products where they rely on engineers.

As always, the role of senior management is to create the framework or organizational structure, including a quality assurance process, that will ensure that the work gets done. However, senior management must have sufficient understanding of the process and the basic concepts to enable them to appreciate the tasks that are involved and provide the required high level supervision. All this is true for information security standards.

This chapter presents a framework for the development and ongoing management of information security standards and describes the related quality assurance process that is required. The chapter also lists the standards that are normally needed, describes their purpose and provides an overview of what they should include.

This chapter discusses the principles:

5.1 Senior management should create the appropriate organizational structure for spearheading the initial development and ongoing management and updating of information security standards.

5.2 Senior management should establish an appropriate structure for quality assurance of information security standards.

5.3 The information security standards should all be structured in a consistent manner that allows them to be applied in a manner responsive to risk.

5.4 Senior management should understand the nature of information security standards that are required and the overall nature and purpose of each one.

5.5 Appropriate transition plans should be in place whenever new information security policies and standards are created.

THE FIRST PRINCIPLE

5.1 Senior management should create the appropriate organizational structure for spearheading the initial development and ongoing management and updating of information security standards.

The sample information security policy set the scene for standards development in its creation of the Information Security Committee. This committee should be comprised of representatives from the major departments, including the head of information security and perhaps other members of the information systems department. However, there should also be representatives from the major line or operating departments that run the business. Properly formed, such a group is an ideal committee to oversee the development and ongoing updating of our standards because the committee:

- includes people who understand information security as well as overall internal controls, and
- also includes representatives from the major departments who will ensure that the standards can be effectively applied throughout the organization.

If an information security committee does not exist, then a similar group needs to be formed, at least for the initial creation of the standards.

STRATEGIES
FOR SUCCESS

The responsibility for the initial development and ongoing updating of security standards should be delegated to an information security committee, or similar group, comprised of representatives from the major departments and including the head of information security and perhaps other members of the information systems department.

Standards development teams

In carrying out its responsibilities to ensure that standards are developed and updated in a priority order, the Information Security Committee will need to form appropriate teams to actually draft or update each standard.

How should the committee determine the composition of these teams? Some standards will be more technical in nature, such as those that spell out the activities that should be in place at all computer sites. Some will be more oriented to overall internal controls and information risk management, such as those that deal with information classification or how we obtain assurance on information security procedures in outside service bureaus. While the balance may shift, all standards need to reflect a detailed knowledge of internal controls and a technical appreciation of information security. Thus team members should be selected so that the group as a whole will have the necessary balance of knowledge and skills.

Furthermore, it is best if the development of all standards is led by one individual department or person. This leadership will help ensure consistency of layout and format in all of the standards and reduce the likelihood of duplications or gaps.

STRATEGIES
FOR SUCCESS

It is essential that the development of standards be led by a person or team, usually the information security group. This leadership will help ensure that the layout and format of the standards are consistent, that the standards are easy to understand and apply and that duplication and gaps do not occur.

The standards should be developed by a team that includes people who have sufficient knowledge of internal controls and of information security. In this way, they will be able to develop well rounded standards that integrate with overall internal control systems and which are responsive to risk.

The process of standards development

When drafts of a particular standard are being developed or updated, they should be widely circulated for comment before they are presented to the Information Security Committee for approval. This is an important step as it will allow us to check whether the standards can meet the needs of many departments and can be applied, where they affect computer sites, to the wide range of computer sites in size and complexity that the company may have. Circulating the draft standards for comment and, of course, ensuring comments are properly acted upon, means that the team that creates the standard can be small and therefore able to work efficiently.

Comments need to be gathered not only from operating departments, but also from administrative departments. Some standards may have an impact on personnel policies and will need to be referred to human resources; others may have legal implications and should be reviewed by the legal department, etc.

STRATEGIES
FOR SUCCESS

Each team responsible for drafting a new or revised standard should circulate the draft for comment and assess and act on the comments before presenting it to the Information Security Committee for final approval. This circulation should include major operating departments, owners of computer sites of various sizes and complexity, and administrative departments such as human resources and the legal department, as appropriate in each instance.

THE SECOND PRINCIPLE

5.2 Senior management should establish an appropriate structure for quality assurance of information security standards.

The key elements of the quality control process are already in place: we have ensured that:

- the teams writing the standards have the requisite knowledge
- the Information Security Committee is responsible for the review of standards, and
- the composition of that committee reflects the various businesses the company is in and members have sound knowledge of internal controls, information security and business processes.

However, there are other steps that we can take to ensure quality control.

First, we need to recognize that some of these standards may be quite technical in nature. We may not have all of the knowledge we need within the company or be aware of what best practices are in a particular area. Thus we should have an approach in place to gather additional knowledge as required. This may include the use of outside consultants with specialized knowledge, a survey of best practices as to what other companies are doing, and research through books and publications to make sure that we have thought of all matters that should be covered and of all techniques that might be included within the standards.

Second, we should make use of the talents which may exist in the EDP audit speciality group within our internal audit department. If there are internal auditors who have specialized EDP audit knowledge, then we should ask them to review the standards as they are being developed and make their suggestions and recommendations before the standards are issued.

Third, we should consider involving the suppliers of the particular hardware and operating systems that we use to help in either the creation or review of the more technical standards we are developing. These suppliers can contribute their knowledge of the particular strengths and weaknesses of their products from a security perspective.

All of these quality assurance steps are summarized in the following chart.

Exhibit 5.1

Development of standards – quality assurance

Quality assurance over the development of standards should include the following steps as appropriate:

- the teams that develop the standards should have the appropriate knowledge of the business processes, internal controls and information security
- standards should be widely circulated for comment and reaction before they are put forward for approval
- the approving committee should include representatives of all major business departments as a means of ensuring that the standards can be effectively and efficiently applied throughout the organization
- research should be done to determine best practices for a particular standard, including contacting other companies to assess their standards
- the use of outside consultants should be considered
- the talents and abilities of EDP audit specialist in the internal audit department should be drawn upon, and
- hardware and operating systems suppliers should be contacted for any advice and guidance they may be able to provide.

STRATEGIES
FOR SUCCESS

Quality assurance procedures should include, as appropriate, the use of outside consultants with special expertise, surveys of practices in other companies and advice from internal EDP audit specialists and suppliers of hardware and systems software.

THE THIRD PRINCIPLE

5.3 The information security standards should all be structured in a consistent manner that allows them to be applied in a manner responsive to risk.

As this principle deals with a very key area, we will discuss it thoroughly.

The following example is a framework for reviewing the key issues. Below are three activities, the first two of which are drawn from the standard on logical security and the last one from the telecommunications standard. Intentionally, the first two activities are not technical in nature while the third one is fairly technical.

As you will want to refer to this example throughout the discussion of this principle, examine it carefully. As well, the discussion that follows will help you understand its contents.

Exhibit 5.2

Example of standard set up

Standard	The given standard **or a compensating control which achieves the same objectives** should be applied whenever any one of the primary objectives is classified as:											
	Integrity				**Confidentiality (including privacy)**				**Availability (or continuity)**			
	Vital	**Highly valuable**	**Valuable**	**Of lesser value**	**Regis-tered confidenti al**	**Confi-dential**	**Internal**	**Public**	**Critical**	**High**	**Medium**	**Low**
Logical security **1. Employee access rights are reviewed periodically by management**	Monthly	Quarterly	Annually	N/A	Applies	Applies	Applies	N/A	–	–	–	–
	Manager	Manager	Supervisor	N/A								
2. Additional access rights for individuals are approved	Systems owner & depart-ment head	Systems owner & depart-ment head	Depart-ment head	Supervi-sor	Applies	Applies	Applies	N/A	–	–	–	–
Telecommunications **3. Appropriate transmission methods are used**	Use message authenti-cation control	Use message authenti-cation control	Use message authenti-cation control	N/A	Data encryption required. Private lines to be used	Secured lines to be used	Public lines may be used	N/A	–	–	–	–

Before using this example as a basis for discussing the suggested structure for standards, we will first explain its content.

The first activity, “employee access rights are reviewed periodically by management,” is an important detective control. Over time, an employee’s access rights may become inappropriately wide. For example, when an employee transfers to a new job within the organization, new access rights may be given without regard to cancelling the old ones. Or, access rights for an employee who has left the company may still be in effect and should be cancelled.

The second activity, “additional access rights for individuals are approved”, relates to keeping all access rights to the minimum necessary for an employee to do his or her job. You will recall that we have defined everyone’s basic access rights as flowing from their job description, with everyone doing that job having the same access rights as shown on an access matrix. But, from time to time, there will be individuals who need additional access rights. This activity sets a framework for determining who can approve these additional rights.

Sample activity 3, “appropriate transmission methods are used”, is taken from the telecommunications standard. It focuses on the need to use an appropriately secure network and related methods for each type of data that may be sent or received.

In this activity, the term “MAC” refers to “message authentication controls” that help ensure that a message is not altered during its transmission. This, of course, relates to integrity. The columns under privacy and confidentiality refer to encryption, use of secure lines and use of public networks. These are means to protect privacy and confidentiality; encryption is the most powerful and the use of public networks, the weakest.

The structure of information security standards

Of course, each standard will be made up of several activities or procedures as are necessary to achieve our security objectives. The example illustrates only two activities from the standard on logical security and one from the standard on telecommunications.

If we simply provided a list of activities or procedures with no further guidance, then it would *not* be possible to apply them in a way that would be responsive to the nature and degree of risk. We would simply have a list of activities that must be in place, regardless of the circumstances. If the standard addressed only the most demanding category, i.e., vital, the result would be overkill; if the standard addressed only "average requirements", the result would be totally inadequate protection in some circumstances.

The example is based on the logical assumption that each standard would list all the activities that might be required. We then indicate which activities are needed for each classification category.

STRATEGIES

FOR SUCCESS

Each standard should list all the activities that may be required under any circumstances and then indicate which standards are applicable and how they are to be applied for the various categories in the classification structure.

On closer examination of these matters, we see that it is not only the activities that change depending on the level of risk, but also the frequency of their application and the seniority of the person performing the activity. This only makes sense; the more frequently a control is applied, the better the protection. The involvement of more senior people strengthens control as a more senior, experienced individual is focused on the task.

Thus we achieve the maximum flexibility in our standards and fine-tune them to varying levels of risk when we vary three factors:

- the manner in which the activity is implemented
- the frequency with which the activity is applied, and
- the seniority of the person performing the activity.

Let us see how our example addresses these matters.

For activity 1, review of access rights, we can see that this is applicable in all cases where integrity is vital, highly valuable or valuable. The N/A, not applicable, is indicated where integrity is of lesser importance. For this standard under privacy and confidentiality, we can see that it applies in the same way across the four categories. Under continuity and availability, the dashes indicate that this activity makes no contribution to these objectives.

Thus we now know the risk levels which, if present, should result in this activity being applied.

Now look at the contents of the boxes under integrity. We can see that this activity should be performed monthly, quarterly or annually depending on the level of integrity risk. The same thoughts apply for the four categories of privacy and confidentiality.

Activity 2, approval of additional access rights, can be interpreted in much the same way, except here the content of the boxes provides directions regarding the level at which the approval should take place, ranging from the department head down to a supervisor.

Some activities vary by frequency and some by the level of authority that carries them out, depending on their nature. Indeed, we can conceive of activities in which both the frequency and the authority level might vary, being "performed daily by the department head" for high risk and "yearly by a supervisor" for the lowest risk.

Activity 3, the use of appropriate networks, illustrates the final dimension. Messages go across the network at all times. *The element that varies here is the manner in which the activity is implemented.* Thus, to maintain integrity as messages are transmitted, we use message authentication in all circumstances except for the lowest level of risk. We use encryption, secure lines or require neither in order to address the various levels of privacy and confidentiality risk. Other activities supporting this standard would include when and how various encryption schemes might be implemented and the activities around them, the standards for secure lines, and so on.

STRATEGIES
FOR SUCCESS

Standards and the activities which support them should be formatted and documented in such a way that the reader can tell how to implement them in a risk responsive way. This means the standards should show for each level of risk in the classification:

- *the activities which should be applied*
- *how the nature of the activity may vary if required*
- *the frequency with which the activity should be performed if germane, and*
- *the authority or seniority level of the person doing the activity, if this should vary.*

The format of the example provides two other advantages.

First, we can see which activity relates, or at least makes some contribution, to the various objectives of integrity, privacy and confidentiality, and continuity and availability. Thus we can pull out of our standards all the activities for a particular system or computer site that support a particular objective. This will assist us in reviewing security procedures for each objective, making it easier to integrate security with the overall system of internal controls.

Second, our structure is so designed that it could easily be put into a database. This would allow users and designers to ask and receive answers to many questions such as:

- What kinds of activities would I need if confidentiality has a risk assessment level of x?
- What are all the activities that help with integrity at site x?

As information security grows in importance and as we develop more sites and applications, the ability to access a database of standards and activities can be a practical tool for designing cost effective business processes that are responsive to risk. It can also give a user quick access to the part of the standards that he or she needs to work with in a particular situation.

STRATEGIES
FOR SUCCESS

Standards and their component activities should be formatted and organized so that they can be stored in, and accessed through, a database.

Developing guidance materials for classifying data and information

Systems owners and those that assist in classifying data will need guidance material to provide direction on the three dimensions of classification: integrity, privacy and confidentiality, and continuity and availability. This guidance material should be straightforward and descriptive; the material itself should be provided as part of the standard on information classification.

No matter what form this guidance material takes, it should contain a description of each level or category of risk for each of the risk classification dimensions. In this way, it will communicate the general nature of each category for each of integrity, privacy and confidentiality and availability and continuity. The descriptions should be written so as to reflect the nature of the company's business and might even include one or two examples of data that would fall into that category to illustrate the concept.

The following illustrates three classification examples, one for each of integrity, privacy and confidentiality, and availability and continuity.

To provide variety in the examples, the one for integrity is the second highest ranking, the one for privacy and confidentiality is the highest, and the one for continuity and availability is the second lowest.

Exhibit 5.3

Integrity

Classification of data: 2 – highly valuable

Data and information placed in this category requires a high degree of integrity.

Risk: Includes data where a loss of integrity would give rise to financial loss, liability or would seriously disrupt our ability to serve customers.

Examples include all data having monetary values or which relates to assets that could easily be converted into cash such as, bank accounts, receivables and inventories. Also data used to make payments, such as accounts payable and payroll data, would normally also be included here.

As regards customer service: As the maintenance of correct prices and "ship to" addresses are vital to order entry, shipping addresses and price lists are also examples of data that would fall into this category.

Exhibit 5.4

Privacy and confidentiality

Classification of data: 1 – registered confidential

Data and information placed in this highest category includes those items where the need for privacy and confidentiality is very significant.

Risk: Includes information which if disclosed would cause severe loss of competitive advantage or would severely damage customer relations through disclosure to others of data or information in our possession about customers.

Examples include corporate planning documents, plans for new products and profits and earnings forecasts and budgets.

As regards customer service: The nature of our business normally does not result in our having customer-supplied information which if lost would severely damage or embarrass our customers. Thus most of our data concerning customers would be placed in some lower category.

As regards personnel: Our union agreements contain clauses requiring strict confidentiality concerning certain employee information such as health data in the company medical clinic. These responsibilities may result in some employee data being placed into this highest category.

Exhibit 5.5

Availability and continuity
Classification of data: 3 – medium Data and information in this category would not be needed for up to two weeks should there be a disaster to our computer resources. Risk: Data and information in this category is generally not referred to on a day-to-day basis to support customer service or to process transactions. It is not required to safeguard our liquid assets such as cash and accounts receivable. Rather, its use is periodic and we can tolerate some delay in the timing of its next scheduled use. As there is a long time period for recovery from a disaster, data and information in this category would not be vital on any particular business day and thus would also be low risk from an availability perspective. Examples include fixed assets records and human resources databases and some of our office automation tools and underlying records.

Organizing the classification guidance material

One good way to organize our guidance material is to provide a list of risk factors and indicate which ones generally affect which dimension of integrity, privacy and confidentiality, and availability and continuity. Alternatively, risk factors could be grouped by classification level, showing the nature of the risks that would normally result in that classification level being chosen.

The key point is that we are developing guidance material, not a rigid framework that when applied in a standard manner will produce a definitive answer. Instead, through the description of the categories already discussed and the developing of the supporting guidance material, we provide factors and issues to be considered in making these classification decisions.

The more common approach is to list the factors that would put a particular type of data or information in a category. The following sample list of factors for assessing if data relates to the two highest categories for integrity illustrates this approach.

Exhibit 5.6

Classifying data

Vital

To determine if data should be classified as vital, consider:

- Does the data contain individually significant values so that even one or a few errors could cause major financial loss?
- Is the computerized data directly used to pay or disburse money with little or no human review of supporting documents? (i.e., is the data highly trusted?)
- Is the data a key element in the provision of information used for the most important management decisions?
- Is the data used to manage logical security or otherwise plays an important part in information security? (e.g., password files, encryption keys)
- Does the data relate to secret processes or business methods that are a core element of competitive advantage?

Highly valuable

To determine if data should be classified as highly valuable, consider:

- Would a lack of integrity lead to direct financial loss?
- Is the data used to help safeguard assets?
- Is the data directly used to prepare financial reports?
- Would corruption or inaccuracy in the data give rise to legal liability?
- Is the data or system used to conduct business or accept or act on a transaction without human intervention? (e.g., EDI transactions)
- Is the data or information used to make daily operational decisions?
- Is the data used to measure achievement of critical success factors?

STRATEGIES
FOR SUCCESS

Systems owners and those that assist in classifying data and systems should be provided guidance material to assist them in the classification of information. This support material should define the various risk categories and list the risk factors that are the most important in allocating data and information to each category. As a quality assurance measure, classification decisions should be carefully reviewed, usually by the information systems department, before being acted on.

THE FOURTH PRINCIPLE

5.4 Senior management should understand the nature of information security standards that are required and the overall nature and purpose of each one.

Certainly, it is not the job of senior management to write the information security standards. However, top management must fully understand the areas for which standards are required and appreciate the purpose and overall nature of each standard. Specifically, it is senior management who will:

- assign responsibility for the development and ongoing maintenance of the standards, and
- put a quality assurance process in place to ensure that proper and cost effective standards are developed.

For these reasons, senior management must develop a knowledgeable appreciation of the areas for which standards are required and the fundamental nature and purpose of each of those areas.

While generally senior management will direct the development of standards rather than actually create them, there are two exceptions where senior management must have a more hands-on involvement in their development:

- information classification standards, and
- roles and responsibilities, including contracting with others in the company.

These key standards and the reasons for senior management involvement are discussed later in this section.

We will first review the areas where standards may be required and then follow this with a brief discussion of the nature and purpose of each of the standards.

What a standard should contain

Like our policy, standards should provide only an appropriate level of detail. A good standard will spell out the precise nature of activities that are required by the standard but will *not* provide an exhaustive explanation or statement of precisely how each activity is to be performed. If this concept is not followed, standards will literally start to fill volumes and lose their functionality.

We set the scene for this in the information security strategy that was developed in *Chapter 4* and summarized the layers of policies, standards and administration manuals as shown in the exhibit below.

Exhibit 5.7

The information security strategy

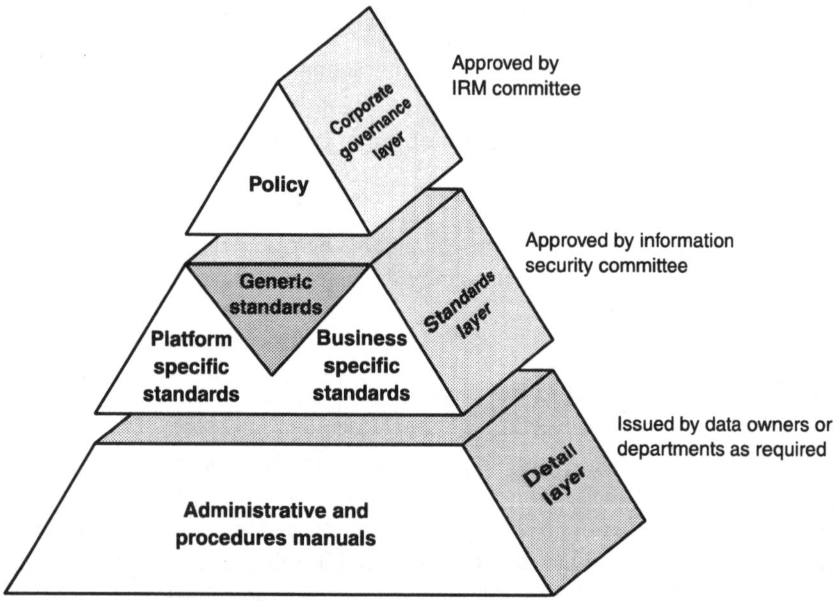

Thus in writing standards, we should recognize that we can and should support them with detailed administrative manuals, checklists of detailed procedures and, of course, training. This third level of administrative procedures was provided for in the information security strategy discussed in *Chapter 4*. As you'll recall, the information security strategy is a brief, overview document that defines the layers of policy, standards and procedures and how they support each other. This should now be kept in mind for the following discussion.

Typically, most companies find that a typical standard is 4 to 5 pages long and all standards taken together require to 40 to 60 pages.

The number and nature of manuals that a company will need to create will vary with a number of factors, including the complexity of the activities involved, the size of the company and whether it is centralized or decentralized, the skill sets and knowledge of the employees who perform the activities and so on.

STRATEGIES
FOR SUCCESS

Standards should focus on the activities that are needed to achieve their purpose and intent under the various risk scenarios that can be envisaged. Details of the administrative methods and procedures needed to carry out each activity can be set forth in administration and procedures manuals. These supporting manuals can be developed as the need for them becomes apparent. This approach will ensure that the standards are focused, reasonable in length, and easy to use, and avoid the mire of unwieldy detail.

Determining the standards required

The specific standards that are needed will vary from company to company in relation to factors such as how large and complex the organization is, the way it is organized and the technologies that are used.

The list of standards provided and then discussed below are typical of those needed by most fairly large organizations. If your company has especially complex or specialized needs, further standards may need to be developed.

The focus here is on the generic standards that will be useful across all types of business processes and for all computer sites across a variety of hardware and operating systems. As discussed in *Chapter 4* under the "information security strategy", it may be desirable to develop platform specific or business specific standards which reflect specific hardware and software environments or business processes.

However, the platform or business specific standards should *not* be used to dilute or avoid a proper level of information security. They should retain all the activities called for in the generic standards and simply be reshaped to fit a particular circumstance. In this way, the activities will still achieve the same level of security and control called for in the generic standard.

STRATEGIES
FOR SUCCESS

Generic standards should be developed first which are applicable across all business processes and various computer platforms. Platform specific standards and business specific standards can then be created from these generic standards where appropriate, as long as these specific standards fulfil the same intent and requirements. They should be reviewed and approved in the same manner as any other standard.

The generic standards which are normally required fall into three major groups:

- standards which set forth needed user activities as part of overall information security (or in which users play a major role)
- technical standards that will be used by computer site owners and technical personnel (these provide for proper internal controls over all computer sites and related technical activities, including the development of application systems that meet user defined security requirements), and
- process standards for certain key processes that we want to have performed in the same manner across the organization, such as use of the Internet, virus prevention and detection, etc.

Note that the policy and standards written from a user point of view apply to all departments, including management of a computer site and the management of the information systems department. Thus, as a department head, the person in charge of a computer site needs to fulfil all department head responsibilities set forth in the policy document. The information systems department should also follow all standards, regardless of the category we have placed some of them in. For example, access matrices should be developed for all jobs within the information systems department, not because these people enter transactions but because we must have a proper division of duties concerning the powerful access privileges that are used by technical specialists. The standards on systems development apply just as much to the systems analysts and programmers as they do to the user. Thus we should not let this grouping of standards, designed to assist understanding, cloud the fact that all departments must adhere to all standards, and this includes the information systems department.

The exhibit below lists the standards that will usually be required. But again, these will have to be tailored to meet the needs and activities of an individual company. These are later discussed in detail. Of course, in some circumstances, there may be other standards that are required; in other situations, some of the standards suggested may not be needed.

Exhibit 5.8

Three major groups of standards

I Standards that relate principally to user activities

i) Information and data classification, including an appendix providing guidance for the decision process of this activity

ii) Roles and responsibilities, including contracting with others in the company

iii) Systems development

iv) Access matrices

v) Requesting and reviewing access rights

vi) Use of third party suppliers

II Standards that relate principally to computer site owners and other technical activities

i) Physical security and protection

ii) Systems software

iii) Logical security

iv) Networks and telecommunications

v) Application programming change control

vi) Computer operations

vii) Database management

viii) Backup and recovery

ix) Disaster recovery

III Standards for key processes

i) Cryptography standard

ii) The internet

As stated earlier, senior management is normally not involved in the creation of the standards; however, there are two standards where they should be more deeply involved and actively work with others to shape the standards.

The first of these is the standard on information classification. This is a key standard in that it is the means by which we make information security responsive to risk. Furthermore, the classifications arrived at using this standard should be used and reflected in the overall system of internal control over each business process.

The second one, the standard on roles and responsibilities, is used to define the roles of various groups in greater depth than was covered in the policy. As the defining of roles and duties is also a key factor in achieving corporate-wide information security, top management should be directly and actively involved.

STRATEGIES
FOR SUCCESS

Senior management should be directly involved in shaping the standards on information classification and on roles and responsibilities. These standards help to ensure that information security processes and indeed overall systems of internal controls are responsive to risk and also assign roles and responsibilities across the company at a more detailed level than was provided for in the policy document.

I Standards that relate principally to user activities

i) Information and data classification

The content of the information security policy was restricted to a focus on the need for information classification, the responsibility of the systems owners with the cooperation of others to do this, and the need to classify data and information along the three dimensions of integrity, privacy and confidentiality, and continuity and availability. The rest of the guidance on information classification should be put in this standard.

By placing the details in this standard, it will be far easier to make amendments as time progresses and the work of classifying our information will lead us to better ways of doing it.

As already explained, information classification is an essential ingredient in making our security processes responsive to risk and creating a balance between the cost of controls and the nature and extent of risks which need to be managed. Thus, it is one of the few standards that merits senior management's close attention and involvement.

Classification is the linchpin by which users define their security requirements and their systems developers and computer site owners provide what is required. These relationships are illustrated in the exhibit below.

Exhibit 5.9

Creating and using data classification

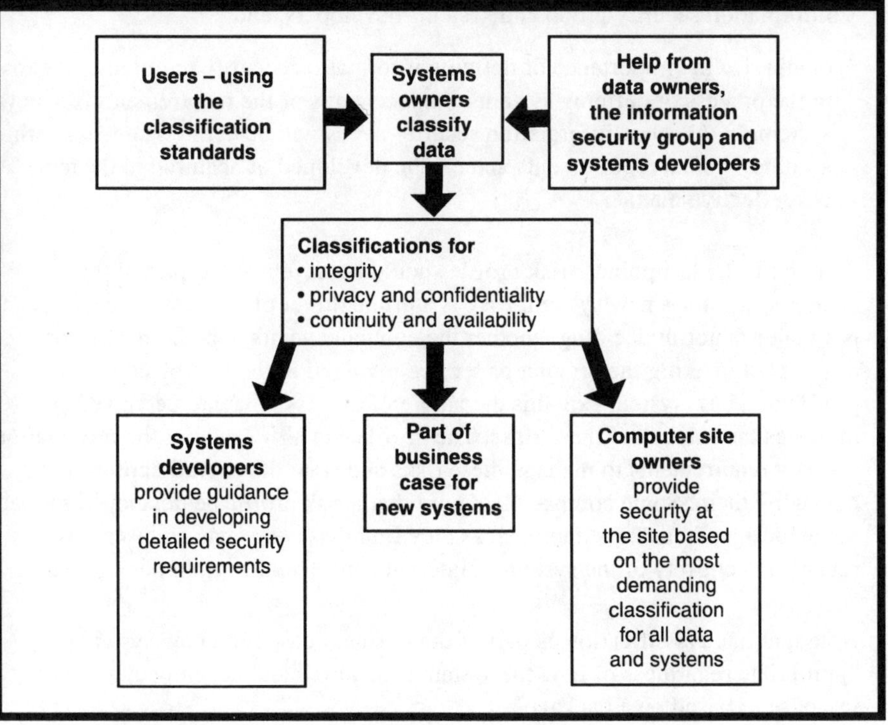

The information classification standard should normally:

- explain the format and layout of all standards so that the reader can see how the standards have been designed to implement security activities that are risk responsive
- state and explain each of the categories we use for risk classification under the headings of integrity, privacy and confidentiality, and continuity and availability
- be referenced to the guidance material that is designed to assist systems owners and others in making classification decisions; the guidance material itself attached to the standard as an appendix
- explain precisely how and by whom classifications should be used to attain information security that is responsive to risk
- reiterate the primary responsibility of systems owners to classify information, but point out that in doing so assistance may be required from data owners, the information security group and systems developers, and
- emphasize the importance of defining information security requirements early in the process of defining systems enhancements or the requirements of a new system. In this way, information security needs will be defined up front with all other system requirements and can be developed or acquired in the most cost effective manner.

As regards the last point, a risk profile should be developed as part of the business case for a new system. Risk is a prime driver of the costs of controls and is a major factor in deciding whether the company wants to be in this line of business of offering the product or service involved in the first place. A risk profile of a new system explains the nature of the risks that are perceived and indicates the sources of these risks. The profile can also spell out the information security requirements to manage these risks and state the overall approach to managing them. Some companies require that a risk profile be developed for each newly designed business approach as they find these concepts are useful as regards the entirety of the system of internal controls that would be required.

Note that risk classification as part of the business case for a new system is appropriate regardless of how the system is acquired and developed, whether in-house or based on a package.

STRATEGIES
FOR SUCCESS

A risk profile should be prepared for each new business process or system being acquired, setting out the classifications, the nature and source of risks, and the approach that will be used to manage these risks. This risk profile should be part of the business case for the system and ideally will cover all risks and requirements for overall internal controls, instead of focusing only on information security.

In a moment, we will discuss the standard for systems development and see how classification decisions will be used when acquiring new systems or making systems changes.

In a later section, when we discuss standards that relate principally to computer site owners, we will see how classification decisions are taken into account in applying these standards.

ii) Roles and responsibilities

This is the remaining standard that may be of direct concern to senior management and which will merit their detailed attention.

Much has been said in the information security policy about roles and responsibilities. However, details as to responsibility assignments or the mandate of various committees and groups have been left for inclusion in the standard so that these more detailed responsibilities can be reassigned or amended when business circumstances or organizational structures of the company change over time.

We can use this standard to provide further detailed statements of responsibility for any of the groups mentioned in the information security policy. The responsibility areas which are most frequently further defined at the standards level include:

- the mandate of the Information Security Committee, in order to spell out the additional mandates and responsibilities top management may wish to assign

- where many computer sites exist within the organization, a clear definition of the role of the chief information security officer and the reporting relationships (often of a dotted line nature) between the information security officers in the various sites and the chief information security officer
- the means by which systems owners and systems developers should ensure that information security requirements are dealt with in an integrated fashion with all other requirements whenever a system is enhanced or a new information system required, and
- the exact kind of information which should be supplied whenever an exemption from policy or an exception to standards arises.

As mentioned throughout the book, it is vital that every system and every computer site have a systems owner or a computer site owner. Because of the extensive responsibilities and authorities concerning systems or computer site ownership, others in the organization often have to know who owns a particular computer site or system in order to dialogue or work with those owners. Thus, many companies use the roles and responsibilities standards as a repository for the current list of systems and computer site owners. Whenever there are changes or additions to this list, a new appendix can be issued to all concerned to attach to the back of the standard.

At the policy level, we discussed the importance of providing for "contracting" within the organization. In this way, a particular business unit or department assigned responsibility as owner of a computer site or a computer system can gain assistance and help from others within the organization for those particular matters they may not have the skill sets to address. At the policy level, it was stressed that such internal contracting should be documented and accepted in writing by the other party. Often, top management wishes to provide additional guidance on exactly when this contracting out might be appropriate and may feel it is important to keep a list or an overall repository to keep track of such contracts that may exist. Where further explanations are required on this contracting out process, the roles and responsibilities standard is an excellent place to do this.

STRATEGIES
FOR SUCCESS

The roles and responsibilities standard should be used to define in detail various responsibility roles such as the mandate of the Information Security Committee and the chief information security officer. It can also be used to define precisely how ownership roles are defined and how exemptions from policy and exceptions to standards should be requested, approved and documented.

iii) Systems development

We saw in *Chapter 1* how many information security procedures are implemented within each application system, which cannot be addressed on an overall basis for the computer site taken as a whole.

Thus the methodology we use to acquire or develop systems needs to cover the definition and implementation of these security requirements in an integrated manner and at the same time, as for all other system requirements.

The purpose of this standard is to integrate information security into the overall systems development process. This standard should:

- explain how the classification categories selected by the systems owner should be used as a guide in developing detailed security requirements
- explain how information security requirements should be defined as part of the overall requirements definition for new systems or any major enhancements and the various roles that systems owners, data owners, and systems developers play in this definition process, and
- assist the reader in understanding how all activities to define, implement and test information security procedures should be intertwined with and performed in conjunction with the detailed systems development methodology used by the information systems department.

Information security includes people-performed procedures and is not merely a question of software. Thus, this standard should spell out the responsibilities of systems and data owners to develop the people-performed procedures and to document them to the extent required in detailed procedural manuals.

This standard can also be a good place to reinforce that information security is part and parcel of a larger overall system of internal controls over the business process. The standard can also reinforce the importance of designing information security as part of an overall internal control process and explain how this should be done in conjunction with the information security policy and the other policies and procedures regarding internal controls that the company has established.

STRATEGIES
FOR SUCCESS

Detailed security requirements for each application system should be defined, documented, implemented and tested in the same way as all other systems requirements whenever new systems are required or existing systems modified. Classification categories for data and systems should be used as a guide in defining these requirements.

---

iv) Access matrices

We have already discussed the importance of access matrices as a means of defining an appropriate division of duties and then communicating this division of duties to systems developers and other technical people so that logical security both of the systems software and application level can be properly designed and implemented. In other words, it is through the access matrix that systems owners spell out the division of duties that is required so that technical people can create the appropriate access rights.

Thus, this standard should:

- set forth the format for and the minimum contents of access matrices
- include a useful example of an access matrix and through an explanation of the example, illustrate the format and the minimum contents which are required

- require that the matrices cover all access rights, including the ability to read and the ability to write on or change files, and
- reinforce that access matrices are not just for employees. Matrices should also be created for each class or type of customer as a means of ensuring that the access we want to supply to our customers is carefully considered and communicated.

v) Requesting and reviewing access rights

User management has a key role to play in the development of the standard for requesting access rights and in making sure that those access rights are changed or cancelled as required when people change jobs or leave the organization.

This standard is a natural continuation of user management's responsibility over access rights flowing from the creation of an access matrices referred to above. This standard can usefully spell out:

- how access rights are requested for each employee
- how these rights must be approved
- the processes to approve additional rights beyond that provided for the access matrix made for any particular employee, and
- procedures for a periodic review of access rights by departmental management for the employees in that department as well as a review from time to time by systems owners and data owners of all access rights to their systems and data.

STRATEGIES
FOR SUCCESS

The responsibilities and procedures to create access matrices, which detail the division of duties to be enforced by information security processes, should be well defined. The means by which access rights are granted, amended and cancelled for all employees and third parties should also be clearly defined.

---

vi) Use of third party suppliers

The use of third party suppliers is growing. In their efforts to achieve greater efficiencies and economies, many organizations are frequently outsourcing key elements of information systems operations to third parties.

As stated earlier, the nature of computer operations which we outsource to service bureaus or facilities managers can vary considerably. On the one extreme, some companies may simply rent computer time at a large outside service bureau and then, by remote access, have company employees carry out all tasks related to the running of the its data centre which is physically located in a third party environment. In this case, the outside supplier is really only providing physical security together with the necessary processes to prevent physical damage through fire, etc. On the other end of the spectrum, they may outsource the entire management of the data centre to the third party as well as the provision of the application software which is used to process transactions.

Regardless of the scope of the arrangements, the key concern from an information security perspective is that, for all activities the outside service bureau performs on the organization's behalf, the third party should have processes in place that fulfil the requirements of our information security policies and standards. There are two key mechanisms by which this assurance can be obtained:

- first, make appropriate contractual arrangements which require the outside party to meet the company's information security policies and standards, with specific reference being made in the contract. The contract should also provide that our internal or external auditor may from time to time conduct an examination at the data centre to provide assurance that the necessary internal control processes have been designed and are being followed to meet our policy and standards needs, and
- second, visit the data centre and review their procedures to see that they meet our policies and standards. In addition, conduct tests at the data centre to see if these controls are being respected and complied with on a day-to-day basis. This usually requires the involvement of the EDP audit specialists from the internal audit group. Alternatively, ask the information security group to review and test the controls at the third party service bureau.

As this work can be time-consuming and requires specialist knowledge, consider having the third party supplier provide an auditor's report as defined in Section 5900 of the *CICA Handbook*. This report process is used to determine that the third party's internal controls have been effectively designed to provide reasonable assurance that control objectives are being met and that these controls are being complied with. This approach requires first negotiating the control objectives, and perhaps the supporting control procedures, to be covered as part of the contract and ensuring that the coverage of the objectives is sufficient to meet the organization's needs.

The purpose of the third party standard is to spell out how the company wishes to address all of the above, together with the assignment of responsibilities for all stages of the process including:

- the appropriate involvement of information systems and information security specialists in the definition of the contract
- the fixing of responsibilities of internal auditors, the information security group, external auditors or others to evaluate procedures at the service bureau in the first place to determine that they adequate to meet the organization's policies and standards, and
- the procedures for determining that the third party's internal control procedures are being adhered to on an ongoing basis.

This is a complex and technical area which will require the involvement of information security specialists and any EDP internal audit specialists that may exist in the internal audit group. The complexity can be best understood by reflecting on the fact that all procedures used at a data centre to manage data centre activities have a major impact on internal controls. We will need to address how the outside data centre has designed and is adhering to control procedures to meet all of our standards for activities they perform on our behalf.

STRATEGIES
FOR SUCCESS

When using outside service bureaus to provide applications or computer sites, the need to ensure the company's information security policies and standards are effectively applied at the external sites is the same as for internal company sites. Contracts with such suppliers should require them to meet the requirements of the company's policies and standards and accordingly provide for their controls to do to be evaluated and regularly tested. Responsibility for this should be formally assigned by designating an employee or department as the computer site owner for each external site.

II Standards that relate principally to computer site owners and other technical activities

We will now discuss the standards for internal controls over all activities at a computer site. All of these external controls have a major impact on information security and thus all these standards should be considered as part of our information security standards.

The standards are applicable regardless of whether we are considering the major corporate computer centre or computer sites such as LANs being managed by an operating department. As explained above, these standards also apply to third party computer sites where company data or programs are stored or processed. Of course, there should be a designated computer site owner for each and every computer site.

Our need for control does not vary with the location of the computer site. However, it does vary depending upon the requirement for security for all programs and data residing at that site. As previously explained, it is the responsibility of each computer site owner to apply all these standards in a manner that is commensurate with the most demanding classification for all data and systems as defined by the systems owners.

i) Physical security and protection

The physical security and protection standard:

- outlines the activities that are required for each risk category to control physical access to the computer site, and
- provides for physical means to avoid damage to the site that could disrupt continuity and availability of computer resources.

All risk categories are touched to some degree by physical security. Integrity is protected as we restrict access to devices of a powerful nature such as master consoles which could be used to alter data without leaving any trail of the changes.

We also restrict access to the computer sites and the tapes and disks stored there to prevent a loss of privacy and confidentiality through theft or copying of such tapes and disks. Physical protection measures to avoid damage through fire and smoke and procedures to ensure ongoing availability of electric power tie very closely into continuity and availability objectives.

This standard also requires a great deal of flexibility in that a company's physical sites may range all of the way from local area networks which are located within an office environment through to major data centres. For this reason, it may be useful to develop two sets of standards, one for dedicated physical premises for major computer sites and the other for local area networks or other computer sites that are included in an office environment.

As previously mentioned, this standard has two principal purposes:

- to control physical access, and
- to prevent a disruption of service to the extent appropriate to the most demanding classification of data and information at the site.

Each of these is briefly discussed below.

At a major data site, the physical security will concern itself with controlling access to the building for employees, contractors and visitors. Security measures will include such things as the use of security badges to be displayed at all times, locked doors and the alarming of these doors, physical control over access to the computer room itself and to tape libraries and areas where information is printed, procedures used to receive and dispatch tapes and other computer media.

For a local area network, it will be necessary to restrict physical access to the file server, not just for reasons of security in the narrow sense but also to reduce the risk of damage due to spilled coffee and other hazards within the office. Other considerations include where and how and how often backup tapes and other computer media are stored off site and whether this storage is sufficient, not just for continuity and availability purposes but to protect this material against theft.

In a major data centre, protection against disruption in service will require some very expensive equipment and incur ongoing costs to maintain that equipment. Often fire extinguishers or automatic fire sprinklers are considered, as well as burglary alarms, computer systems that monitor the atmosphere and temperature control over the computer room for the mainframe computers, the use of diesel generators to supply electrical power in the event of short term disruption to the normal electrical power source, back up of computer networks coming into the data centre, etc.

If a local area network processes applications of major significance to the company, the company may wish to store the file server in the data centre. On the other hand, there should be a minimum set of standards in place to provide some degree of protection against disruption in an office environment. Today, it is feasible to buy uninterruptable power supplies for the file server in case of a power disruption or to "clean" the electrical current to prevent spikes or drops in voltages from interfering with the operation of the local area network. Other protection measures to be addressed include such matters as using dust covers and keeping the file server and other microcomputer equipment away from sources of electrical magnetic energy such as large photocopiers.

ii) Systems software

This standard deals with the procedures for authorizing the addition of new system software for use on a particular computer site and the process by which this change is implemented so that both quality assurance and a proper division of duties are ensured.

Systems software includes:

- the operating system itself, including upgrades and changes thereto
- any additional software that is used to provide for logical security and expand the capabilities of the operating system in this regard, and
- any specialized program tools used by the computer site technical staff to manage the computer resource, such as scheduling packages to help manage the scheduling and production of computer runs, special utilities to provide for the high speed copying of data for backup and other purposes, and numerous other special software tools that may be used for managing and tuning databases and other system software packages.

As explained in *Chapter 1*, systems software is the core of information security: *If we lose control over our systems software, we lose control over security.* Many types of systems software need, and thus have the ability, to directly alter files and programs and usually do *not* create any audit trails. Generally, systems software provides a host of powerful privileges to the person authorized to use it. Indeed, it is the systems software that provides all logical security capabilities. In many ways, an individual who has the ability to change systems software is akin to the locksmith who can change the lock on any door or gain entry with a master skeleton key.

The power and flexibility of systems software programs make them a high security risk. The powerful capabilities of specialized program tools can be either the means by which security is created or the means by which the user of such tools circumvents the normal security processes. If I can find the way to get at systems software, then I have the ability to add new passwords and access rights or use special programs that can go directly at data and programs. Often these changes can be made without leaving any audit trail.

Thus, the systems software standards must address procedures for:

- approving the acquisition and implementation of new system software
- examining each new system software package or any upgrades to existing system software to determine the security risks it may possess due to its extensive capabilities
- controlling the addition of new systems software programs and changes to existing programs, and

- identifying weaknesses in systems programs and making changes to plug holes in security that would exist if the new systems software programs were used "as is" from the supplier.

Controlling systems software changes

Working with information security specialists, the designated technical specialist for each system software program should determine:

- how and under what circumstances the system software could be used
- who should have access to it, and
- what audit trail reports should be generated for follow up.

Every change to any computer program, including systems software, requires a change control process. Clearly, we cannot allow anyone at any time to add or amend systems software or any other computer program. This not only threatens the integrity of our programs, but also allows those with such a privilege to place routines in software which could represent serious security breaches. Remember that programs are able to read, write and alter data. Thus, if I can slip in an unauthorized program or an unauthorized routine into a large complex program, this can give me a trap door or hole through which I can manipulate and change data in an unauthorized manner at a later date. Security specialists and hackers refer to these as "back doors", "trojan horses", "logic bombs" and many other terms depending on the way they work.

The division of duties over amending or adding new software of any type is referred to as change control. Change control normally requires that there be a basic division of duties between:

- those who create and approve changes, and
- those who are able to move new or changed code from a test environment through into the environment used to actually run computer processes and process business (called the production environment).

Ideally, the change control officer making these moves has no other duties concerning the acquisition, testing or approval of new system software. Instead, the duties of the change control officer would be limited to seeing that all other necessary approvals are made, and are on file, before instituting a change.

For computer sites that require a very high level of information security, the company may even wish to produce audit trail reports from the security software of changes that have been made to any systems program and, on a sample basis, have someone else other than the change control officer make sure that such changes were approved. In this way, there will be some assurance that the change control officer himself has not slipped in unauthorized, spurious changes. In addition, wherever possible, final testing of a change should be done by someone who was not involved in creating the change and in a manner that protects the code against further changes either during or after final testing.

It is clear from the above discussion that this whole standard is highly technical in nature and requires highly technical people to define the activities and how they are performed in relation to various categories and levels of risk. The quality assurance of these standards may require the use of some outside expertise, either through having a highly qualified EDP internal auditor review these standards or hiring an outside consultant.

STRATEGIES
FOR SUCCESS

As regards systems software standards, senior management must take careful note of whether appropriate quality assurance procedures are being applied. For a major data centre, the activities required under this standard can be expensive and errors in matching risks and controls can be disastrous and expensive.

iii) Logical security

This standard is the technical heart of information security standards. As explained in *Chapter 1*, logical security consists of software capabilities to appropriately restrict access to computer resources including *all* programs, data, networks, terminals and devices. The logical security software that achieves these objectives is either found within the operating system for the computer hardware, or may be found or supplemented by special logical security software. These two things together are referred to as logical security or logical security software, all of which is part of the systems software we discussed in the last standard.

Logical security software:

- protects all computer resources
- authenticates anyone making a request to read or write (alter) any computer files or programs, and
- authenticates users before it allows an attachment by a remote device, such as accessing a local area network through a public telephone line on a microcomputer.

Besides being the primary means by which we mobilize preventative controls, logical security should also set the scene for detective measures. Thus, logical security should:

- provide audit trails to fix accountability and permit investigation of attempted violations of security
- permit us to produce understandable reports of access rights of customers and employees for review by supervisors as regards the employees that work for them and for review by system owners
- be set to search for and report unusual activity, allowing us to review whether somebody has penetrated our logical security by enabling us to look for patterns of unusual changes or behaviour, and
- produce exception listings disclosing the use of powerful access rights so these may be reviewed and followed up on.

In writing the logical security standard, the organization must keep in mind the four primary goals of this standard:

1. Unless authorized, no one should be able to connect with or gain access to the company's computer resources in any way (e.g., keep out hackers).

2. Employees and others who are permitted access to the company's computer resources are only able to access resources in a specified and authorized manner. In other words, their access rights are restricted specifically to files that they are allowed to read or change or programs they are allowed to execute. Ideally, only technical personnel managing the computer site should be able to directly access programs or data. Normal users should record or read data *only* through the use of approved application programs that provide for proper controls, further support a detailed division of duties and produce audit trails.

3. The computer site owner is the custodian of data and provides a high level of assurance that data can not be changed except by authorized individuals using authorized application programs to do so. When technical personnel have to change data to correct errors or technical problems, these changes are reported to the data owners and all normal controls applied as soon as possible after the fact.

4. The computer site owner holds all applications programs unchanged except for those changes that have been communicated and agreed to by the systems owners. The same exception would have to be made here for programs that have to be changed in an emergency; these would be reviewed and reported to users as soon as possible after the fact.

The logical security standards should set forth specific activities concerning at least the following areas:

- the basic requirements of passwords including their length and composition, how often they must be changed, the encryption methods used for the password file, etc.
- the activities to be used for other access methods in addition to passwords, such as access by voice recognition, smart cards, one time password techniques, the provision of encrypted signatures, etc. and whether these access methods are in addition to or are a replacement for passwords
- the precise manner in which logical security or the operating system is to be set and used in order to provide strong logical security. Where possible, the various perimeter settings or choices as to options which logical security provides should be stated in the standard
- the audit trail reports which should be kept concerning accesses made, with special emphasis on the use of powerful privileges given technical personnel in relation to system software and how and by whom the use of these powerful privileges should be reviewed
- the additional controls which should be placed over access rights and passwords which provide for powerful privileges and the ability to change data and programs without leaving an audit trail, including how such passwords should be guarded, how their use should be reviewed, etc.
- the need to maintain an access matrix for all information systems personnel and the procedures which will be followed to make sure that all access rights are in accordance with this matrix or that additional privileges for individuals are reviewed and approved and reassessed periodically and appropriately

- the nature of reporting that should take place when a breach of security occurs and the escalation procedures to involve more senior executives and outside technical software suppliers to contain such a breach
- the procedures which are to be followed by the information security officer in granting and amending access rights. Where information security activities are decentralized to allow others in other departments to grant or alter certain access rights to files[1], the limitations of ability to be extended to these departmental information security officers should be described, and
- the procedures to be used to review and test check the activities of information security officers, as a check on the quality of their work and a safeguard of some limited value on whether they are only adding access rights as approved by others.

STRATEGIES
FOR SUCCESS

The logical security standard requires a high level of technical expertise. For quality assurance purposes, senior management should ensure a highly qualified EDP internal auditor or an outside consultant reviews these standards for completeness and appropriateness.

1 Often this is used to allow a department to add access rights for new employees in that department, but only to the extent of the specific access rights in accordance with the access matrix, without additional privileges. In other words, these departmental information security officers are restricted to adding a new person to a group with pre-defined and already existing access rules or deleting a person from same, as distinct from the broader abilities of the overall information security officer for the site who can design any type of access for any individual or create access rights for new groups or job profiles.

iv) Networks and telecommunications

This standard should cover all of the activities required to approve connection to new networks, either public or private, or to add new messages or transmit additional transactions over existing networks. The standard also ensures that a computer site having a "high level" of security is not inadvertently connected with a computer site that has a "low level" of security. If "high" and "low" must be connected, additional measures are required to ensure that overall security requirements are still being met.

The standard spells out the procedures for choosing networks and message formats that are responsive to risk. Thus the standard set forth procedures concerning:

- the approval process for adding new network connections or for sending or receiving new types of messages over existing networks
- when private networks should be used, when dedicated lines are required and when dial up lines might be used
- the various encryption methods that the company uses and guidance as to when encryption should be used and if so which method
- guidance as to how messages should be formatted to ensure that they do not become garbled or are subjected to accidental or purposeful alteration during transmission, and
- the approval process for adding new devices to the network such as terminals, printers and other peripherals.

All of these activities have important information security consequences. The use of new networks, the transmission of new types of data and messages across networks or the addition of devices to existing networks all represent means by which access to our computer files and data is further extended. Thus, a process is needed not only to manage the additional costs which will be incurred and the shape and nature of the overall enterprise architecture, but also to ensure that the extended ability to access the existing computer sites is being properly managed and controlled from an information security perspective. When wider connections are permitted, we may need to strengthen our logical security procedures referred to in the previous standard.

STRATEGIES
FOR SUCCESS

When developing the networks and telecommunications standard, consider including in this standard a definition of the circumstances under which the information security specialists in the company should be involved in these activities and whether their approval or only their involvement is required for various circumstances. Remember that the more use the organization makes of networks, the stronger the logical security processes must be.

v) Application programming change control

The management of the quality and logical correctness of computer programs is a wide and important field and beyond the scope of this book. However, certain aspects of the development and the implementation of computer programs have a high impact on the quality of information security, so we will focus on these attributes.

At the same time, it is clearly important that all standards and activities as regards information security aspects of program development should be closely interrelated with and interwoven into the systems development methodologies which the company uses to develop all new systems or make changes to those that already exist.

First, much of the logical security may be implemented at the application system level. As explained in *Chapter 1*, the operating systems and other logical security by itself will not provide all the security we need to fully segregate duties. Generally, at the operating system level, we can only control who has access to a particular program. Thus, at the application level, we must build in the additional security capabilities that segregate activities that are enabled by the application. For example, within an accounts receivable system, the application must be designed so that those who can record cash receipts cannot record credit notes and vice versa. The operating systems and logical security layer cannot do this; generally it can only control who can access and use the application totally.[2]

Thus, the application system must:

- implement requirements for information security that will be provided by the application software itself (such as appropriate division of capabilities across computer screens etc.), and
- provide for the production of data and information such as control reports, edit exception listings and transaction listings which are required to enable users manually to perform other important control activities that contribute to data and information integrity.

The other key element of application programming changes from a security perspective is to carefully control the changes to existing applications or new applications that can be put into active use. Application programs are able to create, write and alter data and, in today's modern systems, often actually generate much of the data or transactions directly. Thus, new application programs or changes to existing programs may represent a security hole; the programmer can accidentally or on purpose add code to alter data or create additional data which could cause errors of be the basis of a fraud. Or, the programmer can create an undocumented, unauthorized back door or hole which can be exploited by a knowledgeable person at a later date to get at and alter data when supposedly using the program as an authorized user. If the programmer wants to be malicious, he or she can write code that will destroy files or change values at random at some future date.

These examples, written in pseudo code, show how these things can be done:

- If the employee number is x, then double the amount of salary for the pay period.
- If the logon identification is Fred Smith, then allow access to all screens and functions of the program.

---

2 See discussion that follows on databases and the related standard; sometimes these further segregations of capability are enforced by the database management system rather than the application program.

- If the system date supplied by the operating system is on or after January 1, 2000, then change all accounts receivable balances to zero.

Note that a programmer could bury these nefarious routines in a large program which he or she was asked to change, or he or she could simply write an extra program to do these things and put it into the computer to be executed along with all other programs. Thus we have to control new programs that have been authorized, as well as ensure that unauthorized programs or unauthorized changes to existing programs are not added.

Three key areas of activity that should be in place to help prevent or detect such misuse of programs and which should be covered in the standard are:

1. A separate environment should be provided for programmers to use in the development and the initial testing of programs. This should be completely partitioned off from the computer environment used to contain actual live data and the programs which are in actual live use (often called the production environment). Thus, the concept is that a programmer working in the test environment should not have access to live programs or live data.[3] These test environments are important as they prevent the programmers from having access to live data and live programs.

2. An activity should be put in place to review the code which programmers have produced[4] and to ensure that code cannot be changed when it is undergoing the final stages of testing. In this way, there is an independent testing and review of program code which might detect code designed to fraudulently manipulate data or to accidentally or on purpose provide holes

---

3 Where information security is a major concern, companies will create not only test and production environments which are segregated from each other, but will also create intermediate staging environments such as integrated testing environments and user acceptance testing environments.

4 These review processes have to be carefully designed or the review process will be huge and unmanageable. Most computer programs contain thousands of lines of code and thus it is hard to review them in detail. Code comparison software can be used that highlights for review those lines that have been added, deleted or altered. This speeds up the review. As well, these reviews can be carried out on a sample basis, with no programmer knowing whether or not his or her current change might be selected for review.

or back doors to data or other programs. Making the code inaccessible to programmers while these activities are going on makes it harder for programmers to make changes to the code after such an independent review and testing has occurred but, before the code has been promoted into production. In other words, a division of duties between the creation of application programming code and its final review and testing should be enforced.

3. There should be a change control process to move finally approved and tested code from other environments into the actual production environment where it will be used live to process the company's business. In this way, we limit the number of individuals who can actually change the programs which are in use and can help ensure that all approvals and tests have occurred before such a promotion into use takes place.

The above procedures are very much the same as those previously described for systems software, reflecting the reality that almost all computer programs can potentially create, alter or destroy data.

When a large number of application programs are in use, it is very hard to keep track of the various versions of programs as they are undergoing development in the various test or production regions and to ensure that programs are not altered after testing but before they are put into production. Thus, special packages known as library management systems, are often used to keep track of programs undergoing change and their various versions and status[5]. Indeed, in a large organization it may not be possible to keep effective control over all of these factors without the use of a library management system. This library management system provides an additional layer of logical access control over all these activities to complement and further enforce the overall logical security already discussed.

5 In large complex environments, library management packages are also used to control changes to systems software.

STRATEGIES
FOR SUCCESS

Application program change controls should be designed to reflect the reality that the ability to change a program is also the ability to create and alter data.

When a library management package is used to keep track of programs undergoing change, the application programming standard should describe the key activities which are needed to make it effective. Indeed, the standard should call for the use of such library management software where there is a high requirement for integrity and information security.

---

vi) Computer operations

In a computer site of any size, some individual or group will be assigned responsibilities to issue instructions to the computer to process certain jobs, run certain batch processes on an overnight basis, assign and reorganize disk space, etc. These tasks will often be performed with specialized and powerful system software tools which, through their necessary power, present challenges for maintaining logical security and in preventing accidental or purposeful alteration of data.

Thus, standards need to be developed for the operations personnel, data storage technicians and others who are using powerful system software such as job schedulers, storage management tools and other powerful privileges. The standards should describe:

- who can use these tools (e.g., an appropriate division of duties)
- how the powerful access privileges are to be protected, and
- how their use is to be logged and reviewed on a regular basis.

vii) Database management

Everything just said about the operations activities and the technical people who manage operations applies with equal force to database management technicians.

In the overall technical management of the database, there are very powerful tools that will enable the database managers to directly access and alter data. Thus, the database management standard must cover:

- an appropriate division of duties
- the control of powerful password privileges, and
- a reporting and review of their use.

Furthermore, depending on the overall architecture of the systems, some of the logical security functions previously described as being implemented through the operating system or through application programming may actually be managed through the database management software. In these circumstances, the standards should address:

- how logical security is to be implemented at the database management level
- what the parameter settings should be to control various database operations, and
- how rules or processes which provide for logical security protection, etc. are to be changed in a controlled manner.

STRATEGIES
FOR SUCCESS

The standards for operations and database management should include processes to control and review the use of powerful access privileges which technical personnel need to perform these tasks.

---

viii) Backup and recovery

Backup and recovery focuses on the ability of a computer site to recover from a minor disruption in service, as distinct from a disaster which makes the computer site unavailable and unusable for an extended period of time. For example, there could be problems in reading the data and information on a particular disk pack which would make certain applications and data unavailable until corrective steps are taken. Or, through the failure of a particular network controller or a network line, certain users may be unable to access the computer site through their terminals for a period of time.

A backup and recovery standard has two fundamental parts:

- activities that reduce the likelihood of these minor disruptions occurring in the first place, and
- those procedures which should be used to minimize the impact of any disruption when it does occur to a time frame that meets user requirements.

For example, we might log all transactions at the time they are received on line at the data centre; this would avoid users having to re-enter transactions that have occurred during the business day prior to a particular disk pack becoming unreadable. Alternatively, we might keep a complete copy or mirror image of the databases in question, so that in the event that a disk pack or device becoming unavailable we could switch to the backup disk drives and disk packs with little disruption to availability.

This standard should also describe the procedures for:

- managing the library of computer tapes and disks
- backing up data and information, and
- storing tapes and disks both at the computer site and at an off site storage location.

These procedures are not only important to be able to restore data and information after a minor disruption but, through the regular dispatch of backup copies of data and programs to an off site storage location, are a foundation for being able to recover from a disaster, as discussed below.

ix) Disaster recovery

The goal of this standard is to describe the activities that are required to develop, document and test a disaster recovery plan as well as define the minimum contents of the plan.

The standard should have sufficient flexibility to deal with the recovery of a local area network in an office environment through to a fast-paced recovery of the company's major data centre. For all the reasons discussed under physical security, it may be appropriate to create two disaster recovery standards, one for the recovery of major data centres and the other for the recovery of local area networks.

More often than not, for major data centres, disaster recovery plans require arranging major contracts with third party suppliers for the use of alternative "hot sites" which the company can use to process information and data for specified time periods should a disaster occur. It is best if the standards set forth be minimum conditions and clauses which should be present in any such contract and also provide direction and guidance as to how the contract should be reviewed and who may sign it.

There is a great deal of detail which needs to go into a well documented disaster recovery plan, including:

- procedures to declare a disaster
- the ways of alerting all of the people within the organization and its technical suppliers
- how these people are to be contacted
- the specific steps that are needed to install operating systems, systems software, applications and data at the outside third party site, and
- how alternate computer networks may have to be used to connect to the hot site.

A host of other factors should also be addressed in the plan. The key point is that the standards should set forth the minimum contents or provide a table of contents for a disaster recovery plan.

However, a disaster recovery plan that has not been tested has little worth. It is through the testing of our disaster recovery plan that we find out whether it is workable and whether all of the steps and activities which need to be taken in an emergency have been carefully thought through and documented in advance. (Of course, the test will also tell us if these plans really work!) Because of the importance of testing, the standards should provide guidance as to:

- how frequently the disaster recovery plan should be tested

- who should conduct these tests
- how the results should be reviewed, and
- how any problems which the testing will inevitably disclose should be addressed and dealt with.

STRATEGIES
FOR SUCCESS

As back up and recovery procedures and disaster recovery processes are closely intertwined, there is no assurance they are sufficient and complete unless they are regularly tested. Accordingly, standards for these areas should define the frequency of testing and how test results are to be reviewed and plans adjusted to correct any deficiencies revealed.

III Standards for key processes

This final category of standards is designed for those particular activities where the organization perceives special guidance may be needed. The standards in this category will indeed vary considerably from company to company. For purposes of illustration, this section discusses two sample standards which are often required these days, one on cryptography and the other on the Internet.

i) Cryptography standard

The cryptography standard should set forth:

- the cryptographic methods, and
- the protocols to be used by the company for different categories of risk.

This standard reflects the reality that there are dozens of cryptographic methods available in the marketplace which vary in costs, complexity, the amount of protection they afford and the cost of implementing and using them. Thus, the standard should reflect the company's decision on what cryptographic methods are to be used for various levels of classification.

The use of cryptography involves far more than simply choosing a cryptographic method and installing the software. The standard should also address protocols and procedures that are required to deal with such things as:

- the maintenance of the keys and the algorithms
- procedures for dealing with exceptions such as the receipt of garbled messages
- the means of coordinating the use of cryptography with customers and other third parties where that is appropriate, and
- the minimum contractual terms that should exist in contracts with such third parties.

ii) The internet

This standard could be thought of as a platform specific standard as previously described in the information security strategy. Thus we would take all of our generic standards that relate principally to the computer site owners, as listed in the Information Security Policy, and interpret them in terms of how these standards are to be applied to our Internet server computer site and use of the "Internet network". Some of the particular areas requiring careful attention for the Internet are described below.

Undoubtedly, information security methods for the Internet will continue to improve and evolve with time. However, for the foreseeable future, we can always envisage a debate as to the nature and value of financial transactions if any, which should be sent or received, accepted and acted upon over the Internet. Thus, the first thing the standard should set is to define the nature of the transactions and business events if any which can be conducted where the Internet is involved.

Even where the Internet is used for general purposes such as the provision of web pages to provide marketing information, to interconnect the company with others through the Internet for E-mail, to join the company's electronic mail systems with those of the Internet or to make available price lists or order forms, some degree of information security control is required. We obviously do not want to have our computer marketing information or price lists changed or hacked; clearly if we allow the Internet to be used to connect our electronic mail systems with the worldwide Internet, cautions and safeguards must be in place to ensure that this does not open up a huge hole in information security. And as the Internet is inherently insecure from a confidentiality perspective, very rigorous standards are needed regarding the content and nature of E-mail and documents that can be exchanged on the Internet.

Thus, the standard would also:

- define the logical security that should exist for any Internet site, including the various types of firewalls which should be selected and implemented for various categories of risk; and
- set forth the precautionary steps and careful considerations that all employees should follow when making use of the Internet.

THE FIFTH PRINCIPLE

5.5 Appropriate transition plans should be in place whenever new information security policies and standards are created.

Whenever we create a new policy and set of standards, or more likely rewrite and upgrade those that already exist, we have to face the possibility that some of our current practices will be offside with these new requirements. Thus we have to consider what transition plans will be needed to get everything on side.

The first and perhaps most important issue from a top management perspective is the cost impact of the new policy and standards and whether they provide the flexibility needed so that customer service and employee efficiency will not be unduly constrained.

The quality assurance procedures we have put in place throughout the development process is our principal safeguard to prevent problems of this nature. This is why we have involved all major departments in the development of policies and standards in the first place. Hopefully we have been wise enough to put in place a means for exemptions and exceptions so that we can deal with any situations in a controlled manner where the policy and standards would unduly drive up costs or give rise to administrative problems.

We also need to remember that our policies and standards are designed to be responsive to risk. In particular, our standards should be created to require less control measures when the level of risks are lower and thus less control is required.

In view of all of this, it is best as a final step to gain a measure of what the impact of the new policies and standards will be. This impact has two key elements:

- the initial one-time cost of their implementation, and
- the change in ongoing costs they will generate.

Of course, the management of the various computer sites and the heads of major departments will be the ones who should be making these impact estimates. However, the internal audit department is a wonderfully useful resource for pulling these estimates together and reviewing them. The internal auditors have an in depth knowledge of the quality of all internal controls, including information security. They are in a highly informed position to assess the differences between what is currently being done and what the new policies and standards will require.

STRATEGIES
FOR SUCCESS

Before finally approving and implementing new policies and standards, the company should have a reasonable measure of the one-time costs to make the transition to them as well as an assessment of their impact on ongoing costs. While these assessments should be made by management, the internal auditors have a broad knowledge base of existing controls and can provide help in reviewing these estimates for reasonableness.

Ongoing costs

The ongoing costs are perhaps the easier of the two elements to assess. The impact, if any, will be centred around an increase in personnel needed to apply any additional controls that we now require and to administer information security matters. Thus we should survey our computer sites to see if the new standards for all activities at the data centre will require any of them to increase their personnel complement and we should ask major business departments whether they will need any additional employees to manage and administer their responsibilities.

The area where personnel increases are most likely is in the major, central information security group. They may need additional personnel to monitor and report on new and emerging security methods and software developments, create or amend standards as circumstances change, provide advice to other computer sites and departments on security issues, etc. They may also require additional ongoing resources to support the Information Security Committee in its activities.

Those who are asked to provide these estimates should be reminded that the policies and standards are flexible. There may be, and indeed usually are, instances where the new policies and standards will reduce control as some current sites and systems may now be over controlled. Furthermore, by centrally administering information security for the LANs in several departments through remote access, we may be able to reduce personnel costs.

One-time transition costs

Estimating the one-time costs of transition requires first reviewing what the major transition activities are.

Typically, the major transition activities will include:

- creating the Information Security Committee and defining its mandate and composition (as this committee can provide oversight and make decisions as required as the transition activities unfold)
- ensuring that owners have been designated for all systems and computer sites, and making decisions as to ownership allocations as necessary
- ensuring that ownership responsibilities within the company are assigned for all systems and computer sites provided by outside suppliers
- classifying any data and information that has not been previously classified
- revising arrangements with third party suppliers who process data or run computer sites for the company

- creating and delivering security awareness programs for all employees, and more detailed continuing education for those small number of employees such as systems analysts, user personnel who liaise with the information systems department and others who will need a detailed knowledge of the new policies and standards
- reviewing and revising internal controls at all computer sites to meet the requirements of the standards, and
- reviewing existing applications and the people-performed internal controls and procedures manuals used in the departments and determining what steps will be taken to deal with any shortfalls in comparison with the requirements of new policies and standards.

As most of the costs of transition and problems occur in the last step, we will look at this area in some detail.

It is much cheaper to create capabilities in computer software in the first place than to make changes to an existing system. Thus where we run into problems that the application systems is designed in such a way that the new standards are not being met, we need to pause and reflect. We should not jump to the conclusion that the software has to be changed. For example:

1. The company may be planning to replace or significantly enhance the system in one or two years and could, at that time, bring it onside with the new standards. In the meantime, it might be able to address the problem or at least reduce any unacceptable risk by designing compensating controls to be performed "around" the system.

2. The company may in fact be able to create and implement new people-performed procedures and these compensating controls would offset any weaknesses in the application and ensure that information security is sufficient as part of the overall system of internal controls over the business process. The cost of these compensating controls is less than the cost of amending the software.

3. Given that changing software is much more expensive than creating it in the first place, the company may decide to do the best it can with compensating controls and then live with the residual risk, recognizing it is not fully able to comply with policy and standards.

In exploring all of these routes, consider making use of the knowledge and expertise of internal audit and seek their advice as to the compensating controls that could be developed and how or whether these would solve the problem.

The first and second examples above require using compensating controls to ensure that the overall systems of internal controls reduces risk to an overall, acceptable level. This illustrates the key importance of exceptions and why a route for exceptions was built into the policy in the first place.

The third and most difficult example illustrates a situation where the limitations of the existing software, without expensive modification, will not permit us to have the level of information security we want, no matter how creative we are in considering compensating controls. In this case, effectively we have a breach of policy as risks are not being managed as required. Thus we should apply for an exemption to policy, a procedure which will bring the problem to the attention of top management for review and consideration.

It is important to understand that the new security policies and standards are *not* creating these problems, but rather are bringing to our attention that problems exist. We would have these weaknesses whether or not we had written new policies and standards. The advantage is that the problems are now known and can be addressed explicitly, in a controlled manner and with key decisions on balancing risks and costs being made by senior management.

In some of these cases, top management may decide to accelerate plans to acquire a new system to deal with information security concerns, or may change the order in which new systems will be acquired. In these situations, the focus will be on the fact that information security is indeed part and parcel of the service that the organization provides to its customers and that it should be seen, for some systems at least, in this light.

STRATEGIES
FOR SUCCESS

Where it is evident that existing systems and internal control processes do not meet the requirements of the new policies and standards, senior management should carefully assess each situation and then deal with each through documented exceptions and exemptions as provided for in the information security policy. In this way, management can make explicit decisions on these matters. It is important to recognize that these problems have always existed and were not created by the new policies and standards; rather the new policies and standards have brought them to light so they can now be managed. In this way, existing systems can often be amended over time as part of the process of acquiring systems for overall business reasons. Compensating controls can often be used in the meantime, so that the overall system of internal controls reduces the risks to an acceptable level.

The need for a transition plan

From the preceding, it is obvious that there are many activities that are required and that they will not occur all at once. Indeed, the transition to a new set of policies and standards may take several months and involve many departments. Thus we need a plan for the transition and should appoint a project manager to manage and report on progress.

The logical choice for the project manager is the chief information security officer. The plan itself should be approved by the Information Security Committee and this committee should receive progress reports and monitor achievements. The Information Security Committee can play a most helpful role as it is in a good position to gather the cooperation needed from many areas to complete the transition plan.

STRATEGIES
FOR SUCCESS

A project plan should be drawn up for the transition. A project manager should be appointed and a steering committee should monitor and guide the completion of all activities. Usually these roles can be filled by the chief information security officer and the Information Security Committee.

Communicating transition plans and activities

Department heads, systems owners and computer site owners will have logical concerns as to how they will deal with transition problems. They will be concerned that existing processes do not meet the new requirements and will want to know the expectations of senior management as to how they are to address the shortcomings and the time and resources they will have to do so. Thus it is important to announce a transition plan and spell out expectations.

These issues should not be addressed in the policy itself as this policy is designed for use over a number of years long after the transition has been successfully managed. Instead, decisions must be made about the transition period and then announced with the transition plan.

The best way to deal with transition is to provide a grace period of, say, three to six months. This gives all those concerned sufficient time to make the changes needed to adhere to the new policies and standards or to identify exceptions and exemptions that they may wish to apply for during this grace period. Thus at the end of this grace period, all should be in compliance or have approved exceptions and exemptions.

Exemptions and exceptions can be used to manage the process as the organization moves forward. For example, we can grant an exemption to the policy but restrict it to one year as we feel that the issue can be addressed in this time period or will be taken care of as systems are being acquired in the normal course of business.

The security awareness training and education programs are good places for explaining the transition plans. And of course, announcements can be made in the company's normal internal bulletins.

STRATEGIES
FOR SUCCESS

The transition plans should be announced to all those affected and should provide for a grace period to make the needed adjustments to adhere to the new policies and standards or request exemptions and exceptions as policy provides.

Remember, our goal is to make a transition to better information security which provides competitive advantage and increased efficiencies. It is an evolution we are leading, not a revolution.

Overview

Chapter 5 – Tailoring security measures to the organization's needs

5.1 Senior management should create the appropriate organizational structure for spearheading the initial development and ongoing management and updating of information security standards.

5.2 Senior management should establish an appropriate structure for quality assurance of information security standards.

5.3 The information security standards should all be structured in a consistent manner that allows them to be applied in a manner responsive to risk.

5.4 Senior management should understand the nature of information security standards that are required and the overall nature and purpose of each one.

5.5 Appropriate transition plans should be in place whenever new information security policies and standards are created.

STRATEGIES
FOR SUCCESS

The responsibility for the initial development and ongoing updating of security standards should be delegated to an information security committee, or similar group, comprised of representatives from the major departments and including the head of information security and perhaps other members of the information systems department.

It is essential that the development of standards be led by a person or team, usually the information security group. This leadership will help ensure that the layout and format of the standards are consistent, that the standards are easy to understand and apply and that duplication and gaps do not occur.

The standards should be developed by a team that includes people who have sufficient knowledge of internal controls and of information security. In this way, they will be able to develop well rounded standards that integrate with overall internal control systems and which are responsive to risk.

Each team responsible for drafting a new or revised standard should circulate the draft for comment and assess and act on the comments before presenting it to the Information Security Committee for final approval. This circulation should include major operating departments, owners of computer sites of various sizes and complexity, and administrative departments such as human resources and the legal department, as appropriate in each instance.

Quality assurance procedures should include, as appropriate, the use of outside consultants with special expertise, surveys of practices in other companies and advice from internal EDP audit specialists and suppliers of hardware and systems software.

Each standard should list all the activities that may be required under any circumstances and then indicate which standards are applicable and how they are to be applied for the various categories in the classification structure.

Standards and the activities which support them should be formatted and documented in such a way that the reader can tell how to implement them in a risk responsive way. This means the standards should show *for each level of risk in the classification*:

- the activities which should be applied
- how the nature of the activity may vary if required
- the frequency with which the activity should be performed if germane, and
- the authority or seniority level of the person doing the activity, if this should vary.

Standards and their component activities should be formatted and organized so that they can be stored in, and accessed through, a database.

Systems owners and those that assist in classifying data and systems should be provided guidance material to assist them in the classification of information. This support material should define the various risk categories and list the risk factors that are the most important in allocating data and information to each category. As a quality assurance measure, classification decisions should be carefully reviewed, usually by the information systems department, before being acted on.

Standards should focus on the activities that are needed to achieve their purpose and intent under the various risk scenarios that can be envisaged. Details of the administrative methods and procedures needed to carry out each activity can be set forth in administration and procedures manuals. These supporting manuals can be developed as the need for them becomes apparent. This approach will ensure that the standards are focused, reasonable in length, and easy to use, and avoid the mire of unwieldy detail.

Generic standards should be developed first which are applicable across all business processes and various computer platforms. Platform specific standards and business specific standards can then be created from these generic standards where appropriate, as long as these specific standards fulfil the same intent and requirements. They should be reviewed and approved in the same manner as any other standard.

Senior management should be directly involved in shaping the standards on information classification and on roles and responsibilities. These standards help to ensure that information security processes and indeed overall systems of internal controls are responsive to risk and also assign roles and responsibilities across the company at a more detailed level than was provided for in the policy document.

A risk profile should be prepared for each new business process or system being acquired, setting out the classifications, the nature and source of risks, and the approach that will be used to manage these risks. This risk profile should be part of the business case for the system and ideally will cover all risks and requirements for overall internal controls, instead of focusing only on information security.

The roles and responsibilities standard should be used to define in detail various responsibility roles such as the mandate of the Information Security Committee and the chief information security officer. It can also be used to define precisely how ownership roles are defined and how exemptions from policy and exceptions to standards should be requested, approved and documented.

Detailed security requirements for each application system should be defined, documented, implemented and tested in the same way as all other systems requirements whenever new systems are required or existing systems modified. Classification categories for data and systems should be used as a guide in defining these requirements.

The responsibilities and procedures to create access matrices, which detail the division of duties to be enforced by information security processes, should be well defined. The means by which access rights are granted, amended and cancelled for all employees and third parties should also be clearly defined.

When using outside service bureaus to provide applications or computer sites, the need to ensure the company's information security policies and standards are effectively applied at the external sites is the same as for internal company sites. Contracts with such suppliers should require them to meet the requirements of the company's policies and standards and accordingly provide for their controls to do to be evaluated and regularly tested. Responsibility for this should be formally assigned by designating an employee or department as the computer site owner for each external site.

As regards systems software standards, senior management must take careful note of whether appropriate quality assurance procedures are being applied. For a major data centre, the activities required under this standard can be expensive and errors in matching risks and controls can be disastrous and expensive.

The logical security standard requires a high level of technical expertise. For quality assurance purposes, senior management should ensure a highly qualified EDP internal auditor or an outside consultant reviews these standards for completeness and appropriateness.

When developing the networks and telecommunications standard, consider including in this standard a definition of the circumstances under which the information security specialists in the company should be involved in these activities and whether their approval or only their involvement is required for various circumstances. Remember that the more use the organization makes of networks, the stronger the logical security processes must be.

Application program change controls should be designed to reflect the reality that the ability to change a program is also the ability to create and alter data.

When a library management package is used to keep track of programs undergoing change, the application programming standard should describe the key activities which are needed to make it effective. Indeed, the standard should call for the use of such library management software where there is a high requirement for integrity and information security.

The standards for operations and database management should include processes to control and review the use of powerful access privileges which technical personnel need to perform these tasks.

As back up and recovery procedures and disaster recovery processes are closely intertwined, there is no assurance they are sufficient and complete unless they are regularly tested. Accordingly, standards for these areas should define the frequency of testing and how test results are to be reviewed and plans adjusted to correct any deficiencies revealed.

Before finally approving and implementing new policies and standards, the company should have a reasonable measure of the one-time costs to make the transition to them as well as an assessment of their impact on ongoing costs. While these assessments should be made by management, the internal auditors have a broad knowledge base of existing controls and can provide help in reviewing these estimates for reasonableness.

Where it is evident that existing systems and internal control processes do not meet the requirements of the new policies and standards, senior management should carefully assess each situation and then deal with each through documented exceptions and exemptions as provided for in the information security policy. In this way, management can make explicit decisions on these matters. It is important to recognize that these problems have always existed and were not created by the new policies and standards; rather the new policies and standards have brought them to light so they can now be managed. In this way, existing systems can often be amended over time as part of the process of acquiring systems for overall business reasons. Compensating controls can often be used in the meantime, so that the overall system of internal controls reduces the risks to an acceptable level.

A project plan should be drawn up for the transition. A project manager should be appointed and a steering committee should monitor and guide the completion of all activities. Usually these roles can be filled by the chief information security officer and the Information Security Committee.

The transition plans should be announced to all those affected and should provide for a grace period to make the needed adjustments to adhere to the new policies and standards or request exemptions and exceptions as policy provides.

Index

A

ABM . . . 43
Access . . . 269
  audit trail reports . . . 313
  customer . . . 96
  matrix . . . 214, 228, 269, 294, 302, 313
  method . . . 269, 313
  profiles . . . 133
  remote . . . 243
  route . . . 52
Access rights . . . 24, 44, 50 to 53, 55, 84, 137, 214, 269, 282, 303, 309, 314
  customers . . . 43, 96
  granting . . . 314
  information systems department . . . 56
  reports . . . 312
  reviewing . . . 303
Accountability . . . 35
Accuracy . . . 19, 22, 86
Administrative
  controls . . . 136
  procedures . . . 292
Amendments to standards . . . 297

Application programs 22
change controls 320
ATM 3, 28, 35, 40, 43, 128, 217
Audit
committees 7
department, internal 327
internal 330
Audit trails 84, 230, 309
logical security 312
reports 311
reports, access 313
Authentication 19, 28, 86
controls 135
methods 29
Authority of VP of information systems 235
Authorization 19, 24, 86
Authorized application programs 22
Automated banking machine, *see* ABM
Automated teller machine, *see* ATM
Availability 270
continuity and 288
definition of 128

B

Back doors 310
Backup and recovery 321
Believed systems . . . . . 4, 39 to 41
Biometrics 55, 136
Boards of directors 7
Bombs, logic 310
Breach of security, reporting 314
Business
continuity 88
continuity plan 83, 88
resumption plan 88, 270

C

Calling cards 28
Canada Deposit Insurance Corporation (CDIC) 81
CICA Criteria of Control Board (CoCo) 81
CEO, *see* Chief executive officer
CFO, *see* Chief financial officer
Change control 310
  application program 320
  officer 310
Changes, audit trail reports 311
Chief
  executive officer 7
  financial officer 8
  information security officer 331
  technology officer 159
Classification
  data and systems 121
  decisions 153, 201
  information 120, 201
  three dimensions of 286
CoCo, *see* CICA Criteria of Control Board
Compensating controls 329
Competitive
  advantage 3
  disadvantage 16
Completeness 19, 21, 86
Compliance 270
  department 78
  with laws and regulations 83
Computer
  criminal 5
  operations 320
  processes 18
  third party systems 209
Computer sites 39, 151, 270, 300
  determining ownership 207
  management of 154
  owners 95, 116, 150, 270
  responsibilities of owners 150, 226
Computing, personal 176

Confidentiality
  definition of 126, 270
  privacy and 2, 26, 38, 77, 87, 125, 132, 282, 284, 287
Continuity 30
  availability and 19, 30, 128, 288
  definition of 128
  goods and services 2
Contracting internally 300
Contractual arrangements 304
Control reports 84, 134
Controls
  administrative 136
  authentication 135
  compensating 329
  detective 135
  general and environmental . . . . . 152 to 153
  internal 271
Corporate
  ethics 78
  governance . . . . . 33 to 34, 82, 180
  objectives 16
Costs
  disaster recovery 130
  transition 328
Criteria of Control Board (CoCo),
  see CICA Criteria of Control Board (CoCo)
Cryptography 237
  standards 324
  techniques 136
Customer-initiated
  data 44
  transactions 24, 44

D

Data
  classification, creating and using 297
  customer-initiated 44
  owners 139, 271
  primary systems 155

responsibilities of owners 140, 221
secondary users 142
security officer 51
versus information 37
Database management 317, 320
Department heads 8, 114, 294
responsibilities of 115
Detective controls . . . . . 57, 134 to 135, 282
Determining ownership of computer site 207
Development methodology, systems 272
Digital signatures 54
Disaster 18, 30
Disaster recovery . . . . . 30, 130 to 131, 147, 322
arrangements 42
costs 130
plan 323
planning 271
Division of duties 132, 271, 302
DOS 48
Duties, division of 132, 302

E

E-mail 35, 59, 195, 326
EDI 35, 41, 217
EDP audit 278
EFT 35
Electronic commerce 6, 16, 29
Electronic data interchange, *see* EDI
Electronic funds transfer, *see* EFT
Electronic mail, *see* E-mail
Emergency change 271
Employee responsibilities 166, 225
Encryption . . . . . 29, 62 to 63, 284, 315
Enterprise architecture 158, 271, 315
Environment, production 310
Environmental and general controls . . . . . 152 to 153

Exceptions 93, 163, 271, 332
lists 84, 312
management of 196
procedures 199
Execute privilege 47
Exemptions 93, 163, 271, 332
management of 196
procedures 198
External auditors 9
Extra transactions . . . . 24 to 25

F

Facilities manager 13
Faxes 194
Fingerprints 55
Firewall 60
Fraud 32

G

General and environmental controls . . . . 152 to 153
Generic standards 294
Granting access rights 314
Guidance materials 145
standards 286

H

Hackers 5, 21, 312
Human resources department 182

I

Information assets
threats to 4
Information classification 120
categories 121
decisions 153, 201
standards 296, 298
three dimensions of 286
Information resources management committee, *see* IRM committee
Information resources management policy, *see* IRM policy
Information security
achievement of corporate goals 18
chief officer 331
direct benefits 14
four pillars 83
glossary to sample policy 269
policy 6
purpose 17
quality assurance standards 278
responsibilities of department heads 115
responsibilities of systems owners 119
standards 282
strategy 175, 178, 181, 292
Information security committee . . . . 91 to 92, 94, 102, 109, 112 to 113, 159, 233, 275, 328, 331
chairperson 109, 111
composition 110
mandate 299
responsibilities 113, 211
Information security group 93, 145, 159, 233, 328
mandate 163
reporting relationships 164
responsibilities 160, 162, 231
Information security policy
assignment of ownership 205
authority 191, 195
e-mail 195
exemptions and exceptions 191
faxes 194
internal contracting 206

interrelationships . . . 188
principles . . . 187
printed material . . . 192
sample . . . 253
scope of . . . 190
table of contents . . . 184
third parties . . . 205
Information service providers . . . 103
Information systems committee . . . 90, 94
Information systems department . . . 56, 156
access rights . . . 56
authority of vice president . . . 235
head of . . . 159
responsibilities of . . . 157, 229
Information systems steering committee . . . 91, 107 to 108
Inherent risk . . . 122
Integrity . . . 271, 284, 287
Internal
audit . . . 330
audit department . . . 327
auditor . . . 9
contracting . . . 300
laws and regulations . . . 78 to 79, 84
Internal control . . . 32 to 34, 39, 56, 62, 76, 81, 83,
. . . 85, 90, 101, 120, 132, 140, 271
procedures . . . 79
systems . . . 32, 34, 298
third party . . . 305
Internet . . . 3 to 6, 12, 29, 35, 43, 58 to 59, 61 to 62, 238, 243, 325
address . . . 59
enterprise architecture . . . 59
server . . . 59 to 60
Intranet . . . 12, 58, 64
IRM committee . . . 73, 90, 94, 108, 180, 196, 207
roles and responsibilities . . . 210
IRM policy . . . 6, 71 to 72, 74 to 75, 101, 107, 117, 204

K

Key processes 324

L

LAN 5, 39, 45, 49, 116, 155, 208, 223, 233, 308
  administrator 39
Laws 77
  regulations and 217
Legal
  department 182
  responsibilities 26
Library management system 319
Local area network, *see* LAN
Logic bombs 310
Logical security 46, 272, 311
  audit trails 312
  software 312
Logicality 19

M

MAC 282
Mainframes 45, 116
Malicious acts 32
Management consultants 10
Management of a computer site 154
Message authentication 284
Message authentication controls, *see* MAC
Microcomputers 6, 38, 176
  policy . . . . . 176, 240 to 242
Midframes 45

N

Networks 6
  telecommunications 315

O

Objectives, corporate 16
Officer, change control 310
Operating system . . . . . . 47 to 48, 272
Outages 30
Outside service bureau 13, 156
Outsourcing
  third party contractual arrangements 304
  third party suppliers 304
  third party, testing controls 304
Ownership
  responsibilities 112
  roles 220

P

PACES 2, 15
Pass phrases 136
Passwords . . . . . . 25, 27, 29, 47, 50, 55, 84, 134 to 136, 309, 313
Personal computing 176, 272
  microcomputer policy . . . . . . 241 to 242
Physical security 46, 272
  standards 307
Policy
  information security sample 253
  microcomputer and personal computing . . . . . . 176, 241 to 242
Policy, information security, *see* Information security policy
Primary data systems 155
Printed material 192
Privacy 77, 272
  confidentiality and . . . . . . 2, 19, 26, 77, 83, 86 to 87, 125, 132, 282, 284, 287
  definition of 125

Process standards . . . 294
Production environment . . . 310
Programs on individual microcomputers . . . 244

Q

Quality
- assurance . . . 15, 19 to 20, 161
- assurance gateway . . . 20
- control process . . . 23
- service . . . 15

R

Read access . . . 26 to 27, 47
Regulations . . . 77
- laws and . . . 217

Remote access . . . 243
Reporting, breach of security . . . 314
Reports of access rights . . . 312
Responsibilities
- of computer site owners . . . 150, 226
- of data owners . . . 140, 221
- of department heads . . . 212
- of each business unit . . . 204
- of employees . . . 166, 225
- of information security committee . . . 211
- of information security group . . . 160, 162, 231
- of information systems department . . . 157, 229
- of secondary data users . . . 142, 222
- of systems developers . . . 144, 230

Risk
- classification . . . 146
- inherent . . . 122
- profile . . . 299

Routine changes . . . 148

S

Sample microcomputer policy . . . 176
Secondary data users . . . 142
  responsibilities of . . . 142, 222
Securing information assets . . . 4
Security
  awareness programs . . . 93, 161, 239, 333
  detective controls . . . 134
  logical . . . 46, 272
  physical . . . 46, 272
  reporting breach . . . 314
  software . . . 49
  walk-through . . . 138, 141, 146
Service
  bureau . . . 13, 156
  providers, information . . . 103
Shareware . . . 64
Smart cards . . . 54, 136
Software, logical security . . . 312
Standard set up . . . 281
Standards
  access matrix . . . 302
  amendments to . . . 297
  application programming . . . 316
  backup and recovery . . . 321
  computer operations . . . 320
  computer site owners . . . 306
  content . . . 291
  cryptography . . . 324
  database management . . . 320
  determining requirements . . . 293
  development . . . 276
  disaster recovery . . . 322
  division of duties . . . 302
  generic . . . 293 to 294
  guidance material . . . 286
  information classification . . . 296, 298
  internet . . . 325
  key processes . . . 324
  logical security . . . 311

networks and telecommunications . . . 315
physical security . . . 307
platform specific . . . 293
process . . . 294
purpose of . . . 290
roles and responsibilities . . . 299
system software . . . 308
technical . . . 294
three major groups of . . . 295
typical length . . . 292
Steering committee . . . 182
Strategic planning . . . 69
Strategy document, *see* Information security strategy
Super user . . . 50
Suppliers, third party . . . 304
Suspense files . . . 134
System software standards . . . 308
Systems
developers . . . 144, 149, 182, 300
development methodology . . . 145, 272
owners . . . 103, 119, 133, 141, 149, 154, 272, 300
responsibilities of developers . . . 144, 230
responsibilities of owners . . . 119, 218
software changes . . . 310
Systems of internal control . . . 151

T

TCP/IP protocols . . . 59
Technical standards . . . 294
Telephone calling cards . . . 28
Telephony . . . 29
Third party
computer systems . . . 209
internal controls . . . 305
software . . . 95
suppliers . . . 304
Threats to information assets . . . 4
Three dimensions of classification . . . 286
Timeliness . . . 19, 23, 86

Transactions
extra . . . . 24 to 25
unauthorized 25
Transition
costs 328
plan 326, 331
Trojan horses 310

U

Unauthorized
alteration . . . . 16 to 17
transactions 25
UNIX 60
Utility programs 22
Utility software programs 22

V

Virus protection 243
Voice prints 55

W

WAN 5, 45, 116
Wide area network, *see* WAN
Windows 48
Windows 95 48
Worldwide web, *see* WWW
Write access 47
WWW 59